THE ECONOMIES OF THE MIDDLE EAST

By the same author

TRADE AND INVESTMENT IN THE MIDDLE EAST

THE ECONOMIES OF THE MIDDLE EAST

Rodney Wilson

M

First published 1979 by
THE MACMILLAN PRESS LTD
London and Basingstoke
Associated companies in Delhi
Dublin Hong Kong Johannesburg Lagos
Melbourne New York Singapore Tokyo

Photoset, printed and bound in Great Britain by
REDWOOD BURN LIMITED
Trowbridge & Esher

British Library Cataloguing in Publication Data

Wilson, Rodney
The economies of the Middle East
1. Near East—Economic conditions
1. Title
330.9′56′04 HC410.7

ISBN 0–333–22043–9

Contents

List of Tables

Acknowledgements

In preparing a work such as this I have incurred an enormous debt to many friends, teachers and colleagues, whose ideas I have absorbed in discussion or in reading. As with my earlier study, I again must express my gratitude to Dr Dick Lawless, head of the Middle East Documentation Centre in Durham, for the help he has given me in collecting material. Without the valuable collection of source material on the Middle East that he has managed to amass at the Centre, my task would have been much more difficult and time-consuming. I would like to thank Professor Walter Elkan, formerly of the Department of Economics of Durham, and now of Brunel, for his helpful comments on the chapter on Iran. Dr William Hale of the Politics Department of Durham offered useful advice on the chapter on Turkey, while Dr Clive Sinclair, Shell Research Fellow in Economics at Durham, read and commented on the chapter on the Yemens and Oman. My work has in general without doubt benefited as a result of the discussions I have had with Professor Denis O'Brien, head of the Department of Economics in Durham.

No amount of time spent studying the Middle East from the outside can be a substitute for actually visiting the countries of the region, and maintaining direct contact. The people I have met during my frequent visits to the area are too numerous to mention, but I must acknowledge the assistance of Durham University's Middle East Travel Fund for making many of those visits possible. In addition I would like to thank Lovaine Ord for the care taken in typing and correcting the manuscript in the midst of her many office duties. Lastly, but quite the opposite of least, I would like to thank my wife Barbara for her help and encouragement, though it is impossible to express adequately in words all that I owe to her.

March 1978 R.W.

Introduction

With the phenomenal development of the countries of the Middle East during the last decade, there has been an accompanying proliferation of literature on their economies. It was with some trepidation, therefore, that I embarked upon a further study to add to this literature. Apart from a few general works of reference, however, most of the studies deal with particular countries rather than the region as a whole. Thus there seemed to be a need for a guide to the economies of the Middle East which was wider in its coverage than the studies which had hitherto appeared. At the same time much of the existing literature was of a descriptive rather than an analytical nature, often not written by economists. Where economic theory was applied in a Middle Eastern context, it was usually a particular model, rather than economic principles in their more general sense. It was these deficiencies in the literature that prompted me, as a practising economist, to start work on this present volume.

Admittedly it is an extremely ambitious task for one author to attempt to cover the entire Middle East on a country-by-country basis, but in my view such a comprehensive approach can have many advantages. First, when only one person is involved, it is easier to adopt a consistent treatment and maintain a unity of style than is the case with a team of authors. Second, it is possible to make comparisons between countries, where appropriate, throughout the text, because of the conspectus of the region as a whole. Third, as there is no need to compromise with other members of a team of writers, a more critical, and perhaps controversial, approach can be adopted.

In this study, I have concentrated on those aspects of development in the Middle East which to my mind will be crucial in determining the future shape of the region's economic activity. It is therefore a highly personalised view, but that of one who has some little experience of the area and its problems. My aim has been to enable the educated but non-specialist reader to distinguish what is significant in the wealth of material and data that is now available on the area. This is not apparent from the more general works of reference on the Middle East, which adopt an uncritical and largely factual approach, but give the reader little insight into how the economies of the region actually function. For those with a basic knowledge of economic theory, it is hoped that the work will prove of particular interest, for I try to illustrate how this theory can be applied in the context of some of the world's most rapidly changing societies. For those involved in the field of development studies, it should suggest which aspects of their subject are valid in the Middle East, and which have less relevance. However, this book is primarily intended for the business reader who wants to obtain an understanding of the workings of the economies of the Middle East, without having to plough through the numerous studies of individual countries and all the economic and commercial publications which are now available on the subject. Usually businessmen dealing with the region have to cover several countries, and it is a time-consuming task for them to acquaint themselves with even a small part of this material. Nevertheless, a lack of background knowledge can be a severe impediment to fruitful business relations. This study provides that essential background information. At the same time, it indicates the vast range of material dealing with the Middle Eastern economies which is now available from commercial publishers and government sources. Most of the main country studies are cited in the references at the end of the book; and the growing number of periodicals and journals dealing with the region as a whole, or with particular countries, are referred to in a separate appendix.

Geographically this work encompasses the entire Middle East, including the so-called northern tier non-Arab states of Turkey and Iran. All the Arab world is covered apart from the Magreb countries and Mauritania, which can hardly be considered as part of the Middle East. The same applies to Somalia which, although a member of the Arab League, is best dealt with in the context of East Africa. Eighteen countries are covered, the five most economically significant in separate chapters. Of these, Iran, Egypt and Turkey owe their importance to their large populations, although Iran is also significant because of its substantial oil production. Saudi Arabia has only a small population, but as the world's largest oil exporter it must be accorded a chapter to itself. Israel is also treated separately, partly due to its unique position amongst the states of the Middle East, but also because it is the most highly developed country in the region, with highly specialised and technologically advanced industries.

It clearly makes sense geographically, as well as economically, to treat the sheikhdoms and emirates of the Gulf together, since Kuwait,

Qatar, Bahrain and the United Arab Emirates have much in common. Less obvious are the similarities between some of the other states which I have grouped together, for a geographer would be unlikely, for instance, to pair countries such as Libya and the Sudan, or the Lebanon and Jordan. Both the latter have been bastions of private enterprise, which sets them apart from the other state-dominated economies of the Middle East, and means that they share many common economic features. Libya and the Sudan are, of course, African states, unlike the other countries considered, but in addition there are many parallels in their economic experiences, especially since the 1969 revolutions in both countries.

Iraq and Syria profess similar economic ideologies, as both countries are governed by Baathist socialist regimes, which makes the political hostility between the Baghdad and Damascus governments rather surprising at first sight. Despite their contiguous territorial frontier the resource endowments of the two states differ considerably, however, for Iraq is a major oil exporter, unlike Syria. North and South Yemen and Oman have more in common geographically on account of their situation at the periphery of the Arabian peninsula, but the similarities go deeper than that: in all three territories the struggle between political forces of left and right has been more intense than elsewhere in the Middle East, and large numbers of their citizens have first-hand knowledge of what Marxian economic systems are like in practice. The chapter on the Yemens and Oman, like the others in this volume, should help demonstrate how diversified the economic experience in the Middle East has become. Nevertheless, a main premise of my investigation has been that certain general economic principles remain constant, and that local variation serves merely to emphasise rather than undermine this precept.

1 Iran: from Third to First World

> Especially in a country with such venerable traditions as ours, rapid change naturally brings its strains and stresses, these are the price we must pay for Westernization and modernization. But I do not propose that we should abandon our great heritage. On the contrary, I have every confidence that we can enrich it. Religion and philosophy, art and literature, science and craftmanship—all will prosper more as we develop our economy . . .
>
> The Shah of Iran, *Mission For My Country* (1960)

Since most economic observers agree that Iran offers the greatest development potential in the Middle East, it seems appropriate to treat that country first in this present work. Its development experience during the last thirty years illustrates how a medium-sized state with a population of 34 million can be transformed economically, provided ample financial resources are available. Iran is, of course, fortunate in having substantial oil revenues, as it is the second largest producer in the Middle East after Saudi Arabia, with annual revenues averaging almost $20 (US) billion over the 1975–7 period.[1] Unlike Saudi Arabia, however, Iran has the necessary complementary resources, both in terms of manpower and land, to ensure that the financial boom resulting from oil exports is translated into real domestic economic growth. Consequently the country is rapidly being modernised along Western lines as economic diversification gathers momentum, and by the 1990s Iranian living standards may not be far short of those prevailing in Western Europe. The Iranian government has in fact become obsessed in recent years with the question of development, since they feel they must modernise quickly, before their oil resources become depleted in a couple of decades' time.

It would nevertheless be misleading to regard Iran as underdeveloped historically, as it has always been an important trading country with considerable indigenous economic enterprise. The cities of Tehran, Isfahan, Shiraz and Tabriz have long been established as major trading centres, serving not only their localities, but also more distant markets at home and abroad. As a result of its geographical situation the Persian Empire was the crossroads for trade between the Orient and the West, at least until the sea routes to the East became opened up. Well before the time of Marco Polo in the thirteenth century the country flourished through its trading links, and the skills of its local craftsmen were renowned throughout the civilised world. Persia itself was one of the most developed of the ancient civilisations, with a strong, centralised administration as a result of its stable monarchy.[2] Under these conditions the economy prospered, and the country boasted perhaps the widest range of goods available anywhere at that time.

Iran's failure to modernise in the eighteenth and nineteenth centuries may perhaps paradoxically have reflected the success of its craft economic activities. These amply provided for the consumption needs of a society where tastes were largely unchanging, and where the majority of people were not constantly striving for new material goods. When the overland trade routes declined in importance, and the nations of Western Europe traded mainly by sea, Iran was to a large extent bypassed, and its citizens did not realise what was happening elsewhere in industry and agriculture. Techniques of production therefore remained the same, while those of Europe changed, and there was no attempt to enlarge existing enterprises or to set up new ventures to take advantage of economies of scale and specialisation. In any case, as the fine handicraft industries served mainly a small domestic élite, the limited extent of the market precluded expansion. The only large organisational units which existed were in agriculture, but this was a result of the inegalitarian distribution of land tenure, with landlords controlling thousands of acres, where their tenants worked hard for pitiful rewards. Urban craftsmen therefore tended to associate large enterprises with social inequality, and did not want to see the experience of the rural areas reflected in the cities. They were content to see craft activities organised as family businesses, where the relationship between reward and effort was readily apparent. Paradoxically, however, the market for the high-value craft products manufactured by these artisans was dependent on the income inequalities associated with a feudalistic society.

INDUSTRIALISATION AT ANY PRICE

Modernisation of industry to take advantage of new technological developments really only started in Iran in the twentieth century, and progress was at first extremely slow. Tabriz was the main centre, with two cotton textile plants, a sawmill, two match factories, a knitting plant and a soap factory, all of which were established between 1900 and 1925, but together they employed only 3500 workers.[3] It was really only when increasing oil revenues enabled the state to play a major role in industrial promotion that more rapid expansion became possible. Thus between 1934 and 1938 there was a 250 per cent increase in industrial employment,[4] largely accounted for by new state-financed factories producing sugar, cotton textiles, matches and cement. Many of these industries were entirely state-owned, while the others, although in private ownership, received substantial state grants and tax concessions, without which they could not have continued in production. Even with state subsidies from the growing oil revenues, costs were high, and producers were only able to sell in the Iranian domestic market, where there was substantial tariff protection against competition from overseas manufacturers.

By the late 1930s the drive to industrialise was already causing overheating of the Iranian economy, with supply bottlenecks becoming evident in labour markets. As the population of Iran was only 14 million at that time, of which less than 3 million lived in urban areas, manpower constraints soon made themselves felt, especially through the supply of skilled labour.[5] Consequently wages were bid up, which helped to fuel inflation. Inflation was also caused by increases in cost resulting from the escalating rate of tariff protection, and the monopolistic position that the new industries enjoyed in the domestic market scarcely helped matters, as it enabled them to charge higher prices than would otherwise have been the case.

Most inflation, however resulted from excess demand rather than from increases in cost, as government spending and investment had increased sharply in order to facilitate the expansion of industry. By 1938 the government was forced to cut back its spending in order to control inflation, but by that time the industrial expansion had gained a momentum of its own. A high demand for imports of machinery and spare parts continued, but when the Second World War started communications with the main European suppliers were disrupted. As a result prices of those supplies that were available in Iran soared, and the wholesale price index rose by one third in 1941, while by 1942 there was hyperinflation, causing wholesale prices to double.[6] As far as Iran was concerned, this was to be a portent for the future, as the experience of the 1970s displays many distinct parallels in the sequence of economic events. It highlights the problems of trying to achieve too much too quickly.

From 1940 to 1955 was a bleak time from the point of view of the development of large-scale industrial establishments in Iran. There was no wartime boom similar to that in Egypt, which had become the main supply centre for the Allied troops stationed in the Middle East. The economic recovery in the immediate post-war period proved short-lived, as the Iranian government soon came into conflict with the Anglo-Iranian Oil Company over the question of royalty payments. The government desperately wanted finance for industrial expansion and the oil industry was the obvious source, for by the late 1940s it already contributed almost one-third towards government spending, and oil exports covered 60 per cent of import payments.[7] As the multinational companies which owned the Anglo-Iranian Oil Company were reluctant to set a precedent and pay higher royalties to the Tehran authorities, their assets were nationalised in 1951. Even before then they had been running down production to demonstrate their power to the Mossadeq government, but after nationalisation production virtually ceased. The Iranians were unable to run the oil installations themselves, and no more oil revenues were forthcoming until a fresh agreement was reached with the Western companies in 1954.

Due to the budgetary crisis no new industrial developments were started between 1951 and 1954 and the existing plants, especially in the textile industry, were on the verge of bankruptcy, since the government could no longer afford to subsidise their operating losses. It was clear that Iran's growth was far from being self-sustaining, and in fact the first development plan covering the 1949–56 period virtually collapsed through lack of finance, as Table 1.1 shows.[8] Industry was to receive the largest single share of investment expenditure under the plan, and it was therefore industry above all else that suffered when the oil revenues were halted. It was only when oil revenues started coming in again in 1955 that industrial expansion was renewed, although finance remained a constraint, as the agreement which the oil companies made with Mossadeq's successor was much less generous than had been originally hoped for. The oil companies, in fact, expanded production in the Arab Middle East at Iran's expense, and consequently any gains made through being able to take half of all profits were more than offset by the losses through production being substantially less than it otherwise would have been.

During the second and third five-year plans there was a marked increase in actual expenditure on industrial development, although, as

TABLE 1.1. Investment expenditure under Iran's Development Plans

	First 7-year plan (1949–56)	*Second 7-year plan* (1956–62)	*Third 5-year plan* (1962–7)	*Fourth 5-year plan* (1968–73)	*Fifth 5-year plan* (1973–8) (revised version)[a]
Total planned investment ($ million)	351	1160	3067	10,854	37,214
Actual investment undertaken ($ million)	68	979	2728	6757	40,397
Actual investments by sector					
	%	%	%	%	%
Agriculture[b]	19·6	22·2	23·1	8·1	14·0
Communications	29·5	39·6	26·3	14·1	17·4
Industry	47·0	9·5	8·4	22·3	14·5
Social services[c]	3·9	13·7	22·4	14·5	14·5
Fuel and energy	—	—	15·6	15·7	21·9

[a] All sectoral figures related to actual investment expenditure, except those of the fifth plan, which are projected target levels.
[b] Only major sectors included in investment breakdown. Expenditure on items such as government buildings, tourism, culture and arts excluded.
[c] Social services include education, health and housing.
Sources: Central Bank of Iran, *Annual Reports* and Plan Organisation Reports.

Table 1.1 shows, industry's share of total investment was small in relation to other sectors. Infrastructure improvements received the largest share of investment funds, for the planners realised that the development of a modern manufacturing sector based on heavy industry would be impossible without an adequate communications system, including surfaced highways and efficient ports. The planners were in any case pessimistic about Iran's industrial prospects during the 1960s because of weak domestic demand conditions. Thus funds allocated to industry during the 1956–67 period were mostly for modernisation of the textile plants established back in the 1930s, and the improvement of other existing manufacturing equipment. The major new departure was the creation of a small manufacturing sector producing consumer durables for the local market, the most notable of which was the car assembly industry.[9] This industry was originally established under a licensing agreement with the Rootes Group of the United Kingdom, whereby Hillman cars were assembled in Iran using British made components. The agreement has been continued with the American Chrysler company who took over Rootes, and today the main models produced are family sized Hillman Hunter and Avenger cars, called Paykans in Iran. By the late 1970s locally assembled cars accounted for over four-fifths of the Iranian market, including not only Paykans, but also Jyanes, a locally produced version of the Citroen Dyane, and the Chevrolet Iran Royal, a higher-income market car based on the Opel Commodore.

A factor helping the promotion of new industry was the creation in 1959 of the Industrial, Mining and Development Bank (IMDBI), a joint venture formed with the participation of foreign banks and the Iranian government. This organisation not only provides finance for industrial expansion, but also carries out local market studies on behalf of clients to determine which industries are feasible.[10] Amongst the successful companies which it helped to launch were the Arj Company, producing refrigerators and coolers, and the Pars Electric Manufacturing Company, which made television and radio equipment, both of which now dominate the local market. A sister organisation helping medium-sized ventures is the Development and Industrial Bank of Iran, though its capital is much smaller, at only $150 million, compared with over $2000 million for the IMDBI.

In recent years the emphasis in Iran has been on the creation of large-scale industrial establishments, rather than assisting smaller ventures. As large-scale industries are usually of a capital-intensive nature, the amounts of investment funds required are much higher, not merely because of the size of total output, but also in terms of each unit of output.

In other words, the average capital:output ratio is higher, as well as the amount of capital in relation to other productive inputs, including labour. This accounts for the greatly increased spending on industry under the fourth and fifth development plans, as Table 1.1 shows, with industry accounting for over 22 per cent of actual investment during the 1968–73 period compared to only 8.4 per cent during the previous five years.

Iran's first heavy industries were, not surprisingly, in the fields of oil refining and petrochemicals. The Shahpur Chemical Company, located on the Gulf, was one of the earliest ventures, as it has been producing ammonia and urea for fertilisers since the late 1960s. This plant is being expanded, and in addition a new giant fertiliser plant at Shiraz run by the state-owned Iran Fertiliser Company is due to come into production by 1980. Now that Iran has become virtually self-sufficient in fertiliser production, efforts are being made to establish other petrochemical industries. These include the manufacture of polyester and acrylic fibres in a $110 million joint venture shared by the IMDBI and Du Pont of the United States, and a venture with Chemie Linz of Austria to produce melamine for the local furniture market.[11] At present all Iran's man-made fibres and modern furnishings have to be imported.

There is state participation in all of Iran's new heavy industry, for local private businessmen were both unable and unwilling to be sole investors in such large-scale ventures. Even apart from the initial financing considerations, most private entrepreneurs doubted whether heavy industry would be economically viable, and in practice these doubts appear to have been well founded. The case of the iron and steel industry illustrates the problems in trying to make a new heavy industry viable. Although work on Iran's first iron and steel plant at Aryamehr near Isfahan was started under the fourth five-year plan, there were serious delays, so that the plant only became operational in 1973, two years later than originally scheduled. The plant, a conventional one built with Russian technical assistance, uses coking coal for its blast furnaces. Iran's factor endowment is unfavourable for conventional plants, however, as the coal for the plant has to be imported from the Soviet Union, and the iron ore as well. Although there are iron ore deposits at Kerman, these apparently are not rich enough in ore to be suitable for the plant. As a consequence the savings on the balance of payments through establishing this first import substitute steel plant were negligible, especially when the initial capital costs of the plant were taken into account, since all the equipment was brought in from abroad. In addition Iran is no more self-sufficient than before, for at least hitherto it could buy its iron and steel requirements in a competitive international market. Now, in contrast, at least as far as the Aryamehr plant is concerned, Iran is tied to the one supplier for its inputs for the steel industry.[12]

If instead of rushing ahead with the Aryamehr plant in the late 1960s Iran had waited a few more years before establishing its first steel plant, new technology more suited to the country's factor endowment would have become available, though of course this could not have been predicted. It is possible to make steel through the gas reduction of iron ore, and, as Iran has abundant supplies of natural gas, this process is obviously preferable to using non-indigenous energy for the industry. When the Iranians embarked upon the expansion of their steel-making capacity in the course of the fifth development plan, it was therefore decided to use this new gas-reduction process. The first steel plant using the process opened in 1977 at Ahwaz, with a capacity of 300,000 tons of sponge iron, which it is hoped to raise to 2·5 million tons eventually.[13] The capital costs involved in the new process are, however, high. The Ahwaz plant cost $650 million, with the Swedish firm Thyssen undertaking most of the work. A further plant planned for Isfahan using a gas-reduction technique developed by the British Steel Corporation may cost $1 billion by 1980, when it is due to come on steam, while the estimated costs of the third gas-reduction plant at Bandar Abbas have escalated to over $3000 million,[14] which has meant that the Iranians have been forced to delay the project due to a shortage of funds. This delay may turn out for the best, because when using new technology it is usually wise to proceed cautiously, and avoid becoming overcommitted. It is typical of the 'act now, think later' approach of the Iranian planners that they have wanted to embark upon three gas reduction plants, rather than trying one first and evaluating the results. Technology in this field is developing rapidly, and the Iranians may find themselves paying a high price for trying to do everything at once. The lesson of the Aryamehr experience of steel-making has obviously not yet been learnt.

A WORKSHOP ECONOMY

Although much of the emphasis in Iran's recent development plans has been on the development of large-scale enterprises, the numbers actually employed in industries such as iron- and steel-making or petrochemicals are relatively small. To a large extent this reflects the capital-intensive nature of these heavy industries, as the amount of capital invested per job created can be as high as $1 million. Thus if the Iranian government wanted to use its oil revenues to maximise the creation of new employment opportunities in manufacturing industry, the investment strategy adopted was hardly the way to achieve this. Those few Iranians who do work in the modern sector industries enjoy high wages, however, as productivity levels are also high in terms of output per man, reflecting the capital intensity of the plants. Meanwhile many of those engaged in the key positions within the new ventures are Western expatriates rather than Iranians, as there are few local citizens who have the necessary qualifications or experience.

Iran's problem is not that it has a low level of skills, but rather that the skills that its labour force do possess are not well suited to the needs of modern industry of the Western type. Unlike most Third World countries Iran is highly urbanised, the towns and cities accounting for over 43 per cent of the total population.[15] Large numbers of people are engaged in traditional handicraft industries, among them silversmiths, coppersmiths, carpet weavers, leather and wood workers, as well as numerous others. Traditionally manufactured consumer goods range from the luxury class to those for the lower-income mass market who cannot afford imported goods or their local substitutes made in the modern sector. These industries, constituting Iran's industrial inheritance, are part of what economists now call the informal sector, but which can perhaps be more aptly described as the bazaar sector in the Persian case, as it is in these urban markets that most of the establishments are located. Although trained artisans only comprise a small proportion of those engaged in the informal sector, they nevertheless represent a substantial reserve of skills in relation to the numbers with skills in the modern sector.

A notable feature of the traditional manufacturing sector is the small size of the majority of establishments. Table 1.2, presenting data from a 1972 survey, shows that over 97 per cent of establishments employed less than 10 persons, yet, as there were over 219,000 individual enterprises in this category, they accounted for over 600,000 workers. This constituted two-thirds of Iran's total industrial workforce at the time, and it seems likely that the position has remained much the same since. Thus it appears that the nation's typical industrial worker is either self-employed, or engaged in a family business, where he will usually be a close relative of the owner.[16] Naturally, advantage cannot be taken of economies of scale in such small establishments, but this is unimportant in traditional handicraft industries, where there is little need for modern machinery, and where there are few indivisibilities in production.

Because those who work in Iran's multitude of small establishments

TABLE 1.2. Urban industrial establishments by size in Iran

Establishments in which are working	*Number of establishments*
1–9 persons	219,240
10–49 persons	5230
50–99 persons	282
100–499 persons	243
500–999 persons	61
1000 or more persons	34
Total	225,000

Source: Ministry of the Economy, *Industrial Survey* (Tehran, 1972). Cited by Walter Elkan, 'Employment, Education, Training and Skilled Labour in Iran', *Middle East Journal*, vol. 31, no. 3 (spring 1977) p. 176.

either own the businesses, or are likely to inherit them, there is often a willingness to work steadily for long hours, despite the relatively modest reward. Such dedication to work, and loyalty to the business, is seldom found in the larger establishments in the modern sector, where management and workers are often divided, and industrial unrest is always likely to occur over wage rates. In contrast in the smaller businesses the workers directly perceive the relation between reward and effort, as any profits either accrue to the family, or are ploughed back into the business. A further incentive factor is the absence of any middleman or retailer profit margin, for the owners of these bazaar workshops usually sell direct to the public.

As their costs and therefore their prices are kept down, Iran's small businesses have not required the massive assistance from the state that the new infant industries in the modern sector have obtained. There is no infant industry tariff protection for the craft industries, yet for modern textile plants the rate of effective protection can be as high as 74 per cent, while for the car assembly industry it is 86·6 per cent.[17] The modern sector industry therefore occupies a monopolistic position in the domestic market, whereas the traditional sector is strongly competitive, not only because of the absence of tariff protection, but also simply because of the large number of producers in each sphere of industrial activity. Sellers of handicraft products therefore find themselves in the position of price takers rather than price makers, although, because of the skill of the bazaar merchants in bargaining, prospective purchasers often obtain the contrary impression.

One of the chief merits of Iran's numerous small workshops is that they do not impose any financial burdens on the state, as they are entirely self-sufficient, unlike the modern sector industries whose initial high capital costs the state normally underwrites. Apart from direct state grants, the modern sector industries also receive subsidised credit through the organisations already mentioned, I.M.D.B.I. and the Development and Industrial Bank of Iran. Although the latter caters for medium-sized firms, the workshop sector is excluded, for medium size is taken to mean firms with at least 100 employees. Instead the workshop owners have to borrow, either from the private banks at commercial rates, or from traditional moneylenders, who demand extremely high interest charges.[18] This discriminatory treatment against small establishments in the provision of credit seems strange, given their relative efficiency and the major contribution they make to economic activity. If only a fraction of the funds that are advanced for heavy industry were reallocated to help these workshops, then the returns could be very high indeed in terms of overall economic development.

On welfare grounds a policy of helping small establishments would also have considerable merit, as large numbers of people would benefit, as opposed to the small élite of highly paid employees who work in the modern sector. Any extra income generated in the workshops immediately helps the many others employed in the bazaars, such as the local traders, and those offering services of all types for a low-income market. In other words the domestic multiplier effects are considerable, whereas most of the funds spent on large-scale projects ultimately find their way abroad, either directly through the importation of foreign capital equipment, or indirectly through the spending of the expatriate workers, or the local élite, on expensive imported consumer goods. Therefore, while the bazaar workshops are closely integrated with the rest of the Iranian economy, the local links of the new capital-intensive industries are extremely tenuous in terms of both demands for productive inputs and employees' expenditure.

Unfortunately recent economic developments in Iran have started to affect adversely the country's small workshops. Although few job opportunities are available in modern sector industries, there has been an enormous increase on the size of the government bureaucracy in Iran, which now accounts for over 770,000 jobs.[19] As a consequence of rapidly rising salaries, civil service employment is drawing many of the abler people away from occupations in the bazaars, especially the young; hence the average age of those still in handicrafts is steadily rising. There is little doubt what young people will decide when faced with the choice of a well-paid government job in pleasant conditions for short hours, or work in the bazaar for long hours for much less remuneration. It is not surprising that many of the younger boys who in former times would have become apprentices in their family's workshop now go into secondary and even higher education, in a quest for the paper qualifications so valued by the government.

One of the most undesirable consequences of Iran's oil boom must be its threat to the workshop economy. If this ultimately collapses then the country will have lost its most self-reliant economic sector. It is ironic that it is the drive to develop modern activities in the cause of economic independence that may in the end make the country more vulnerable to outside pressures. High-cost economic lame ducks may replace viable competitive activities, and the whole economy may become dependent on the preservation of monopolistic markets and increasing government handouts for its modern industries. This is certainly not the economic destiny of Iran which the Shah perceives, but it may well become the reality. In addition, as these new industries age, and the plants need to be replaced, neither these, nor the technology for second generation plants, are likely to be available locally, yet as the oil revenues will then have dried up, replacement may be precluded. At least handicraft industries are not prone to this type of technological obsolescence.[20]

THE WHITE REVOLUTION

A further problem of Iran's current industrialisation strategy is that it is leading to growing economic inequality and social imbalance, and therefore many of the fears that the Shah has about the detrimental side-effects of modern capitalist development are being increasingly realised in his own country. Those engaged in the modern industries, whether as workers or managers, represent a new élite, as already mentioned, while the rewards of business owners and managers are extremely high, even by Western standards, which makes them way out of line with the earnings of most Iranians.[21] Despite the high earnings of the workers in the modern sector, industrial relations problems are emerging, as the large size of the establishments results in a lack of communication between workers and management. In contrast, disputes over working conditions and earnings rarely occur in Iran's small craft workshops, and any problems that do arise are quickly cleared up by direct discussion.

In order to give employees in the modern sector a greater sense of indentity with establishments in which they work, the Shah announced in 1963 the introduction of new profit-sharing laws. This legislation constituted part of the so-called White Revolution, which was the Iranian alternative to the Red Revolution, for through measures such as profit sharing, it was hoped to avoid the contradictions which the Tehran government, like its Marxist opponents, believed were inherent in Western capitalism.[22] But, although revolutionary in name, these measures in a sense represented no more than an attempt to extend the harmonious industrial relations that characterised the craft industries into the new manufacturing industries. In other words, if the revolution succeeded, then this would be due to uniquely Iranian circumstances, and the craft traditions in particular, and could not easily be repeated elsewhere in the Middle East.

Under the profit-sharing laws employers were obliged to work out with workers' representatives a collective agreement to pay bonuses proportionate with gross profits, reduction of costs, reduction of wastage, or a provision of a share in the net profits, or a combination of two or more of the above'.[23] In practice most enterprises agreed on a system of revenue sharing based on gross production, as that was the easiest variable to calculate, and the least likely to be subject to dispute. True profit sharing in the sense of distribution of a proportion of net profits to the workers accounted for only 12 per cent of the agreements registered. Despite all the attention given to the methods of distributing profits, and the widespread publicity given to the law, its impact on urban income distribution was minimal. Although over 1100 agreements were signed by mid-1967,[24] the legislation had much less effect on the large and medium-sized enterprises covered than was originally envisaged.

This partly reflected the fact that the amounts set aside for distribution to company employees was only the equivalent of 20 per cent of gross profits,[25] and in any case, as this related to the share of net profits after depreciation rather than gross profits, the system could be easily abused by tampering with depreciation allowances. By agreeing to use total production as a proxy for profits it was of course hoped to overcome this. However although this would prevent renewed tampering over time after the initial agreement was made, it only exacerbated the situation if the initial agreement itself was suspect. In addition, a further problem of using production as an indicator for profit sharing was that firms would be tempted to hold output down, and charge more, thus increasing profits without increasing the distribution to its employees. As most of Iran's modern industries enjoyed monopolistic privileges in the domestic market through tariff protection, as has already been mentioned, the temptation to behave in this way was clearly considerable.

The growing income inequality in Iran's urban areas has been accompanied by a concentration of economic power in the hands of a few influential families such as the Khayemmis, the Ladjevardis, the Rezais, the Akhavans and the Farmanfarmians.[26] This has occurred despite the objectives of the White Revolution, which aimed to stop the development of the types of vast business empires which these families control. It seems that the monopolistic forces present in the Iranian economy were such that profit sharing and other similar measures were insufficient to prevent concentration of ownership. Nor did the much-heralded opening of the Tehran Stock Exchange in 1966 contribute much to the diversification of share ownership, as many of Iran's leading industrial undertakings remained unquoted in family hands, while share dealings in the exchange were mostly monopolised by the country's richest families in any case.[27]

The Iranian government viewed the concentration of economic power as an unwelcome development, especially since once a particular group increases its economic power this usually means it also acquires more political muscle. There was concern that this growing political strength on the part of an interest group might rival the Shah's own power internally, as the owners of the means of production are usually one of the main forces to be reckoned with in internal politics anywhere, and the Tehran authorities realised that if they appeared to be acting in the interests of the new wealthy classes this would only drive a wedge between them and the mass of the Iranian people, which could in the long term undermine the regime if the workers became alienated. Therefore in July 1975 new measures were announced providing for the distribution of 49 per cent of the shareholdings of Iran's 320 main companies to the public in order to give more people a share in the ownership of the country's basic means of modern production.[28]

This represented an important new stage in the White Revolution, and a major step forward from the earlier profit-sharing laws, for employees were given first options on the shares of their own enterprises before they were offered to the public generally. By March 1976 the 102 largest companies had already sold 20 per cent of their shares,[29] and, by the 1978 deadline laid down by the government, it seems that the 49 per cent target may have been reached. The remaining 218 medium-sized companies covered by the measures have been moving more slowly, and the deadline has been put back for them, but by the early 1980s they will have to comply by offering their shares. Despite these delays, however, one indicator of the early success of the scheme is that by 1977 over 72,235 industrial employees had for the first time a stake in the ownership of the companies in which they worked.[30]

Initially, when the Law for the Expansion of Industrial Ownership was announced it was feared that it would lead to a crash in share prices. Consequently there was a loss of confidence on the part of investors, and it is estimated that Iran's richest families switched funds worth over $2 billion abroad during 1975 and 1976.[31] In reality the effect on share prices was much less adverse than was feared, for the compensation awarded by the government was generous, and in line with the market values of shares before the measures were announced. The prices paid by the government-affiliated Financial Organisation for the Expansion of Ownership of Productive Units were in fact well in excess of those paid by workers buying shares in turn from that organisation.[32] Yet as the amounts paid out in compensation have been large, this has also meant that the liquid funds which former shareholders received were also considerable. With limited investment opportunities in Iran, they have little choice but to acquire overseas holdings. This outflow of funds has been accentuated by the squeeze on profits, as the government brought in rigorous price controls to prevent profiteering from the oil boom, but did not control wages or the costs of other factors of production. In terms of investment outflows, it seems therefore that a high price has been paid for the diversification of industrial ownership.

AN ACHILLES HEEL

The original measures introduced in the name of the White Revolution applied not only to industry, but to agriculture, which until the 1960s was much more significant than manufacturing in terms of its contribution to national output, and which still is of greater significance in terms of employment.[33] Sweeping land reform measures were introduced for the first time in Iran in 1960, their aim being to break the power of the large landlords.[34] Prior to the reform over 70 per cent of the country's fertile land comprised large estates, usually owned by absentee landlords who were either high officials, tribal and religious leaders, or merchants.[35] As with the ownership expansion measures governing industry, the main motivation behind the land reform was essentially political, as the Shah wanted to break the power of the feudal chiefs, whom he viewed as a threat to his own position. The large landlords were also seen as an obstacle to progress in the rural areas, for they resisted any change, at a time when the Shah hoped to expand agricultural production in order to meet the ever-increasing food requirements of the country's population, which was increasing at almost 3 per cent per annum.[36] At the same time the Tehran government wanted to increase its hold over all areas of its vast country, and pre-empt any secessionist moves, by winning popular support from the peasants themselves even in the remotest regions.

The 1960 land reform restricted land ownership to 400 hectares of irrigated land or 800 hectares of unirrigated land. However, as there has been no cadastaral survey of holdings, and there is no official record of farm sizes, it proved impossible to implement these measures. Therefore in 1962 the law was amended, with private landholding limited to one village or its equivalent rather than any fixed land area. Compensation for expropriated land was paid over ten years on the basis of landowners' tax returns, which penalised those who had made false declarations. Land was allocated to sitting tenants, who had to repay the full price over fifteen years. It was the simplicity of these provisions that made the law a success, and ensured rapid implementation. By 1966 over 14,000 villages had been redistributed to an estimated 520,000 farming families, representing over one-quarter of the total rural population.[37] In addition, as a result of further reform measures in 1965 to take account of variations in village sizes, a further 10 per cent of the rural community benefited by receiving land.[38]

Despite the sucess of the land reform measures, agriculture in Iran has lagged behind other sectors, and the country has changed from being self-sufficient to becoming a substantial net importer of food. Imports were amounting to $1500 million a year by the late 1970s, and these may double in the next decade, for food consumption is increasing at 10 per cent per annum with rising living standards.[39] Yet domestic crop production is only rising by 2 per cent per year on average, and the official figure of 7 per cent is regarded by most observers as a gross overestimate. Blame for the poor performance of the agricultural sector cannot be attributed to the land reform measures, as these had minimum effects on farm operations, and any temporary disruptions caused were long since over by the late 1970s in any case. Although the large estates were subdivided, there were few scale economies in farming prior to the land reform, for the holdings were subdivided for operational purposes into small plots. Therefore, if there was a scale problem which was hindering the advancement of Iranian agriculture, it existed long before the land reform, and can scarcely be said to have been affected by it.

From the mid-1960s onwards the Iranian authorities began to think that the major obstacle to farm improvement was the small size of the majority of the country's holdings. If only these were enlarged, it was thought, it would be possible to introduce modern farm machinery and dramatically increase agricultural production. A scheme to consolidate fragmented holdings was therefore started in 1967, although it met with little success. At the same time the Agricultural Development Bank indicated that it would give priority to mechanisation schemes as far as its lending was concerned. In 1969 new legislation was passed providing for the establishment of large farming units, to be run as agro-businesses. These were either to be in the form of joint-stock companies or co-operatives, and usually comprised two or more villages.[40]

A strong economic case for land consolidation can easily be argued. Over four-fifths of the total farming community work holdings of less than 11 hectares, but though these account for 40 per cent of the country's richest agricultural land they provide less than 20 per cent of the marketed supplies.[41] Admittedly a large portion of the produce is for subsistence on these farms, and if food was not supplied in this way the demand for marketed agricultural produce would be much higher. In comparison with medium-sized farms the small holdings are nevertheless inefficient, as holdings of between 11 and 100 hectares provide almost three-quarters of total marketed supplies, yet occupy less than 50 per cent of the country's cultivatable area. These medium-range farms would appear to be the optimum size for Iranian conditions, for when farm size increases further, efficiency appears to decline. Statistics show that farms over 100 hectares provide only 6 per cent of total marketed supplies, although they occupy 12 per cent of the cultivatable area.[42]

Despite the poor performance of those farms with more than 100 hectares, in recent years the Iranian government has concentrated its efforts on assisting large productive units, at the expense of the smaller holdings. The country's first large agro-industrial scheme was the Haft Taffieh sugar cane project, which was started as early as 1961. This project was highly successful: sugar production averaged 12 tons a hectare, a substantial yield by any standard.[43] The Western firm involved in managing the project, Hawaian Agronomics, has since become involved in another scheme at Maghan. Apart from these sugar cane schemes, however, the agro-businesses in Iran have an extremely poor record. The three major ventures for grain production in Khuzestan ran into serious difficulties, and the Western partners withdrew, for they had serious reservations about the long-term viability of the businesses after their own experience of trying to manage such complex undertakings.[44]

The first project to be cancelled involved the Hashem Naraghi Development Company of California, which pulled out of a 20,000 hectare venture early in 1976. Later the same year the Agricultural Development Bank of Iran, a state-financed body, was forced to take over management of Iran Shellcott, for the Western partners, Shell International and Mitchell Cotts, decided to withdraw.[45] Originally Shellcott had planned to develop a 15,000-hectare agro-industry scheme, but irrigation work fell well behind schedule, and by 1975 only one-third of the planned area had the necessary water provision. At the same time land levelling was proving more expensive than foreseen, and the Pahlavi Foudation, which channelled Iranian government funds into the scheme, was unwilling to underwrite these cost escalations. What finally decided Shell and Mitchell Cotts to abandon the scheme, however, was that the data on the land and its cropping potential supplied by a local research station proved far too optimistic in relation to actual yields. With returns less than expected and costs greater, the Iranian government is now left with a project with little chance of financial sucess. The experience of the Iran-California Corporation with another 10,000-hectare agro-business in Khuzestan was similar, and the Tehran authorities have been left with this scheme on their hands as well.[46]

While funds have been channelled into costly agro-business ventures with dubious financial prospects, the potentially much more productive medium-sized farms have been starved of credit. There has been considerable investment in complex agricultural machinery such as combine harvesters, yet, while many of these lie idle due to poor maintenance, there is a shortage of ordinary tractors. The number of tractors in Iran increased by only 10,000 in the fifteen-year period following the land reform,[47] and in the eastern part of the country there are no tractors at all in many areas. Consequently labour productivity in agriculture remains low, and rural living standards stagnate, which has induced many of the most gifted young people to leave the countryside for the cities in search of higher wages. Over 250,000 people a year have been leaving the land in Iran over the last two decades, a rate which, if sustained, will leave rural areas deserted.[48] Nevertheless, with low prices for farm produce which help urban consumers rather than rural producers, this exodus seems likely to continue.

It appears that in agriculture, as with industry, Iran has paid a heavy price for backing grandiose schemes while neglecting the more obvious ways of raising agricultural productivity. What the country's farmers want are more money for irrigation pumps, drainage schemes and fertilisers, as well as ploughs and other simple agricultural implements. Peasants largely welcomed the initial land reform, but the attempts to create farm corporations have been largely unsuccessful from the start, for the peasants have been reluctant to exchange their land for a shareholding in a large company. Smaller-sized units based on family ownership would appear to be a more appropriate organisational form in the Iranian context. Yet, unless help is given urgently to the smaller farms, they may soon disappear like the craft workshops, and all that will be left will be subsistence-orientated peasant plots, and a few large farm corporations that require ever-increasing state subsidies.

2 Egypt: the Ghost of Malthus Lingers On

It may be safely pronounced of Egypt that it is not the want of population that has checked its industry, but the want of industry that has checked its population.

Thomas Malthus, *An Essay on the Principle of Population* (1798)

As the most populous state in the Middle East, Egypt presents the economic planner with an enormous developmental challenge. In view of the economic backwardness and widespread resistance to change that existed in 1952 before the revolution, the achievements since then have been remarkable, however, involving as they have radical changes in the economic structure of this teeming country. A substantial industrial sector has been created in what was hitherto a primarily agricultural economy. Within each sector there has been considerable diversification, and the country's industrial capacity now includes an iron and steel plant, as well as numerous manufacturing establishments producing consumer durables.[1] Major infrastructural developments have been undertaken, the most conspicuous of which is the Aswan High Dam, which has resulted in the provision of electricity in towns throughout the Republic. This, in addition to the country's petroleum reserves, means that there are adequate energy resources for further industrial expansion for the first time in its history.

Despite these fundamental changes in economic structure the long-term development record of Egypt must be viewed as rather unsatisfactory so far. The last quarter-century has not seen any significant improvement in the living standards of the majority of Egyptians. The country remains poor, for its *per capita* gross national product is only \$310, the lowest in the Middle East apart from the Yemens, and well below the level of any other country bordering the Mediterranean. The growth performance is also disappointing, with the average increase in *per capita* gross national product being only 1·5 per cent over the 1960–75 period, and, although this has improved slightly in recent years, the 1973–75 average remains only 1·7 per cent.[2] Given this poor record many question whether Egypt will ever escape from its poverty trap and reach the level of development which Nasser promised at the time of the revolution.

The limited growth that did occur in Egypt was nevertheless sufficient to have raised the living standards for most people had the fruits of development been shared evenly. In practice, however, this was far from being the case and the increases which there have been in gross national product have only benefited certain classes of Egyptian society. *Per capita* income levels in the rural areas are stagnating, as the benefits of development accrue to the urban middle classes.[3] Admittedly, income distribution is much less skewed in Egypt since the revolution, and even the middle classes are far from being well off by European standards. What appears to be happening is that these middle classes are steadily growing in number, and it is this increase which absorbs the extra income, rather than rises in living standards for individuals already in the class. Nasser's Arab Socialism was merely a socialism for his own class: it did little for the Egyptian masses.

A SQUEEZE ON RESOURCES

A major factor holding down living standards in Egypt has been the rapid rate of population increase. Even before the revolution of 1952, the Nile Valley was regarded by many as a classic example of the Malthusian nightmare about to become a reality, with more than 20 million people crowded into a cultivatable zone covering only 5 per cent of the country's surface area. Since then the population has almost doubled to over 38 million, with the rate of increase during the past twenty years averaging 2·5 per cent a year.[4] Fortunately the increase has slowed since the early 1970s to just over 2 per cent per annum, but this is still high by world standards, and is likely to remain so given the trends prevailing in birth and mortality rates.

In Egypt the birth rate has been falling steadily since the 1950s, from 45 per 1000 people in 1952, to 34 per 1000 people today. The decline was until recent years much less, however, than the fall in death rates, from almost 20 per 1000 people in the early 1950s to only 13 per 1000 by the 1970s.[5] It is only during the past five years that the decline in birth rates has more than matched the declining death rates. Despite these declines both birth and death rates remain at high levels. The infant mortality rate in Egypt is still very high, with over 100 deaths per 1000 live births. With improvements in health facilities, especially in rural areas, falls can be expected in this rate. Such declines imply, however, that a relatively high rate of population increase will probably be sustained for the remainder of this century.

The effect of population growth on *per capita* GNP growth is not of course entirely negative. Population growth leads to an expansion in the labour force, and this can have a positive effect from the point of view of output growth, provided the marginal productivity of labour is positive. Of course in so far as there is underemployment of the existing workforce, and the marginal productivity of labour approaches zero, the contribution of additional labour to productivity may be minimal. Thus where factors complementary to labour are in short supply, as in the case of capital and land in parts of the Middle East, additions to the workforce may do little to improve production supplies. The empirical evidence from field surveys of agricultural work suggests, however, that there are actually shortages of labour at peak harvest times, and this must cast serious doubt on the zero marginal productivity hypothesis.[6]

The problem with population growth is that any favourable production effects are lagged, as children are at least fifteen years old before they enter the workforce in a full-time capacity. Admittedly, in Egypt there is a certain amount of child labour, so people may make some contribution to production at an earlier age. Nevertheless the production effect in the short run is likely to be minimal, while the consumption effect of population growth is immediate. More people means increased demand for food, clothing, housing, services and household durables, though consumer demand for the latter is not high in Egypt because of low living standards. But Egypt has a high dependency burden, with large numbers of dependant non-workers in relation to the working population, and all these dependants represent additional consumption demands. In Egypt over 40 per cent of the population is in the under-fifteen age group. If population increases were reduced, the lower dependency burden would mean that everyone could be better off, and per capita incomes could rise.

The high dependency burden in Egypt not only lowers consumption standards, but also has an adverse effect on savings, and hence on the investment upon which economic growth ultimately depends. In Egypt the ratio of savings to GNP is currently below 10 per cent, although it shows some signs of improving. With a high rate of population growth not only are savings supplies lowered, but investment requirements rise. An enormous amount of investment would be needed to provide industrial employment for Egypt's growing population. In reality investment fell steadily in the 1960s from almost 20 per cent of GNP in 1963/64 to only 14·5 per cent in 1966/67, when expenditure on armaments was increased prior to the Six-Day War.[7] Investment was very depressed during the post-war period. It has, however, risen again in recent years to almost 15 per cent of GNP, but much of the new investment is being directed into the Suez area for the reconstruction of the Canal cities. A high proportion of Egyptian investment has therefore been used to replace destroyed capital stock, rather than providing additional permanent employment opportunities for the growing population.

Population growth does not necessarily contribute to the growth of the human capital stock. There is a need to educate the growing population, if the quality of the human capital stock is to rise, or even stay constant. In Egypt illiteracy is actually increasing, in terms of absolute numbers with population growth. The cost of formal education, as well as job training, is a heavy burden. The average quality of the human capital stock, and additions at the margin, may be declining in the rural areas. In Egypt the number of schoolchildren undergoing primary education has been increasing by only 1 per cent per annum, as it has been necessary to hold back expansion of existing schools. State policy has wisely limited class size to an average of forty-two pupils, but as expansion in the system can only come through provision of more schools and teachers, which is necessarily very expensive, this represents a direct cost of population increase. Preparatory and secondary schools face the same problem in Egypt, and some institutions even operate a shift system.[8]

In Egypt's case, as in the Malthusian equation, the most acute and immediate effect of population growth has been felt on food supplies. Table 2.1 illustrates this effect, by contrasting the rate of population increase with the expansion of grain production, the grains cited being the staple foodstuffs in the Egyptian diet. When the index of population increase is compared with the weighted index of grain production, it is apparent that population increase is tending to outstrip food supplies. During the base year chosen, 1966, there were no exceptional climatic conditions which would have adversely affected agricultural production, nor was there any dislocation due to conflict. The agricultural production index used is probably more reliable than a value index, as the latter would have to be deflated by the wholesale price index, which is notoriously unreliable in Egypt.[9] A large proportion of food is sold in

TABLE 2.1. The population and food balance in Egypt

Year	*Population size (in thousands)*	*Index of population increase* (1977=100)	*Grain production (thousand metric tons)*				*Index of grain production* (1966=100)	*Grain imports (£1000 Egyptian)*[a]
			Wheat	*Maize*	*Millet*	*Rice*		
1966	30,139	100	1465	2376	859	1679	100	90,129
1967	30,907	103	1291	2163	881	2279	100	105,700
1968	31,693	105	1518	2297	906	2586	111	74,522
1969	32,501	108	1269	2366	813	2556	105	48,445
1970	33,329	111	1516	2393	874	2604	112	48,591
1971	34,076	113	1729	2342	854	2534	115	80,926
1972	34,839	116	1616	2417	831	2507	113	63,522
1973	35,619	118	1837	2507	853	2274	116	77,389
1974	36,417	121	1884	2640	824	2242	119	310,042

Note: Index of grain production weighted for four crops cited according to the areas planted in the base year 1966, which in a country where land is a very scarce resource, such as Egypt, gives some guide to their relative importance.

[a] £E = $US 2.55 (December 1977).

Sources: Central Agency for Public Mobilisation and Statistics, *Statistical Yearbook of the Arab Republic of Egypt* (June 1972 and October 1975). Computed from data on pp. 7, 26–8, 34 and 248 (1972) and pp. 4, 34 and 215 (1975).

black markets at prices well above the official levels used in the government's price index.[10]

Despite the fact that agriculture remains the largest single economic activity, in terms of both the value of output and employment, for many years Egypt has relied heavily on the importation of foodstuffs to feed its growing population, as is apparent from Table 2.1. Until the 1970s a substantial proportion of the food imports, especially grains, were provided under the United States Public Law 480 programme, whereby American surpluses of agricultural produce were supplied free to needy Third World countries. Increasingly United States grain sales to the Soviet Union meant that this source of aid was halted, however, for the Americans not unnaturally preferred to sell their surpluses rather than give them away. As a consequence Egypt found itself competing in world grain markets as a buyer of ever more expensive foodstuffs, which used up a substantial proportion of its limited foreign exchange earnings. Hence the large increase in recent years in the import bill recorded in Table 2.1. The lack of any apparent relationship between the value of grain imports and domestic production reflects not only volume increases, but also the huge price rises in world markets.

There is a considerable opportunity cost involved in population increase when foreign exchange that could be used to pay for capital goods imports to build up Egypt's productive capacity is used instead to finance food imports. Long-term growth prospects suffer because of immediate consumption needs. Yet in recent years food imports have accounted for over one-third of the country's total import bill, and the situation has become so desperate that even short-term credits have been used for food purchases rather than development projects. Much of the assistance to Egypt from Saudi Arabia and the rich oil-producing nations of the Gulf has been used in this way, and it is fortunate that much of the finance has been in the form of grants rather than loans. This assistance has prompted sellers to charge Egypt more for grain imports, however, as is apparent from the 1974 figure cited in Table 2.1. Apart from the opportunity cost on the import account, Egypt's population pressure also harms export earnings, as the crop area devoted to cotton, the leading export, has been reduced in order to substitute food crops for domestic consumption.[11] Thus it appears that population pressure has led to a serious squeeze on the country's scarce monetary reserves, and has resulted in Egypt becoming more dependent than ever on external economic assistance. Instead of becoming a leader amongst the Arab nations, as Nasser hoped, his country has become in many respects an economic burden on its richer neighbours.

The widespread food shortages in Egypt during the last decade illustrate how critical the supply situation has become, and this has prompted the authorities to deploy more resources into agriculture and raise farm produce prices in an effort to stimulate domestic production. Under Nasser food prices were deliberately held down, in order to keep the cost of living low for urban workers, and hence limit wages. In this way it was hoped to make Egyptian industry more competitive in world markets, although in fact, except for such well-established manufacturing fields as textiles, this was far from being the case. And as a result of the lack of incentives, domestic production of foodstuffs stagnated despite the ever-growing consumption needs. The problems President Sadat inherited were enormous in this respect, for the poor levels of industrial productivity did not justify wage rises, yet the urban workers could hardly be expected to pay more for necessities out of their low incomes. Thus the only way of increasing the prices the farmers received was to introduce government subsidies on foodstuffs, to make up the difference between what the urban workers were prepared to pay and the price the farmers expected to receive if they were to remain in production for the market. More will be said about this later. At present it is sufficient to note that the internal budgetary account is being squeezed as much as the external balance of payments account through population pressure. Ironically, although population pressure has resulted in the government's raising farm prices to stimulate agricultural production, it is also the population increase that contributes to the industrial overmanning that causes low productivity and wages, with the result that the workers cannot afford to pay more for foodstuffs. As long as these countervailing forces persist, the country will never be able to correct its present financial situation.

NEW ORGANISATION, OLD BUREAUCRACY

Egypt's financial burden is accentuated by the need to pay thousands of civil servants, for its swollen bureaucracy is by far the largest in the Arab World. The government's administrative machinery consists of twenty-five separate ministries, with at least one representative from each in the Cabinet, making the latter one of the most unwieldly decision-making bodies in the Middle East, with a minimum of thirty-four members.[12] There is considerable overlap between the ministries, and confusion about where the responsibility of one ministry ends and another starts. Economic affairs, for instance, are divided between the Ministry of

Economics and Economic Co-operation, the Ministry of Finance, the Ministry of Planning, the Ministry of Trade and the Ministry of Supply. Any new industrial project will involve all these ministries, but in addition the Ministry of Industry and Mining, the Ministry of Electricity, the Ministry of Labour Force and Training, the Ministry of Social Affairs, the Ministry of Insurances and the Ministry of Housing and Reconstruction will also almost certainly be involved. If new communications are needed for a project, then this will not only involve the Minister of Communications' department, but that of the Minister of Transport, and possibly the Minister of Marine Transport and Minister of Civil Aviation. Where trained manpower is required then this may fall under the jurisdiction of the Ministry of Education or the Ministry of High Education, or perhaps even the Ministry of Scientific Research and Atomic Energy.

Faced with such a confusing array of Ministries to deal with it is not surprising that foreign investors are reluctant to embark on new projects in Egypt, despite the generous provisions of Sadat's Open Door Policy.[13] This has attracted considerable attention from Western multinational companies, as it provides five-year tax holidays on new investment and free repatriation of profits out of the country, as well as establishing free zones where no import duty is applied on components brought in from abroad.[14] The General Organisation for Arab and Foreign Investments and Free Zones, with which prospective investors have to deal, admittedly trics to simplify matters for foreign businesses, but when dealing with numerous Ministries there are usually considerable delays in obtaining approval for new projects. Foreign residents in the country frequently complain that the Egyptians are their own worst enemies when it comes to attracting funds to stimulate development, since it is pointless to enact liberal investment laws when administrative procedures for dealing with the investments remain so cumbersome. Frequently businessmen, who have been continually passed on from one ministry to the next, give up in exasperation, and decide to base their Middle Eastern operations elsewhere.

Egypt historically has had a relatively large bureaucracy, for central government has always played a major role in economic affairs, originally because it regulated the use of irrigation water.[15] As Egypt's predominantly agrarian economy could not exist in its desert environment without supplies of Nile water, this gave the government control over the commanding heights of the economy. With the development of industry it was fairly widely accepted in Egypt that the state would also want to assert its control, and therefore when Nasser nationalised most of the existing industry in the early 1960s, and decided to establish further state sector industries, there was little domestic opposition. However, the growth of the state sector industries was accompanied by a steady increase in the number and size of the ministries concerned with economic affairs.[16] It appeared that there were nearly as many people engaged within the ministries concerned with industrial affairs as there were in the industries themselves.

In the period from 1959/60, when the state sector industries started being established, to 1964/65, the number of civil servants rose by 250 per cent, yet at that time the new industries had scarcely begun producing. By 1973 almost 2 million people were engaged in 'other services' in Egypt, a category of employment which largely refers to those in the full time civil service, since those in private services are mostly unenumerated. This large figure compares with an industrial workforce of under 1,200,000 in enumerated employment, according to official Egyptian statistical sources.[17] Within the industries themselves a large number of administrators are needed to deal with the constant paperwork coming from the civil servants, and the ratio of white-collar to blue-collar workers in Egyptian industry is consequently one of the highest in the world.[18]

This bureaucratic overmanning in industry was one of the factors which prompted Sadat to reverse Nasser's economic policies of state control, and restore an element of private enterprise in the economy again. President Sadat believed that the competition from the new private sector industries established under the Open Door Policy would not only help widen Egypt's industrial base, but also improve performance in the state sector, which would be no longer in a monopolistic position. Unfortunately it seems that this policy is not working successfully, since there are few new enterprises in evidence, perhaps because, as already indicated, foreign businessmen are put off from investing in Egypt by the country's cumbersome bureaucracy. Ironically, it is therefore as a result of its bureaucracy that Egypt is unable to escape from the economic morass into which it has fallen.

Egypt's complex labour laws, a legacy from the Nasser era, also deter many foreign businessmen from setting up new ventures. First, although Egypt is a low-wage country, this incentive for prospective investors is partly eroded by the high rates of social security contributions which all employers have to pay on behalf of their employees, for these amount to almost one-quarter of the total wage bill. Second, prospective employers are deterred by the fact that it is virtually impossible to dismiss workers, and in Egypt's state sector industries it is customary to retain employees even during periods of slack demand when there is no work for them to do. As a consequence, once workers find employment they tend to regard it as a job for life, and there is little labour mobility. A third factor which deters industrial investors is the 1961 legislation on working hours, which makes employment conditions even more rigid. Each employee's working week is restricted to forty-two hours, and there is a general prohibition on overtime, for the government encourages firms to take on more workers rather than make existing employees work longer.[19] In this way it is hoped to maximise employment opportunities in manufacturing industry. Exemptions can be arranged if an employer applies for special permission, but as this once again means dealing with the government bureaucrats, it can be a lengthy process, which few employers consider worthwhile, as exemptions are only granted for a limited period in any case.

As a result of these deterrents to investment in manufacturing, most of the private capital entering Egypt under Sadat's Open Door Policy has gone into banking and tourism. This has further intensified the bias in favour of services and against the development of manufacturing.[20] Admittedly the tourist industry does have enormous potential, and is a source of useful foreign exchange, but much of the employment created is in the areas where the antiquities are located, often far away from the major centres of population. The foreign banks which have re-established themselves as a result of the Open Door Policy are also a mixed blessing. In their favour it could be argued that they can make funds available to finance new domestic industrial projects. However, despite Egypt's financial difficulties, it is not lack of funds which inhibits investment, but rather a lack of confidence in the country's ability to run industrial ventures profitably, and worries that there may be a return to Nasser's style of socialism at some future date. Hence foreign bank funds have largely gone into property and real estate ventures, or else have been used to help traders with their import finance, so that the growing appetite of Egypt's middle classes for Western consumer goods can be satisfied.

Foreign industries are therefore providing increasingly the goods Egyptians demand, while domestic industrial production stagnates under the weight of its own bureaucracy. Industries are forced to absorb more people than they really need in the interest of employment creation, yet investment remains low. All graduates coming out of Egypt's large university system, which comprises over 276,000 students,[21] are guaranteed employment either in the government administration or in state-run industries. Paradoxically this has the effect of actually lowering industrial investment, as funds are diverted from longer-term capital expenditure to meet the growing current expenditure on wages and salaries. This in turn adds to the vicious circle, as demand increases while the capacity to meet that demand perhaps even declines.

Within the state-run industries there is little incentive to strive for results, in any case, since promotion usually comes through having connections rather than through merit. Those in administrative employment within the manufacturing sector, or in central government, tend to regard their jobs as sinecures, and seldom work even the short 8 a.m. to 2 p.m. day which is customary.[22] Much of their time during these working hours is taken up by tea and coffee breaks, or by reading the daily newspapers, which usually proves more interesting than the tedium of clerical work. Instead of working hard in the morning for little reward, many of these state sector employees devote their efforts to a second job, often in a private trading establishment or a small workshop, which they undertake in the late afternoon and evening. This second job accounts for a large part of their income, but it is less reliable than the steady wage or salary from government employment, which is seen as a form of social security to fall back upon. Naturally, in these circumstances few are willing to take the plunge and go into private employment on a full-time basis, especially as their morning job makes so few demands upon them. In essence, therefore, what the Egyptian bureaucracy consists of is a vast army of part-time workers drawing what amounts to at most a part-time salary, for work which they regard as of secondary importance. It is scarcely surprising that, considering the way the system operates, Egyptian bureaucracy does not function very efficiently.

THE BURDEN OF DEFENCE

Apart from the steady growth of the bureaucracy being a tremendous drain on productive activity, any evaluation of Egypt's economy in recent years must also take account of the enormous costs which the high level of defence expenditure has imposed. Defence spending amounts to 40 per cent of the Cairo government's total budget allocation, representing one of the highest proportions in the world, exceeded only by Israel, the other main belligerent in the Middle Eastern conflict.[23] Unlike Israel, however, Egypt is a poor, developing country, and expenditure on defence implies a direct opportunity cost from the developmental point of view, as it means few resources can be devoted to more productive civilian activities. Unfortunately Egypt does not enjoy a substantial income from oil exports, for its petroleum resources only meet domestic needs, so Nasser and Sadat could not follow the Shah's example and finance defence expenditure in this way.

The sacrifices the Egyptians have made for the sake of the war effort are readily apparent. Despite the emphasis on centralised planning of the economy under President Nasser, only one plan has ever been seriously implemented, yet almost every other Arab state has experience of several, even those that favour free enterprise, such as Jordan. The five-year plan for the 1960–5 period suffered from many shortcomings,[24] but the attempt made to overcome these in the second plan had to be abandoned due to the 1967 war. Similarly when a provisional ten-year plan was drawn up for the decade 1972–82, this was rendered obsolete by the war of 1973. Thus for over a decade, from 1965 to 1976, Egypt was in the bizarre situation of having a large Ministry of Planning and an Institute for National Planning to undertake training and research, but no actual plans. Because of the conflicts and continuing uncertainties over military matters, it was impossible to take a long-term view of development, and even the annual budget proved a difficult exercise. When, finally, a second detailed plan was drawn up for the 1976–80 period, in the aftermath of the Kissinger interim peace settlement, the development expenditure envisaged soon had to be cut back drastically due to problems in rescheduling debts incurred in the purchase of military equipment over a dozen years earlier.[25]

The full magnitude of the burden imposed by Egypt's spending on defence can be gauged from Table 2.2. Between 1963 and 1975 expenditure rose over fourteen-fold, and, although it fell slightly in 1976, it still amounted to $4859 million, a sum even greater than the expenditure by Israel. The close relationship in the trends and absolute amounts of defence spending by the two countries shows how throughout the period both these major parties to the Middle Eastern conflict have tried to keep up with each other in the arms race. Earlier, in the 1950s, the relationship was less close, with Egypt's expenditure consistently higher than that of Israel, as the latter was unable to support such a large burden while at the same time undertaking the necessary civilian expenditure to meet the needs of the influx of Jewish immigrants.[26] As Israel's population is in any case only a fraction of that of Egypt, its expenditure on a *per capita* basis is obviously much greater, as the table shows. Because of Israel's higher living standards, however, the absolute levels of gross national product for both countries show more similarity than might be imagined from the relative population sizes. Thus the proportions of GNP which were allocated to defence spending in the two countries were also remarkably similar, at least until the 1973 war. Since then the Israelis have striven to make their military position stronger, and this is reflected in the fact that one third of GNP has been allocated to defence since 1974. For Egypt the sacrifice, though not quite as large in relation to GNP, is nevertheless considerable, and certainly levels like that of 1975 could not be sustained over a prolonged period.

In addition to the burden imposed on the economy in terms of domestic resource reallocation out of civilian projects, military expenditure also imposes severe strains on the balance of payments. These are particularly acute in the case of a developing country such as Egypt, which produces few armaments itself, and has to rely on imported equipment. Egypt's foreign exchange problems in recent years would have been much worse, however, had it not received substantial military aid from abroad. The question of interest to Egyptians is how much of this aid could be channelled into civilian development programmes in the event of a peaceful outcome to the Middle East conflict. One school of thought suggests that the country's backers from the Arab oil rich nations might lose interest, and stop granting any aid if Egypt ceased to be a 'front line' state. In that case, Egypt would have little to gain from a peace settlement with Israel in foreign exchange terms. Recent Egyptian arms deals have been underwritten by the Saudis and King Kalid has promised to continue Faisal's policy of close co-operation with Egypt. There is strong evidence that Mirage fighters supplied to Saudi Arabia have been put at President Sadat's disposal.[27] The negotiations for the purchase of Western military hardware, to replace Egypt's ageing Soviet-built equipment, could not have been conducted were it not for the promise of Saudi financial backing. Western aircraft salesmen have found that they have had to persuade the Saudis as well as the Egyptians of their equipment's merits, which provides additional evidence concerning how the new arms deals are being underwritten.

The major loss to Egypt as a result of the conflict with Israel was undoubtedly the Suez Canal.[28] Although the major Arab oil producers compensated Egypt after its closure as a result of the 1967 war, the amounts paid were fixed in terms of 1966 revenues. Canal revenues would, however, have grown significantly between the late 1960s and early 1970s. Apart from the losses during the eight-year period before the reopening in June 1975, the closure has also meant long-term losses, for the supertankers built for the Cape route can no longer be

TABLE 2.2. The economic burden of defence expenditure in Egypt and Israel

	Egypt			*Israel*		
Year	Total spending ($ millions)	Spending per capita ($)	Percentage of GNP	Total spending ($ millions)	Spending *per* capita ($)	Percentage of GNP
1963/64	437	16	8·6	271	109	10·7
1968	690	22	12·5	628	224	15·4
1969	805	24	13·0	829	292	18·0
1970	1262	38	19·6	1429	483	19·9
1971	1495	43	21·7	1484	470	23·6
1972	1510	43	20·2	1262	404	20·9
1973	2757	77	31·0	4153	1310	40·8
1974	3117	111	22·8	3688	1173	31·8
1975	6103	163	N/A	3552	1045	35·9
1976	4859	128	N/A	4214	1201	36·3

Source: International Institute of Strategic Studies, *The Military Balance*, successive issues, 1963/64–1976, Part 2, Tables 2 and 3 in each issue.

accommodated in the canal. The maximum draft which the canal allows is 38 feet, which only allows for the passage of ships of up to 70,000 tons when loaded, yet modern tankers can be as large as $\frac{1}{2}$ million tons. Enlargement of the Canal is likely to prove expensive, and even the initial clearing programme with limited dredging is estimated to have cost $300–400 million. The Japanese offered a loan of $140 million for enlargement of the Canal, repayable over twenty-five years at only 2 per cent interest. In exchange they received agreements on petroleum exports from Egyptian fields from the General Petroleum Company.[29] This offer is likely to cover only a small portion of the financial requirements for enlargement. It is debatable whether the enormous expenditure is justified, for the most expensive item in shipping costs is that of port handling charges, with the distance factor much less significant in overall cost.

Sadat's decision to reopen the Suez Canal was undoubtedly courageous, as it meant that Egypt has again much to lose in any future conflict with Israel. The President got some support from elsewhere in the Arab world nevertheless, for the reopening of the Canal benefits not only Egypt, but other Middle Eastern states as well, including South Yemen, Saudi Arabia and the Gulf shiekhdoms. The sea distance from the Gulf states to north-west European ports has almost been shortened by half. The benefits of reopening the Canal are substantial for the Egyptian economy, as the dues in the first year alone (1975/76) were over $200 million, and by 1976–77 the pre-closure 1966–67 figure had been surpassed. In addition, it is estimated that a substantial amount is earned from the sale of supplies to ships, and from expenditure by passengers and crews in Canal towns. Therefore, even without the revenue from the supertanker trade, substantial profits can be made from dry cargo.

The reopening of Suez has helped generate new foreign interest in the proposed industrial, financial and commercial free zones at each end of the Canal. Port Said will be a particularly attractive town, now that its whole area has been declared a free zone. A new $3,600 million plan has been drawn up for the Canal Zone, to be supervised by Mr Osman Ahmed Osman, one of Egypt's leading engineers, who has been appointed to head the Ministry of Reconstruction. The scale of the operation is massive, as the devastation to the Canal cities in 1967, and later in 1969 from constant bombardment, approached that of Berlin or Rotterdam in 1945.[30] Plans for the Port Said free zone include a new airport, a harbour, a tunnel under the canal, an industrial complex, a fertiliser plant and oil refineries. It is hoped that the necessary investment for these ambitious schemes will be forthcoming as a result of the Open Door Policy, although the success of this is already being questioned, as has already been indicated. Clearly, continued peace is a precondition if investment confidence is to be fostered in an area which has until recently been a battleground.

Despite the waste and dislocation brought by war to Egypt's canal cities, the continued military build-up has resulted in some favourable economic spin-offs—although nevertheless these do not to any great extent offset the major losses. Military conscription in Egypt does provide many with a chance to learn not only soldiering, but also trades which are useful in civilian life after leaving the services. The level of skill is unfortunately low in Egypt's 280,000-strong army, but it is much higher in the air force, which comprises over 28,000 men.[31] Handling and maintaining the modern tanks and guided missiles requires a high level of technical competence, though maintenance admittedly leaves much to be desired in Egypt. For the young soldier from the Egyptian countryside, the period with the army may represent his first experience of urban life. This may help prepare people for the type of industrial society which could ultimately result in higher living standards for the majority of the population.

The new industry already established in Egypt includes a small armaments sector producing rifles and machine-guns. In order to achieve a greater degree of self-sufficiency in military equipment, Egypt has helped establish a new body, the Arab Organisation for Industrialisation. This multinational organisation is jointly owned by four Arab states: Saudi Arabia, Qatar, the United Arab Emirates and Egypt.[32] As its contribution Egypt has handed over the four munitions factories established by the Russians in the 1960s, while the rich oil-producing states have provided the financial capital. One of the factories is being used for the maintenance of Egypt's Russian-built equipment, thanks to Western rather than Soviet help, while in another factory it is hoped to assemble Lynx helicopters under licence from Westland Aircraft and Rolls-Royce of the United Kingdom. Egypt also plans to manufacture anti-tank missiles and ground-to-air missiles, as well as jeeps. The latter is in co-operation with American Motors, who are already involved elsewhere in the Middle East.

One major economic externality resulting from Egypt's military activity has been the development of basic infrastructure, including fast road links from Cairo to the Suez area, and modern airports. Construction activity on these roads provided needed employment, while the improvements in communications undoubtedly enhance the long-term prospects for Egyptian industry. When the canal ports were closed industrial exports had to pass through the congested port of Alexandria. Now that port capacity has been built up again in the Canal zone, Egyptian firms can at last take advantage of the improved road links. Thus Sadat's decision to reopen the Canal again will reap even greater dividends for Egypt's balance of payments position, providing peace can be maintained.

CINDERELLA APPROACHES MIDNIGHT

Egypt's enormous spending on imported military supplies has resulted in its falling heavily into debt, but it is only since the mid-1970s that the strains have become severe. The largest debt is to the Soviet Union, which was Egypt's main arms supplier during the Nasser era. The amount outstanding is in excess of $10,000 million, and while its balance of payments remains in a precarious state, with export receipts covering less than half of import payments, the Cairo government is in no position to repay the loans.[33] Many of the loans were originally negotiated with a twelve-year moratorium on repayments, and only interest payments were due before then. Thus until 1979 the repayments were with respect to expenditure incurred before the 1967 war, but, as arms purchases increased substantially after that, the repayments problem will worsen appreciably over the next few years.[34]

The strained relations between the Soviet Union and President Sadat have not helped matters, for the Russians have been unwilling to defer payments. The Moscow authorities hoped that the Arab oil-rich countries which back Egypt would underwrite the debt, and that in particular the Arab Organisation for Industrialisation should play a major role in this as part of its contribution to the struggle against Israel. In this way it was hoped that the Soviet Union could obtain hard currency to finance its own purchases of foodstuffs and investment goods from the United States and Western Europe. Hardly surprisingly, conservative-minded states such as Saudi Arabia totally rejected these Russian schemes, not only because of their anti-communist stance in world affairs, but also because most of the debt concerned represented a legacy from the time of Nasser, whom the Riyadh authorities viewed as an enemy.

Faced with this opposition, the Soviet Union has applied enormous pressure on Egypt, which has caused further problems for the economy. The most obvious pressure was the withholding of spare parts for

Russian-made military equipment, which still comprises over 90 per cent of Egypt's defence supplies. As a consequence the army and air force have been seriously weakened, as much of their equipment is in a state of disrepair, and cannot easily be fixed locally. Efforts by Western aircraft manufacturers to, for example, service Soviet MIG 21 planes in Egypt have been completely unsuccessful.[35] Pressure has also been applied to civilian projects, such as the country's aluminium smelter, which the Russians originally agreed to build, but then tried to delay considerably. Egyptair, the national airline, has been forced to lease American Boeing planes, as its Russian-built aircraft, on which it still owes most of the purchase price, have been grounded because of a lack of spare parts.

Egypt's debt problems involve not only the Russians, however, but also the Western world, including the International Monetary Fund. The IMF has been prepared to finance some of Egypt's foreign exchange requirements, but only on stringent conditions which President Sadat has experienced great difficulty in meeting. Officials at the Fund in Washington want to see Egypt spending its new borrowing on long-term development projects, rather than immediate consumption needs. To ensure this the IMF requested that the Egyptian government reduce its spending on food subsidies, and redirect funds into investment. These subsidies were estimated at $510 million in 1974, and this sum had climbed to $920 million the following year.[36] Clearly some action had to be taken, yet when in January 1977 the Egyptian authorities reduced subsides on several basic foodstuffs and cooking oil, widespread rioting resulted. As a consequence the government was forced to reinstate the subsidies, and call on the Arab oil producers for further subsidies, but even *their* patience is wearing out. The government therefore appears to have reached an impasse, in which all its efforts are devoted to day-to-day survival, and the future is ignored. Meanwhile the effects on the balance of payments are catastrophic, since the subsidies encourage consumption which cannot be met from domestic production, while at the same time the government has to borrow abroad to finance this type of expenditure.

As well as having detrimental balance of payments effects, the subsidies also retard development through causing a misallocation of domestic resources. Internal prices in Egypt, as in other Third World countries, are of course affected by protective tariff policies which enable the newly established infant industries to charge more than they could in competitive markets open to international producers. The infant industries are also able to purchase their input requirements at a much lower price than would prevail in an open market. Thus the Egyptian car assembly industry, for instance, is able to purchase its steel from the Helwan plant at well below production costs, with the government covering the difference. This is justified in the name of infant industry protection to give the new ventures a wider margin between costs and prices until they become more firmly established. Such protection can hardly be justified, for the Egyptian textile industry has now been established for almost seventy years; yet subsidies are still given:[37] cotton, for example, is sold to spinning mills at $679 per ton, compared to a world market price of over $1430 per ton, simply so that the textiles industry's 250,000 employees will not be forced out of work.[38]

The price distortions are not only economically inefficient, but often regressive from the point of view of income distribution. Naturally, urban workers like to see cheap bread in the shops, but the low grain prices undoubtedly have a disincentive effect in the agricultural sector, while, in addition, farm workers are usually much poorer than those engaged in the country's protected industries. As in the Soviet Union, in Egypt there is a system of compulsory procurement of agricultural produce with farmers required to market a substantial proportion of their output through state channels. However, this is inequitably administered, as the quotas for produce do not increase proportionally with farm size, and this means that the larger farmers have a greater surplus which they can sell at high prices to private markets after they have fulfilled their deliveries to the public corporations.[39] In any case, these corporations often have difficulty securing supplies, since farmers avoid keeping records of what they produce. The state dairy corporations are obliged to supply milk to the public at nine piastres a litre, but farmers are reluctant to sell their milk at low prices, and as a consequence much of Egypt's modern dairy processing capacity is lying idle.

A widespread air of unreality seems to have developed in Egypt in recent years, and to some extent President Sadat's Open Door Policy must be held responsible.[40] On the one hand living standards do not seem to have risen at all for the mass of ordinary Egyptians, who continue to live in abject poverty; yet on the other hand there is a new sense of prosperity in Cairo and Alexandria because of the oil boom elsewhere in the Middle East. The thousands of Egyptians who have migrated to the oil-rich Gulf and Libya repatriate a large proportion of their high earnings, which their families use to purchase imported luxury goods from the West. These families of Egyptian expatriates form a new affluent class, together with the Arabs from the oil-rich states, who often reside in Cairo or Alexandria on a semi-permanent basis, flaunting their material possessions for all to see. In addition many of Egypt's indigenous capitalist class, who lived in exile during the Nasser era, have now returned, and are running private businesses, usually of a service nature, to cater for the needs of the new affluent.

It is not surprising that the ordinary Egyptian feels discontented when he sees such affluence around him in which he cannot share. Many who served in the Egyptian forces during the October 1973 war felt it was their efforts and sacrifices which made the oil price boom possible, yet they have received no material benefit despite the promises made by Egypt's politicians at the time. The demonstration effect of the conspicuous consumer spending is undoubtedly detrimental to the poorer classes, for it only makes them resentful, and does not induce any effort to work harder. The new lavish spending is after all essentially generated by rentier income, and the well-paid administrative jobs which educated Egyptians can obtain in the Gulf probably involve less work than industrial employment at home. The ordinary Egyptian's sense of being cheated is made worse by the rampant inflation of property prices and rentals in urban areas caused by the beneficiaries of the oil boom, which means that an average worker's wages is lower than most private apartment rentals. At the same time the flood of imported consumer goods permitted by the Open Door Policy results in less foreign exchange being available to purchase investment goods, which keeps productivity low, and hence holds down wage levels. In these circumstances the gap between effort and reward in Egypt would appear to be wider than ever, which does not bode well for the future for Cinderella may not reach home before midnight, and if not, who knows what the 'ugly sisters' may do.

3 Saudi Arabia: Enigmas of a Rentier Economy

> Rent is a creation of value, but not a creation of wealth; it adds nothing to the resources of a country.
>
> David Ricardo, *Principles of Political Economy and Taxation* (1817)

Although petroleum revenue has been pouring into the desert kingdom of Saudi Arabia for almost forty years, the country remains underdeveloped. Few linkages exist between the modern oil sector and the rest of the economy, which is based largely on subsistence farming and nomadic animal husbandry. Dualistic economies are admittedly characteristic of most of the developing countries of the Third World, but the absence of economic integration merits explanation in a country which has long had the financial means to pursue a more balanced policy. The ease with which Saudi Arabia has obtained its income may paradoxically explain its lack of development, since most of this income has been of a rentier nature, accruing from the possession of one scarce resource—petroleum. Today the country presents an almost perfect example of a rentier economy, a state with high consumption but little production, large incomes but no necessity to work for these earnings.

WEALTH AND WASTE

Saudi Arabia is the richest yet possibly the most enigmatic country in the Middle East, because, although its crucial role in the world petroleum industry is much publicised, much less is known about its other economic activities.[1] The oil sector, however, employs only a small fraction of the country's active labour force, while the majority are engaged in agricultural activities and services.[2] There is little doubt that the fortunate few engaged in the oil sector have benefited substantially from the oil boom, as their salaries and wages are high even by the affluent standards of the world petroleum industry. Those working in service activities, especially civil servants, city retailers and merchants, have also benefited from the oil boom through the multiplier spin-offs from government spending locally, and from the expenditure of those engaged in the petroleum sector. For people outside these occupations, including that half of the population who are not urbanised, any benefits from the increase in petroleum revenue are much less tangible. Their links with the modern sector of the Saudi Arabian economy are extremely tenuous, and they are caught in a similar situation to that experienced by those in the traditional sectors of dual economies elsewhere in the Third World.

Nevertheless, as far as financial resources are concerned, Saudi Arabia's favourable situation bears little resemblance to that prevailing in other Third World countries. The astronomical growth in the value of Saudi Arabian oil exports is depicted in Table 3.1, and these account for over 95 per cent of the country's export earnings. Even before the trebling of oil prices in the aftermath of the October 1973 Arab-Israeli war the rise in export receipts was impressive. Some of this was accounted for by an increase in export volume, as the table shows, which more than doubled over the 1968–72 period. The rise in volume in fact more than offset the decline in prices experienced during the first three years of the period covered, although the most rapid rise came after 1971, when prices were also starting to pick up. From the table it is apparent that government revenue from oil also increased, which consequently eased fiscal constraints, since this revenue accounts for the major proportion of government receipts.

The rise in government oil revenue was even greater than the increase in the value of oil exports. This is because government oil revenues not only reflect the price of oil, but also its share in oil income, and in 1970/71 the tax on oil incomes was raised from 50 to 55 per cent, and by 1974 had risen to 85 per cent. At the same time the royalties which the oil companies paid the government for exploration concessions and production rights rose to 20 per cent of company revenue, although the companies merely added this on to the selling price which the final consumer ultimately pays.[3] The price charged for oil bears little relation to production costs therefore, and in 1974 it was estimated that oil extraction in Saudi-Arabia cost a mere 12 cents a barrel, and, as the selling price was over $11 higher than this, the mark-up has clearly become astronomical. Most of this mark-up accrues to Saudi Arabia, of course, either through income taxes, royalties or oil company profits. That is not to say, however, that this is spent locally, but it does indicate the enormous economic power which the Saudi Arabian rulers can wield.

For the majority of Saudis, the astronomical growth of the petroleum

TABLE 3.1. Saudi Arabian oil exports and revenue

Year	*Volume of exports* (million barrels)	*Price per barrel* ($)	*Value of exports* ($ million)	*Government revenue* ($ million)
1968	1031	1·85	1905	926·4
1969	1085	1·81	1959	949·2
1970	1382	1·78	2296	1214·0
1971	1722	2·25	3651	1884·9
1972	2185	2·50	5459	2744·6
1973	2767	3·27	8994	4340·0
1974	3099	11·36	35,622	22,573·5
1975	2579	11·16	29,579	25,676·2

Sources: Saudi Arabian Monetary Agency, *Statistical Summaries* (Jeddah, 1974/75 and 1975/76) Tables 14, 16 and 20. Price figures computed from Saudi Arabia Monetary Agency, *Annual Report* (Jeddah, 1975) Table 2, p. 21. Exchange conversions at rates prevailing in each year. 1977 rate, 3·5 riyals per U.S. $.

industry in their country has been a mixed blessing, with only the transitory benefits of the Western consumer society to offset the permanent costs arising from the erosion of their traditional way of life.[4] The flood of cheap imported goods has disrupted, and in some instances annihilated, indigenous economic activity. Local beef and camel meat has been replaced by foreign supplies, while fresh fruit and vegetables are threatened by a massive inflow of canned imports. Food accounts for over one-quarter of Saudi Arabia's total import bill, with spending now running at over 1,500 million riyals annually; yet much of this was formerly produced locally. Traditional crafts and skills are also being eradicated, with European furniture and carpets replacing the works of Arab craftsmen. The remnants of the domestic weaving industry have been almost wiped out, while imports of textile and clothing have tripled since 1970.

The principle of comparative advantage may lead us to expect such changing trade patterns, as a result of increased specialisation in petroleum and associated products. Importation 'releases' domestic resources from production, which can then be redeployed into the expanding export sector. This classical trade model does not work in the

Saudi case, however, for the 'released' resources are not reabsorbed into new economic activities. To some extent this reflects deficiencies in the redeployment mechanism, due to skill differentials and labour market imperfections. Those made redundant in agriculture and the traditional crafts lack the skills which modern industry requires. Saudi Arabia's nomads find adjustment to city and town life difficult, and few find industrial employment an attractive proposition. The largest Saudi employer, the Arabian American Oil Company, ARAMCO, therefore has mostly expatriates in skilled occupations, with Americans and Europeans holding the key positions, and Palestinians and Egyptians from urban backgrounds lower down the company hierarchy, in the less skilled jobs. ARAMCO has been slow to replace these expatriates with local Saudi labour, despite its long history of activity in the country since obtaining its first major exploration concession back in 1933.[5] Its expatriate workforce have a vested interest in preserving their jobs, and in restricting the spread of skills associated with the oil industry. Their high earnings represent not only a return for their skills, but also include a quasi-rent element, derived through keeping skills in short supply.

Even if the petroleum industry adopted a more open recruitment policy, and made greater efforts to provide training for Saudi citizens, it seems unlikely that there would be any significant increase in employment opportunities. The oil industry is by nature very capital-intensive, and ARAMCO employs only 13,000 people, despite an annual turnover of $30 billion. There has been little recruitment of new personnel for production tasks, although oil output has doubled since 1970. ARAMCO's parent companies, Standard Oil of New Jersey, Standard Oil of California, Texaco and Mobil, undertake research and development into new production techniques with high-cost American labour in mind, and therefore aim at labour-saving innovations and place less emphasis on capital cost. ARAMCO has in recent years engaged some Saudi nationals in posts with pretentious-sounding titles, but much of this has been window-dressing for the benefit of the government, while in reality these company officials were underemployed. Now that ARAMCO has been nationalised by the Saudi government it seems probable that this type of bureaucratic featherbedding will become more widespread.

CONSUMPTION WITHOUT PRODUCTION

The classical model of international trade is concerned with movements in final goods and commodities, but assumes that factors of production are immobile. In the Saudi case not only do crude oil and refined products move through trade, but also the labour and capital engaged in petroleum production. Wages and profits do not accrue for the most part to factors supplied by Saudi Arabia, and the country receives instead the residual rentier income element as its main gain from trade. This rentier income has grown enormously, especially since the oil price increases of January 1974 brought by the collective action by the cartel comprising the Organisation of Petroleum Exporting Countries (OPEC). Though the flow of oil revenues into Saudi Arabia is now almost 100 billion riyals annually, the country has lacked both resources and the means to absorb this rentier income, or to use it to increase real wealth through the development of the domestic conomy.

Attempts to bolster the agricultural sector of the economy have only materialised since 1970. These have been pitifully inadequate for the most part, while many of the schemes represent a misdirection of resources, and do little to help local agriculture. Millions of riyals have been spent on the Faisal Model Settlement Scheme in the Wadi Jizan, which aims at training Bedouins in the use of modern agricultural machinery and techniques.[6] To date, however, only 500 Bedouin 'trainees' have participated in the scheme, while the model farm is entirely run by German advisors, who alone seem capable of handling the sophisticated equipment. Meanwhile traditional Saudi agriculture is neglected, with producers having to cut prices to compete with imported foodstuffs in local markets. Cereals and fruit enter the country completely free of duty, while the tariff duty on meat and vegetables amounts to only 10 per cent. The upward float of the Saudi riyal has made it more difficult for local agricultural producers to compete. Despite the revaluation of the currency, the government has refused to raise tariff walls, as their main policy objective is to protect urban consumers from the effects of imported inflation. A 400 million-riyal subsidy on foodstuffs has been announced in a bid to stem inflation, but this mostly will apply to imported food which is marketed in the shops. Given this level of subsidy, Saudi Arabian subsistence farmers may be tempted to buy cheap food imports rather than provide for their own needs. The local farming subsidies introduced in 1973 seem grossly inadequate by comparison, and in any case will do little to help Saudi Arabia's rural areas, despite a 45 per cent subsidy on fertilisers, which does prove useful, but barely compensates for recent price rises, especially in phosphates.

Although Saudi Arabia's import bill for manufactured goods currently exceeds 20,000 million riyals, indicating the size of the growing domestic consumer market, the country boasts little manufacturing activity. Most of the new industry is closely linked to oil. There are, for instance, three refineries controlled by the state-owned General Petroleum and Mineral Organisation (Petromin), a fertiliser plant and a sulphuric acid plant. These plants are all of large capacity, but because of the technologically advanced nature of their production processes only a few hundred people are employed in each of them. Until recently the production operations of the Saudi Arabian Fertiliser Company (SAFCO) were run by the American company Occidental Petroleum. Although the plant at Damman had a capacity of almost 2000 tons per day, it was run at less than a quarter of this.

Occidental Petroleum, having persuaded the Saudi government to establish a large plant at a cost of 100 million riyals, was keen only to operate the plant at a low level for local consumption, rather than produce for export. The company feared that if Saudi Arabia became a major exporter of fertilisers it might prejudice the company's chances of establishing similar high-cost plants elsewhere in the Middle East. Fertiliser production in Saudi Arabia, or the lack of it, therefore provides a classic example of how a multinational company succeeded in siphoning off supposed development expenditure through the exercise of monopoly power. In effect the net result was that Saudi rental income from petroleum was recycled into monopoly profits accruing to private Western stockholders, with only a peripheral business interest in the Arab world.[7]

Saudi Arabia's only steel plant is small by Western standards, and its activities are confined to manufacturing metal rods for reinforcing concrete, and girders for use in the construction industry. Construction is booming, and several large multinational companies have landed huge contracts for the construction of new roads, ports and airport facilities. The government is spending over 3275 million riyals extending the road system, and almost half that amount on ports and airports.[8] In addition a new real estate development fund has been set up recently, which under the 1974/75 budget was allocated almost 160 million riyals. The major foreign companies participating in construction projects include John Laing Construction and George Wimpey and Company of the United Kingdom. One joint contract won in 1975 for a new airport in the south of the country at Abha was worth over £20 million. Such massive expenditure on infrastructure will reinforce existing trade patterns, as it serves to make virtually the entire country accessible to goods from the outside world. These developments to some extent parallel the type of growth which occurred within the colonial empires of the nineteenth century, though in Saudi Arabia the financial stakes for today's multinational companies are of much greater magnitude.

In contrast to the amounts spent on building infrastructure to help commerce, Saudi Arabia's housing programme seems hopelessly inadequate. A large proportion of the population is nomadic, living under canvas, and present housing policies do little to encourage settlement. Amongst the poorer Saudis settled in urban areas, whole families usually inhabit one room. Sanitation is primitive, and conditions are as crude as in shanty settlements in low-income Third World countries. Instead of providing low-cost housing, most of the new construction is of luxury apartment blocks. For example, the major housing contract sanctioned in 1975 by the Ministry of Waqfs was for the construction of 53 new apartment blocks in Medina, comprising 700 flats at a cost of almost 120,000 riyals per flat.[9] These are well outside the financial means of even skilled Saudi workers. The only people able to afford such prices are expatriate executives, senior bureaucrats and high-ranking military personnel. An additional major housing development being planned by the Ministry of Finance and National Economy for Medina will provide 2000 villas at even higher prices, on an exclusive development.

Saudi Arabia's main item of budgetary expenditure is defence, estimated at almost 9 billion riyals in 1975 alone, an amount which renders spending on items such as housing paltry by comparison. The defence budget has almost doubled since the oil price increases of January 1974. Since that date major orders for the air force alone include the purchase of Mirage fighters from France valued at $800 million, and U.S. Northrop F-SE Tiger II jet fighters worth $750 million.[10] In addition to this expenditure on aircraft, the Saudi navy has also been expanded from its former insignificance into a modern fighting force through a $500 million deal negotiated with the United States, said to include nineteen destroyers and frigates. The élite Saudi National Guard has maintained its share of the rising defence budget, for in 1975 the United States was awarded a $335 million contract to supply it with Hawk missiles. As well as this direct military outlay, there can be little doubt that much of the expenditure on improving communications has also been undertaken with military considerations in mind. Having established itself as a major economic force in the Middle East, Saudi Arabia also wants to be considered as a military power to be reckoned with. Its military capacity now rivals Iran, whom it confronts across the oil-rich Persian Gulf.

Expenditure on education takes second place to the lavish defence budget. Between 1970 and 1975 almost half of Saudi Arabia's education expenditure was allocated to university expansion, which benefited only a small élite group. In a country where the overwhelming majority of people are illiterate, and most children in rural areas have no access to schooling, this direction of resources into higher education was unwarranted and inequitable. Even the planned school expansion, involving the construction of 2000 new schools, will be insufficient to provide schooling for the majority of the country's children.[11] Most of the curriculum in the country's schools is of a purely academic nature, with an emphasis on religious education, while vocational training is minimal. To date, fewer than 3000 Saudis have received any technical training in vocational centres.[12] As a consequence of the way the education system has developed, most pupils shun technical education, and prefer a traditional academic education which will lead them, they hope, to a white-collar job, preferably in the government bureaucracy.

The health budget is even smaller than education, despite the fact that only the major towns have modern hospital facilities. Although an expansion programme is planned, this will only raise the country's hospital capacity to 20,000 beds.[13] Religious considerations influence even the provision of health facilities, as four of the largest new hospitals planned are to be situated in the Mecca area, so that they can cater for incoming pilgrims who arrive with diseases. The largest single health contract financed by the government recently has been a deal with the Whittaker Corporation of the United States worth $115 million, to provide medical services in armed forces hospitals. Government aid to civilian hospitals is much less adequate. The state provides loans of up to half of the construction costs to hospital contractors, instead of making advance payments. The new general hospital in Medina will have only 500 beds, although the city's population is estimated at over 100,000 people. Despite the country's wealth, there is no national health insurance system. Instead, there is a contributory social insurance scheme, which covers Saudi citizens engaged in new industries and government employees. No provision is made for the large numbers of immigrant workers from Yemen who undertake much of the unskilled work, especially in the port of Jeddah, Medina and smaller settlements west of the Hejaz, and in Assir.

THE ASSET DILEMMA

Securing future income in a world of uncertainty is the main policy objective of Saudi Arabia's rulers. As present income requirements are limited, King Kalid and his royal advisors can either conserve their valuable oil assets as an insurance for tomorrow, or build up the physical assets of their desert kingdom, or instead acquire assets abroad which promise a favourable rate of return.[14] Until 1975, when ARAMCO was taken into state ownership, since it was the oil company rather than the government that controlled production levels the authorities could not pursue conservation policies. The second option, involving the building up of domestic industry and agriculture, has been attempted to a limited degree, as has been already noted, but from the point of view of securing income from non-oil sources, the pay-off is likely to be in the distant future. Increasingly the third option is being taken up, with the Saudi government and private businessmen holding large amounts of assets in the industrialised countries of the West. The trebling of oil prices following the October 1974 war has led to a tremendous increase in liquid funds in the hands of the oil-producing nations, and, with the rentier income from oil amounting to over $25,000 million in 1975 alone, Saudi Arabia's choice concerning the form in which these assets are held has major implications for the Western world.[15]

Saudi Arabia's enormous trade surplus is illustrated by Table 3.2. Exports have exceeded imports throughout the period under consideration, but the gap has grown rapidly, for in 1969 export receipts were two and a half times higher than import payments, but by 1974 were over four times as great. The difference for 1974 and 1975 would be even larger if the cost of insurance and freight (c.i.f.) was excluded from import payments, as it was in earlier years, which are given on a free on board (f.o.b.) basis. Freight costs rose substantially after 1974, largely due to the port congestion resulting from the import boom. Most of these costs are in terms of foreign exchange, as imports usually arrive in non-Saudi ships, and these had to lie idle off the Red Sea and Gulf Coast ports for up to 120 days during the 1974–5 boom, although this congestion has since eased as the handling capacity of the ports has been improved.

At the same time as the trade surplus has grown, the table illustrates just how rapid the growth of exports and imports has been in absolute terms. Export revenues rose over eleven-fold over the 1969-75 period, while import spending increased by a factor of almost seven. Between 1974 and 1975 export receipts contracted slightly due to the decline in demand for petroleum products in international markets as a result of the recession in the industrialised countries of the West. Meanwhile imports rose by almost 70 per cent, and consequently the trade surplus

TABLE 3.2. Balance of payments and reserves of Saudi Arabia (in million riyals)

Year	*Exports*	*Imports*	*Total foreign assets*	*Internationl reserves* (liquid assets)	*Longer-term assets as percentage of total*
1969	8670	3360	3706	2731	27
1970	9770	3200	4308	2979	31
1971	14,770	3670	7303	6487	11
1972	18,720	4710	13,090	10,350	21
1973	28,820	7200	18,040	14,345	21
1974	109,940	13,620*	73,903	50,701	31
1975	97,380	23,020*	139,948	81,850	41

* All import data f.o.b., except 1974 and 1975, which are c.i.f.

Source: IMF, *International Financial Statistics*, vol. XXIX, no. 10 (Washington, October 1976).

was reduced slightly, although it was still over 74,000 million riyals. Foreign assets therefore continued to grow, and most of these are still held in extremely liquid forms, such as foreign currency, gold, Special Drawing Rights or short-term financial assets. The latter, which account for most of these assets, comprise bills such as those issued by the British Treasury—which have a thirty-day or ninety-day maturity—similar government stock issued by other Western governments, or demand deposits with central and commercial banks. It is difficult to quantify the exact amounts of the latter in relation to holdings of government assets in the absence of reliable published data.[16]

As Saudi Arabia accounts for one-quarter of all OPEC oil production, its policy is clearly crucial for the future of the cartel. The world recession of the mid-1970s, which was a consequence of the huge oil deficits incurred by the consuming countries, ironically threatened to undermine the new higher oil prices, as it led to a slackening in demand for oil. The more populous oil-producing countries, particularly Iran, Venezuela and Nigeria, were reluctant to cut back on supply as they did not want to sacrifice the revenue which was needed for development projects. Saudi Arabia, however, took action to conserve supplies to keep the world price steady. This action was inspired by political as well as economic motives. Oil supplies were reduced by closing the pipeline (Tapline) which carries ARAMCO oil to the Mediterranean littoral in Lebanon by way of the Israeli-occupied Golan Heights. This flow of oil has been a source of political embarrassment for Saudi Arabia since the Syrian defeat on Golan, even though Israel has not claimed the pipeline royalties, which still accrue to the Syrian government.

Although Saudi Arabia has been earning foreign exchange from oil for several decades now, it is only recently that the question of recycling a substantial proportion of the oil revenue into longer-term financial assets in the West has been considered by the Ministry of Finance and private Saudi investors. The people in Saudi Arabia who handle the oil revenues lacked financial expertise, and had little knowledge of stock markets in the West. Therefore there was a strong preference for avoiding stocks and shares, except for property investment, which were felt to be a safer security. Instead, assets were held in the form of short-term demand deposits, as already mentioned, with just a few major American and European banks. These banks were reluctant to turn away any business, but such large volumes of demand deposits presented many problems, as they could not be re-lent on a similar short-term basis. The danger of borrowing short-term and lending long-term was exacerbated by the substantial amount of switching of deposits which has taken place, with Arab depositors withdrawing large amounts from one bank and placing it with another. To a large extent this switching was the result of currency uncertainties, especially with the American dollar and sterling, the world's two main reserve currencies. Despite interest being higher on deposits denominated in these currencies, Saudi Arabia lost heavily when sterling was devalued in 1967, and also later as a result of the plight of the dollar in the early 1970s.[17] Countries with strong currencies have been reluctant to receive Saudi investments, as this pushes up their exchange rates, making their exports uncompetitive, and consequently causes unemployment. Hence controls were introduced on the amounts of Arab oil money being exchanged into German marks, while deposits denominated in Swiss francs, and held in Zürich or Geneva, earn negative rates of interest.

There are some indications that Saudi Arabia is starting to acquire longer-term financial assets, although the amounts are small in relation to the vast holdings of short-term securities. Table 3.2 shows long-term capital assets as a proportion of total financial assets, which appear to be increasing since 1972, after a decline before them. Until 1970, and again in 1972, there was a net inflow of capital into Saudi Arabia, due largely to investment from the West in the oil industry, mostly in exploration and production rather than refining. In 1971, however, there was for the first time a net capital outflow on the capital account, and this seems to have been gathering momentum since the oil price increases following the October 1973 war. Longer-term capital investments accounted for almost 58,100 million riyals in 1975, an impressive sum, but well short of the amount of funding from short- to long-term securities which most Western governments would like to see.

The conservatism of the Saudi Arabian monetary authorities is illustrated by the data presented in Table 3.3, which shows the country's official reserve holdings. The Saudi Arabian Monetary Agency (SAMA), as the kingdom's central bank, handles the vast amounts of oil income flowing into state coffers. In its early years of operation it had a strong preference for gold holdings, as this was believed to be the most secure of all assets, and certainly preferable to paper currency. Nevertheless, by 1971 SAMA found itself holding the major portion of its reserves in foreign exchange, since it was difficult to obtain sufficient supplies of gold. The country's growing balance of payments surplus during the period under review was therefore largely reflected in a growth of foreign exchange holdings, mostly in the form of currency, or demand deposits with Western central banks and a few large commercial banks. SAMA was reluctant to hold assets in the form of foreign investments, even those of a short-term nature such as the British government Treasury bills previously mentioned. Hence the agency's

TABLE 3.3. Reserve holdings of the Saudi Arabian Monetary Agency (million riyals)

Year	*Gold*	*Foreign Exchange*	*Foreign investments*	*Total*
1971	574	2909	785	4268
1972	574	5515	764	6853
1973	574	10,833	983	12,390
1974	546	13,094	2293	15,933
1975	546	56,413	20,109	77,068

Source: Saudi Arabian Development Plan 1975–80 (English edition, Riyadh, 1975) p. 40.

foreign investment portfolio actually fell between 1971 and 1972, and, although there has been a rapid growth since in absolute terms, the ratio of investments to all foreign asset holdings has only risen slightly to just over one-quarter. This is a low ratio even in comparison to that found in the most conservative Western central banks. SAMA could certainly at least increase its holdings of short-term foreign government securities, but preferably longer-term investments, without putting the riyal at any risk.

Securing future income by investing in Euro-dollars or other Euro-currencies has thus not proved a simple matter for Saudi Arabia. Although several proposals were put forward for creating special deposit facilities with the International Monetary Fund to aid the recycling of oil money, these were not received enthusiastically by the oil-producing states, as the rates of interest offered were too low to be attractive for countries such as Saudi Arabia. The total amount promised to the IMF by the oil-producing countries together by 1976 was only equivalent to three months' oil revenue for Saudi Arabia alone.[18] Bilateral currency swap schemes have similarly not amounted to much, in spite of the efforts of the oil-consuming countries, as the returns offered have not proved high enough to encourage Saudi participation. Bilateral aid to Third World countries has not been forthcoming to any appreciable extent from Saudi Arabia, except for loans and grants to its Arab neighbours such as Egypt.[19] This aid may yield political dividends for Saudi Arabia's conservative ruling family, but the economic returns to the country are likely to be nil from lending Egypt funds to purchase military equipment or acquire imported foodstuffs for the teeming millions of the Nile Valley.

It seems that much of Saudi Arabian oil revenue reinvested in the West will continue to go through private banking channels, despite the defects of this procedure. The acquisition of overseas assets aggravates the country's exchange rate problems, however, for if it revalues the riyal, then the value of these assets slump. Because of this factor, the last Saudi revaluation amounted to only 2·33 per cent, much less than predicted. The value of the riyal is now fixed in terms of IMF Special Drawing Rights, which are based on a basket of sixteen of the leading world currencies, representing most of Saudi Arabia's main import suppliers. It seems that this has resulted in investment being diverted from those countries whose value tends to be declining *vis-à-vis* SDRs, such as Britain. Instead, oil revenue will be recycled more and more to countries whose currencies are already strong. Through inter-country substitution of recycled funds, the strong get stronger, and the weak bear the burden. The growth of rentier economies like Saudi Arabia has only served to increase world maladjustments in income.

4 Israel: Self-help or Client State?

The promised land—nobody has thought of looking for it where it really is—within ourselves.

Theodor Herzl, *Writings* (1896)

Only one economy in the Middle East can really be considered as developed—Israel. Living standards are high, and compare favourably with European levels, as by 1975 *per capita* gross national product amounted to $4100, well above the United Kingdom figure of $3735.[1] The country boasts a highly diversified economic structure and produces not only goods for immediate consumption, but also so-called 'higher order' goods in the production process, such as components used in local assembly industries, and even machinery. Yet, although most of the new economic activities have only been established for a short time, and in other countries would be regarded as infant in nature, Israeli producers of both industrial and agricultural commodities have managed to keep costs down, and can compete successfully in world markets.

These achievements seem remarkable for a young nation with a mere thirty-year history, much of it spent in conflict with its immediate neighbours. How has such success been managed, and at what cost? In addition to examining these questions, it would be useful to ascertain if the Israeli experience is unique, or whether there are lessons for the other developing countries in the Middle East.

The Israelis are of course a nation of immigrants. Contrary to popular belief these immigrants did not inherit a desert when they arrived in Palestine, but instead started to occupy some of the most productive agricultural land in the entire Middle East.[2] As part of the eastern littoral of the Mediterranean the area receives adequate winter rainfall but, unlike the Lebanon to the north, where the mountains rise out of the sea, much of Israel comprises a wide coastal plain, where farming conditions are ideal. During biblical times the area was an important centre for food crops, and it became the major granary for the eastern section of the Roman Empire. It rivalled the Nile and Tigris-Euphrates Valleys in terms of agricultural production, but, unlike these low-rainfall regions, it was not dependent on irrigation. At the time of the Second World War the area which is now Israel was the hub of the Middle East Supply Centre, which was set up to provide food for the Allied troops taking part in the North African campaign.[3] In order to augment production, there was a considerable amount of reorganisation of agriculture, with new rotation and cropping techniques tried. These innovations undoubtedly laid the basis for the spectacular advances in Israeli agriculture, yet this is often overlooked by modern commentators.

AN ECONOMY UNDER SIEGE

Israel was born in conflict, for once independence was declared in 1948, the armies of the neighbouring Arab countries invaded in order to prevent the emergence of a Jewish state on what they regarded as Arab territory. After a short but bitter conflict, the territory that had formed Palestine was left divided three ways, with the Egyptians holding Gaza, the Jordanians the West Bank, and Israel the remainder, which was however by far the most economically important share.[4] As a consequence of this conflict, all economic links between the new state of Israel and its Arab neighbours were severed, including the railway connecting Tel Aviv and Gaza. From that time on Israel's external trade was to be orientated towards the outside world, rather than with the Middle East on an intra-regional basis.

Despite the Arab boycott the economy of Israel prospered, while both Gaza and the West Bank entered a long period of relative stagnation, even though their links with the neighbouring Arab countries were maintained. This contrast in economic performance must largely be explained in terms of the differing resource endowments of the territories, which were of much more importance than the direction of trade. The West Bank, comprising the highlands of Judea and Samaria, was of limited agricultural potential, apart from sheep grazing and some limited cultivation of olives.[5] Gaza, although a fertile strip, became seriously overpopulated with an influx of refugees, which was totally beyond its capacity to support. In contrast, as already indicated, the provinces making up Israel were very fertile, apart from the Negev, while Galilee was particularly well developed agriculturally. With the exception of East Jerusalem the new state also inherited all the major centres of economic importance in Palestine, including the ports of Haifa and Jaffa, the latter becoming a suburb of Tel Aviv as the Jewish city developed.[6]

To their credit it must be admitted that the Israelis certainly did make the most of the opportunity for development which the favourable physical environment presented. The achievements of Israel's agriculture have been remarkable, with production rising more than 650 per cent between 1950 and 1970, while *per capita* production trebled. This represented not only the most impressive performance of any country in the Middle East, but in fact the highest growth rates in agricultural productivity in the world.[7] This success was partly due to horizontal expansion, especially in the semi-arid area bordering the Negev, as the amount of irrigated land was expanded fivefold. In addition there was notable vertical expansion through intensification, as new crops and tillage were introduced, including hybrid varieties. Animal husbandry steadily improved, and the most up-to-date dairying techniques were employed, with dairy herds trebling over the last two decades. Israel's agricultural methods, especially for dryland farming, have become a model for world agriculture, and the envy of the Middle East.

The innovations in irrigation and water resource management have been applied in many other countries, and Israeli agricultural experts are recognised as being leaders in this field. Recently, for example, the sprinkler irrigation system, which other countries in the Middle East are only starting to introduce, has been declared wasteful by the Israelis. In its place a new method of drip irrigation is being adopted, which uses less than 5,000 cubic metres of water to irrigate one acre of land, less than one-sixth of the amount required by conventional sprinkler systems. This system has successfully turned the southern Arava, the hottest and driest part of Israel's Negev Desert, into blooming fields of crops. Other projects for improving the utilisation of water resources still at the experimental state include trapping the run-off streaming down desert slopes after short but heavy showers, and developing crops which can thrive on brackish groundwater.[8]

In addition to these technical measures to improve water utilisation, economic measures are also being considered. At present water supplies to Israel's farmers are subsidised in order to keep down costs of production in agriculture, and hence the price of food and export crops. There is increasing pressure to remove these subsidies, to make farmers even more conscious of the need to conserve water than at present. The subsidies in a sense act as a disincentive as far as investment in new techniques such as drip irrigation is concerned. It has been suggested that investment in water-saving techniques should be subsidised, rather than the water itself. This would not only include drip irrigation, but also the installation of electronically operated and controlled irrigation systems, which provide water on a programmed basis only when essential.[9]

It is unfortunate that the economic isolation of Israel in the Middle East prevents the dissemination of technical ideas of this sort to other countries in the area, most of which face similar problems in the management of water resources.[10] Even if relations were normalised between Israel and its Arab neighbours, some facets of Jewish agricultural policy could not be emulated. The institutional arrangements as exemplified by the kibbutzim and moshavim organisations could not easily be copied in the Arab world, where the records of agricultural co-operatives have been extremely disappointing. In kibbutzim settlements land is collectively owned, and the members share equally in the revenue but work according to their ability.[11] It seems unlikely that a system in which effort was not directly related to material reward would work on a long-term basis elsewhere in the Middle East. The moshavim could perhaps function better outside Israel, as they combine private ownership of family farms with collective ownership of agricultural machinery, while marketing and the supply of seeds and fertilisers is handled through co-operatives.[12] There is a remarkable lack of bureaucracy in the moshavim organisations, which contrasts strikingly with the co-operatives in Egypt, Syria or Iraq.

Israel's organisational ability has helped not only agricultural production, but also marketing. The Jaffa brand name for citrus is renowned throughout the Western world, reflecting the trebling in citrus fruit exports since the Second World War. The grading, packing and shipping is handled extremely efficiently, and at low cost, in contrast to other Middle East producers whose quality control seldom meets the standards required in Western markets. Since 1970 Israel has been trying to diversify its citrus production to lessen the dependence on Jaffa oranges, which still account for the bulk of citrus fruit proceeds. Old Jaffa groves are being replaced with Valencias, grapefruit and lemons, and Israel actually exports mandarin oranges to Japan, which is of course the major producer itself.[13]

Considerable efforts have been made to determine market requirements and production feasibility before new crops are started. Apart from citrus produce, Israel has become a major exporter of avocadoes, tomatoes and strawberries. The market for avocadoes is so large in Europe that Israel cannot keep up with demand, even though production has risen from almost nothing in 1966 to over 17,000 tons in 1976. Tomatoes have been introduced more recently, but by 1977 Israel was already exporting 3000 tons annually. Most are grown in hothouses near Rafah, where the highest tomato yields in the world have been recorded, using a trickle irrigation system. By the 1980s, using this water-saving technique, Israel will be able to produce 50,000 tons a year for export. Flowers are another of Israel's marketing successes, and in 1976 the country exported 220 million flowers worth $20 million. Because of its climate Israel can grow roses, carnations and gladioli well before Western Europe, even in late winter. The flowers are cut, packed and sent to the airport all in the same day, and then flown out overnight to be sold throughout Europe within twenty-four hours of being picked.[14]

NATIONHOOD FOR WHOM?

Unfortunately the Palestinians living under Israeli occupation have not benefited from a similar agricultural revolution. Admittedly the land tenure system has not helped, as almost half the agricultural holdings on the West Bank are below three acres in size, while three-quarters of the farms are of less than seven acres. This rural overcrowding is partly the result of the high birth rate amongst the West Bank Arabs, but it was worsened by the influx of displaced Palestinians after the 1948 conflict. Those with relatives on the West Bank naturally prefered to live and work on their land rather than reside in refugee camps. In Gaza there was a similar influx of refugees, but the problem was worse there, for a land area of only 140 square miles had to accommodate almost 400,000 inhabitants. Obviously, with such small plot sizes, it is impossible to introduce any mechanised farming methods.

Any commentator relying exclusively on Israeli source material on agriculture in the West Bank and Gaza would gain the impression that since the Israeli occupation there has been a green revolution in these territories. Official sources cite an average annual growth rate in agricultural production of 36 per cent for the West Bank, and 25 per cent for Gaza over the 1968–74 period.[15] These figures are patently misleading, as they use 1968 as a base year, a year when there was considerable disruption of agricultural production in both Arab territories following the Israeli occupation. Most of the more modest rise which actually there has been in agricultural production is accounted for by the introduction of new high-yielding seed varieties, with wheat yields doubling, but this achievement is far from being unique, as hybrid seeds have been introduced in virtually all the countries in the Middle East, including neighbouring Jordan. The improvements in crop production would therefore probably have occurred in any case without the Israeli presence.

In reality the occupation has probably had a detrimental effect on agricultural incomes in the West Bank and Gaza, despite the increases in yields. Arab farmers have experienced great difficulties in marketing their produce, for they are denied access to the local market. There is a real conflict of interest, since Israeli producers fear that Arab competition would drive down prices; but in fact the farmers who suffer from low prices are those in the occupied territories. Field crop prices in the late 1960s underwent a general decline of 7 per cent,[16] while the costs of farm inputs such as fertilisers were well above the prices prevailing in neighbouring Jordan. Arab livestock producers have also been denied access to Israeli marketing channels, with their prices and production suffering as a result.

During the last decade the major change in the agriculture of the West Bank and Gaza has been in the crop mix. The area devoted to export crops—particularly vegetables, citrus and tobacco—has been increased, while the area of melons planted for local consumption has decreased. This change in crop mix is the result of the Israeli authorities doing everything possible to encourage agricultural exports. At first, following the occupation of the West Bank in 1967, the military authorities were reluctant to allow Palestinian Arab farmers to sell to their traditional customers on the East Bank in Jordan. This resulted in widespread protests by the farmers, to which the authorities were forced to yield, and they lifted the trade restrictions. The more perceptive Israeli military administrators soon realised, however, that a continuation of traditional trading links was in their own best interests as well, for the agricultural produce exported to the East Bank earned useful foreign exchange for Israel. In addition the authorities saw that as long as Palestinian Arab citrus fruit growers could dispose of their produce on the East Bank, this would prevent competition with citrus fruit producers within Israel, and keep prices buoyant, thus partially solving the marketing difficulties already mentioned.[17] In this way the 'Open Bridges Policy' was initiated, and trade with the Jordanian East Bank remains at a high level. Much of the agricultural produce exported to the East Bank is not actually consumed within Jordan, but is largely re-exported, mainly through Palestinian merchants in Amman, to Iraq and the Gulf states, including Kuwait.

The Israeli authorities have tried some agricultural extension schemes on the West Bank, but the record of success has been poor in contrast to that on Jewish farms. One sheep-fattening plan sponsored by the military authorities badly misfired, and resulted in a decline in the output of mutton. The newly fattened sheep were more susceptible to disease, and quickly became infected by sheep imported from the East Bank in Jordan. This led to the authorities banning the importation of sheep from the East Bank. However, West Bank farmers had for many years bought these sheep for fattening before selling them in Jerusalem and other urban centres. The halt in imports therefore meant a mutton shortage, and the military authorities were forced to buy sheep from Romania as substitutes.[18] Thus the original modest extension effort had economic ramifications which were much wider than those originally envisaged.

From the economic perspective the occupied territories are mainly viewed by Israel as a source of cheap labour, rather than as being of value agriculturally. Indeed the main contribution which the Arab inhabitants make to agriculture is by working on Israeli farms rather than on their own small fragmented plots. Over 50,000 workers from the West Bank and Gaza are officially employed within Israel's pre-1967 boundaries, representing more than one-quarter of the total workforce from both territories in enumerated employment. In addition many thousands more are hired unofficially by local Israeli bosses, who pay wages well below official levels. Those who hire labour unofficially also benefit by avoiding paying social benefits, which can amount to 50 per cent of wages.[19] Some of these workers commute daily to work in Israel, while others reside in special work camps. The Arabs tend to fill the menial jobs that Israelis, especially the younger generation, find unattractive, such as casual farm labour, refuse collection or work in the tourist industry as hotel waiters and porters.

Arab pay is low in relation to that of Israeli workers, partly because they seldom climb beyond the lowest rung of the promotion ladder, but also due to the low wage rates prevailing in the occupations they work in. The pay differential between agriculture and industry in Israel is extremely wide for a developed country, with remuneration in manufacturing 250 per cent higher on average. Jewish agricultural workers who are members of kibbutzim of course enjoy all the social benefits which these organisations provide—such as low cost, or often free housing and subsidised meals—but this does not apply to the Arab labourers, who do not qualify for membership. Even with low wages workers are still keen to migrate to work outside the West Bank and Gaza, for prices are escalating so rapidly that Arab families need any extra money they can earn in order to maintain their living standards. Over the 1974–6 period, in fact, earnings in the occupied territories lagged well behind price increases, for according to the official index retail prices doubled;[20] and this excludes housing costs, which have risen even more sharply.

Ironically the construction industry is the largest single source of employment for the migrants, and a majority of the building workers in Israel are Arabs. This dependence of certain key sectors of the Israeli economy on Palestinian Arabs worries many Jewish politicians, but economic convenience in this instance does seem to override other considerations. It seems inevitable, moreover, that this dependence on Arab labour will increase over time, given the changing ethnic balance inside Israel and the occupied territories, as illustrated in Table 4·1. Until the 1970s there was a steady increase in the Jewish population of Palestine as a whole, as a result of substantial immigration into Israel, and at the same time emigration of Arabs. The main ethnic shifts occurred in the aftermath of the 1947–8 conflict, and Israel's declaration of independence. In spite of a further exodus of Arab refugees, however, following the occupation of the West Bank and Gaza in 1967, this outflow seems to have been more than compensated by the higher Arab birth rate. During the 1970s the Arab rate of population increase was averaging over 3·0 per cent in the occupied territories and an astonishing 4·1 per cent within Israel's pre-1967 boundaries, while the Jewish rate of increase has declined to 2·7 per cent per annum. Such trends obviously belie the ideal of those in Israel who would like to see the whole of Palestine become a Jewish state, as what in fact already exists is a binational territory.[21]

An Israeli awareness of these demographic trends and how they frustrate the long-term ambitions of some of the founders of the Zionist movement perhaps helps explain the discrimination which Arabs experience in Israel. The most unfortunate group are those with Israeli citizenship, who by 1976 numbered over 550,000, as Table 4·1 shows. Many of these people are highly educated, and a few have even graduated from the Hebrew University of Jerusalem and Tel Aviv, yet they find it difficult to obtain employment commensurate with their qualifications. At the same time, with their Israeli educational background, they also find it impossible to obtain employment in neighbouring Arab states. This group of Palestinians therefore find themselves in a kind of

TABLE 4.1 Population of Palestine by ethnic group

	Israeli citizens (thousands)[a]			*Non-citizen Arabs*[b] *in West Bank and Gaza* (thousands)	*Total population of Palestine* (thousands)	*Proportion of Arabs in Palestine* (%)
	Jews	Arabs	Total			
1931	174·6	476·2	650·8	385·0	1035·8	83·1
1952	1450·2	179·3	1629·5	587·2	3003·9	51·7
1962	2068·9	262·9	2331·8	932·0	3553·8	41·8
1972	2723·6	476·9	3200·5	1030·0	4230·5	35.6
1976	3012·1	551·8	3563·9	1139·4	4703·3	36·0

[a] There were of course no Israeli citizens before 1948, but those counted in this category for 1931 include residents of the territory which became the state of Israel with independence.

[b] The 1948, 1952 and 1962 non-citizens population estimates exclude Gaza, which was not covered by Egyptian statistics. The author has made the following estimates for Gaza, which are included in the total population figure for Palestine: 1948, 170,000; 1952, 200,000; 1962, 290,000.

Sources: 1931 Government of Palestine *1931 Census*, Part II, Table VII, pp. 24–5; for Israeli citizens from 1948, *Statistical Abstract of Israel*, no. 25 (1974) Table II, p. 21; for non-Israeli citizens in 1952 and 1962, Hashemite Kingdom of Jordan, *Statistical Yearbook*, no. 24, (Amman, 1973) Table II, pp. 2–3; for non-Israeli citizens in 1972 and 1976, Israel Central Bureau of Statistics, *Administered Territories Statistics Quarterly*, vol. VI, no. 3 (1976) Table A1, p. 1.

limbo, their citizenship not in doubt like those in the West Bank and Gaza, but their economic and social position very much in question.[22]

THE JEWEL OF THE EAST

There are virtually no Arabs employed in Israel's more highly skilled industrial occupations, and most of those who are employed in manufacturing produce import substitutes rather than valuable export goods. Nevertheless, this reflects not a lack of Arab skills, but rather the nature of Israel's export industries. The largest single export-earner is the diamond industry, which alone accounts for over 40 per cent of the total value of Israel's industrial exports. Its export sales in the 1970s were worth five times the value of those of citrus fruit, although this refers to gross rather than net earnings, as Israel itself is not a producer of diamonds, and the whole industry is concerned exclusively with the polishing of precious gems. In fact about one-fifth of the value added in the making of finished stones is undertaken in Israel, which means the industry earns roughly the same amount of foreign exchange as citrus exports.[23]

The diamond-polishing industry was originally established by Jewish immigrants who came from the diamond centres of Belgium and the Netherlands.[24] Due to the uncertain conditions in Europe in the 1930s when the Nazis were gaining strength, these skilled workers decided to migrate to Israel, but to continue their old jobs if possible. The workshops they established soon flourished, and by the 1940s the industry was firmly established. The skills were passed on to a new generation, and the trade expanded rapidly in the next two decades, so that by 1970 there were 450 establishments, employing almost 10,000 highly paid workers.[25] By that time Israel had already overtaken both Belgium and Holland as a diamond centre, accounting for one-third of the total volume of world exports and employment.

This industrial success owes nothing to any comparative advantage that Israel enjoyed by virtue of its geographical location, for transport costs are minimal in relation to the value of diamonds. Most of the diamonds are flown in from South Africa, and then processed in Israel before being re-exported to the main markets in Europe and the United States. Competitive forces are, in any case, not a major factor determining location in the world diamond industry, for most buying and selling is controlled by the London Diamond Syndicate. This accounts for over 40 per cent of world output through the De Beers Consolidated

Mines of South Africa, and purchases a further 40 per cent through contracts with the major independent producers. As long as the Syndicate is satisfied with the skills of those engaged in Israel in cutting and polishing, then the future of the industry seems assured. In addition an extra safeguard from Tel Aviv's point of view is that a majority of the people involved in the international diamond trade are sympathetic to Israel because of their religious beliefs.

The world diamond-processing industry is best viewed as imperfectly competitive, since the various major centres specialise in cutting and polishing different types of stones. Israel, for instance, is mainly concerned with medium-sized stones; while Belgium, which has the second largest industry, centred in Antwerp, processes smaller stones. The structure of the industry therefore represents a classic case of product differentiation. Israel, in fact, has a near-monopoly of international markets in popular medium-sized 'melees', since it supplies 85 per cent of the world's total output. In contrast to the lack of international competition, within Israel itself the industry is extremely competitive, especially as entry for new firms is so inexpensive, with the fixed investment per worker amounting to only $600.[26] As a consequence of diamond specialists leaving established firms to set up their own businesses, the number of workshops increased rapidly between 1970 and 1974, from the 450 cited earlier to 725. Tel Aviv remains the centre of the industry, with 210 firms, but other towns—including Jerusalem and Netanya, the birthplace of the industry in Israel—are growing in importance.[27]

The growth of Israel's diamond-processing industry has caused several favourable spin-off effects, with significant vertical linkages being established into higher forms of production in the capital goods field. Israel has become the major world centre for diamond tools, with four local firms supplying all domestic needs, as well as exports worth over $1 million annually. Diamond cutters made in Israel are used in all major centres throughout Europe and North America. In addition to these backward linkages, Israel's diamond industry has also established forward linkages embracing services and marketing. In 1974 a new diamond exchange was opened in Ramat Gan, near Tel Aviv, to which dealers from all over the world come to trade. Israel's financial institutions handle most of the credit and exchange arrangements for the country's diamond industry. The Union Bank of Israel specialises in this, handling two-thirds of the finance needed by the diamond trade, worth $1000 million a year. Bank officials have a specialist knowledge of the industry and its requirements, and the bank maintains representative offices in

Antwerp and Brussels. Local insurance firms also provide for the industry's huge requirements in this respect, with Ihud and Peltours doing much of the business. Israel has also become an international centre for apprentices wanting to learn the skills of polishing and cutting. Israeli firms not only train local personnel, but also teach apprentices from Belgium and the United States, who return to their own countries when the skills have been acquired.[28]

MASTER OR PUPPET?

Despite Israel's striking successes in industry and agriculture, the degree to which the country can ever be self-reliant is questioned not only by those Arabs who challenge the state's existence, but also by many loyal citizens of the country itself. Few economies in the modern world can exist in isolation, of course, and indeed international trade theory suggests that it is only through economic interdependence, and the resulting specialisation and division of labour, that living standards can be raised. This only underlines Israel's basic dilemma, because the founders of the Zionist movement did hope to create a self-reliant homeland, and this was the motivation behind movements such as the kibbutz settlement schemes. Yet, as has already been noted, some major sectors of the economy have become heavily dependent on non-citizen labour, while, with increasing education, Israelis themselves naturally do not want to undertake unskilled manual work.

Although this dependence on the outside world is a new phenomenon in the labour field, Israel had always relied heavily on foreign backing for its capital requirements.[29] Without substantial financial inflows, the country would have been in severe balance of payments difficulties, especially in the early years following independence, as Table 4·2 shows. In 1952 for instance, four years after the new state was founded, the import payments for goods and services, represented by the debit column of the table, were almost five times greater than exports receipts, represented by the corresponding credit column. This imbalance was however steadily being reduced in relative terms up to the early 1970s, though not in absolute values. After the October 1973 war the imbalance was again increased slightly, and by 1975 the debit item in the goods and services account was more than twice the credit item, as the table shows.

Fortunately for Israel access to external finance has been relatively easy, and the country has not had to dampen down its growth

TABLE 4.2. Impact of international assistance and restitutions on Israel's balance of payments

	1952	*1955*	*1960*	*1965*	*1970*	*1975*
Movements of capital ($ million)						
Credit	162	106	425	699	1158	3645
Debit	46	30	357	509	553	1453
Transfer payments including restitutions ($ million)						
Credit	192	214	315	330	678	1754
Debit	1	4	7	9	24	4
Goods and Services ($ million)						
Credit	86	144	336	711	1410	3827
Debit	392	432	682	1234	2650	7864
Total transactions balance (Credits = Debits)[a] ($ million)	440	466	1079	1752	3261	9321
Capital flows and transfer payments as percentage of total credits	80·4	68·7	68·9	58·7	56·3	57·9

[a] Allows for a small allocation of $15 million Special Drawing Rights in 1970, and net errors and omissions.

Sources: Statistical Abstract of Israel, no. 25 (1974) Table VII (1), p. 181; *Monthly Bulletin of Statistics*, vol. XXVIII, no. 1 (Jerusalem, January 1977) Table G.1, p. 21.

significantly merely to save foreign exchange, as the other non-oil exporters in the Middle East have been forced to do. In addition, as almost two-thirds of capital inflows have been of a long-term nature, there has not been the risk of speculative short-term outward movements, which can be an extremely destabilising influence on the balance of payments and exchange rate. Over one-third of the long-term capital financing has been in the form of loans from the United States government on extremely generous terms. The favourable interest payments on Israel's overseas debt are indicated by the relatively low debit item shown in the capital account of Table 4·2. Although these charges have grown in absolute magnitude, they still represent less than 40 per cent of capital inflows. In contrast many other Middle Eastern countries, especially those involved in the successive conflicts with Israel, such as Egypt, find that the service charges on money borrowed is crippling their economies.

Israel receives more developmental assistance from the United States than all the other countries in the Middle East taken together. The United States has even been prepared to hold large numbers of long-term bonds issued by the Israeli government, a privilege accorded to no other developing country. As well as this government funding there has also been substantial direct investment in Israel by private individuals, mostly American Jews, who are kept closely informed about the shares of companies quoted on the Tel Aviv stock market. This long-term private investment has accounted for around one-quarter of all financing over the period since the state of Israel was established.[30]

Details of the huge transfer payments which Israel receives are given in Table 4·2. These are partly accounted for by restitutions from West Germany, as compensation for the suffering which European Jews suffered as a result of Nazi persecution.[31] These restitutions are paid by both private West German institutions and the government, with the latter providing the major share. The rise in value of these payments partly reflects the appreciation of the Deutschmark *vis-à-vis* the dollar, which the figures in the table are cited in, but it also indicates the ever-increasing generosity of the West German Social Democratic Government on this issue. At a time when the grant element in aid is falling to developing countries generally, Israel stands out as an exception because of these payments, which involve virtually no servicing charge, as the debit column of the transfer account of Table 4·2 indicates.

As well as the restitutions, there has also been substantial West German direct investment, with German companies now owning over 420 million-Deutschmarks worth of assets in Israel, representing more than the total value of the rest of German investments in Asia taken together. Economic relations between the two countries are extremely close, with over sixty industrial firms in Israel involved in projects with German counterparts, including marketing links, sub-contracting, know-how agreements and joint research and development.[32] One manufacturer of men's clothing has closed down its West German production line due to high wage costs, which in 1976 amounted to $7 an hour per worker, and transferred the plant to Israel, where wages are only $1·25 per hour in the clothing industry. The main product, men's suits, is exclusively for the United States market. This type of employment transfer is the exception, however, as it would be wrong to view Israel as a country suited to labour intensive production techniques given its limited population.

In the Middle East oil-exporting states, governments and industry are interested in joint venture projects, where they supply the finance and a European or American firm supplies the technological know-how, often under a licensing agreement to manufacture a branded product. Israel, in contrast, chiefly wants to participate in joint ventures where it supplies the technology and the foreign partner supplies the finance. This reflects the advanced state of the country's existing industry, and the high level of technical competence of many of its workers. Israelis have been able to master a wide range of industrial techniques, from electronic computers to light engineering. Many of these industries have developed to serve the country's immediate needs for items such as agricultural machinery, irrigation pipes and plumbing equipment, etc.

Israel's largest industrial firm is Koor Industries, which ranks amongst the world's 100 largest firms. Amongst these companies its structure is unique, however, for it is wholly owned by the Histadrut, Israel's General Federation of Labour.[33] This organisation has 1,340,000 members, including skilled and unskilled workers and participants in co-operatives such as the kibbutzim and moshavim settlements. It is politically powerful, as it influences the decision making of the ruling Israel Labour Party. In addition it wields enormous economic power, for it directly employs 240,000 people through Koor Industries and Kupat Holim, the trade unions' own health organisation, which extends medical aid to almost three-quarters of the population of Israel. Koor Metals, the largest division within the Histadrut industries, makes a complete range of materials for the building industry, from wire mesh for concrete, to cranes. In addition it manufactures a large variety of machine tools.

Koor Industries also makes a large portion of the material supplies for the Israeli armed forces. It manufactures aircraft hangars, and provides aluminium and stainless steel components for the local aircraft industry. As a consequence of Israel's desire to be as self-reliant as possible in the provision of military equipment, industries such as aviation have been strongly encouraged by the government. Israel's victories in the 1956 and 1967 wars, and the holding operation in 1973, have to a large extent been due to its air superiority, but this has been with imported aircraft. However, the local aircraft industry is now producing military aircraft of its own, although these are transport aircraft rather than combat planes such as French Mirage and American Phantom jets, which remain the backbone of Israel's air force. Nevertheless, Israel has been so successful in aircraft production that one-quarter of all planes manufactured were sold abroad by 1976, bringing in foreign exchange worth $128 million.[34] Export of component aircraft parts to the United States, such as jet engine blades, is also increasing, and by the mid-1970s over 18,000 people were employed in the aviation industry. As well as exporting aircraft, Israel has also won foreign orders worth $250 million for its Gabriel missiles, and sales of electronic devices to detect infiltrators are also booming.

The military equipment industry is very specialised, and it makes economic sense for Israel to concentrate on fields where it has already achieved some measure of superiority over its competitors, rather than to diversify further.[35] This dilemma also applies to industry generally in a small country, and Israel's position in the diamond industry has already been noted. The country cannot easily hope to achieve the dominant position which it enjoys with respect to certain types of diamonds in other fields of economic activity. Yet unless it can identify comparable fields for specialisation, it is likely to be very vulnerable to world market conditions. As a major centre for citrus fruit exports, there is of course an awareness of this already, but no ready solution comes easily to hand.

Israel's trading position is becoming more vulnerable as a consequence of its becoming increasingly dependent on one external supplier, the European Economic Community, not all of whose members are as sympathetic to Israel as the United States is, for example. France in particular has substantial economic interests in the Magreb countries, while the EEC as a whole is very dependent on the Middle East oil exporters, and this means that they cannot afford to disregard the Arab boycott of Israel. The EEC certainly does not want to be accused of discrimination in favour of Israel, and therefore in trade negotiations concessions to both parties in the Middle East conflict have to be carefully balanced. Israel itself is in a weak bargaining position, for its exports to the EEC amount to less than half its imports. Free entry to the EEC market has been negotiated for Israel's industrial products, in return for a phased reduction of tariffs on the country's imports from Europe, but most agricultural produce is still subject to quota restrictions.[36] Israel's position is not dissimilar to Turkey's in this respect, as Chapter 6 shows. Like the Turks, the Israelis have experienced great difficulties in securing financial assistance from the EEC to help finance their trade deficit. Israel waited three years before receiving a $90 million loan from the European Investment Bank, as agreements with Egypt, Syria and Jordan had to be concluded first, but the loan represented less than one-seventh of the country's annual deficit with the EEC in any case.[37]

In trade as well as financial matters Israel therefore remains to a large extent dependent on the whims of the outside world. Given current trends it seems unlikely that the country will gain freedom of action in the economic sphere to match the degree of political autonomy it enjoys. Ultimately Israel's only hope of greater economic freedom would be the achievement of a Middle East peace settlement, and normalisation of its economic relations with its Arab neighbours. The country could be a major regional trading centre and, in exchange for finance from the oil surplus countries, could provide valuable technological know-how on water-resource management and other matters. In the Middle East context Israel could be a partner amongst equals, whereas as far as its current international economic relations are concerned, it must toe the line with the West to a large extent.

ılthough Dubai is increasing in im-
at more than 250,000 barrels a day.
'ith oil, production there starting in
ves will be comparable to those of
ited Arab Emirates are also richly

5 The Gulf: Absorption for

rves may be greater than any other
e Soviet Union. So far all of the gas
ing built to liquefy offshore gas into
ne. Other plants are planned to har-
habi and Dubai.
Qatar has been less than one-third of
ent years, as Table 5.1 shows. Ex-
atar, for before the Second World

The productivity of resources depenany, now British Petroleum, carried
mentary resources and of a market first exported in 1949, but the valu-
capital as it is of natural resourcesucing in the 1960s; yet now these are
cannot use all the capital to which re fields. Oil production has fallen in
there is an insufficiency of suitable nd the slackening in world demand.
employment of available funds and tent to see this reduction, since they
perience and skill. or import financing, and oil in the

P m of asset-holding. Qatar is follow-
The Economics of started conservation policies from
oil price rises, as Table 5·1 shows. In
is still expanding, as Dubai and

Kuwait, Qatar, Bahrain and the Unihey can perhaps one day rival Abu
enced during the last two decades one c lower Gulf.
formations the world has ever seen. Th
becoming affluent consumer societi
expensive and sophisticated material LITY
has to offer. Their enormous purchasin
capita gross national product levels, tlthe Gulf states resemble those of the
UAE during 1976 being $15,480 and $ica and Australia in the days of the
of the level of even the United States, tury, with the dramatic inflow of
GNP *per capita* is $14,400, these three er spending, the outflow of profits
countries in the world, if GNP is takenuction boom. Admittedly, the new
wellbeing. Only Bahrain, which unl more permanent than those of the
producer of crude oil, has a more modhe authorities fear that in the long-
$2410, but using this criterion of devs like their predecessors of a century
categorised with the developed countrs anywhere of communities whose
nation.[1] tation of one mineral resource that
The remarkable levels of economic omic transition once that resource

became depleted, or was no longer in demand. In the light of this experience the future for the Gulf must be extremely uncertain, especially as the environment is so unfavourable in every respect, apart from the availability of energy supplies.

Sceptical commentators suggest that to see what the future will be like without oil it is only necessary to examine the Gulf states in the past, when they were mere trading outposts, with a few local marine-based economic activities such as pearling and fishing. Although this view may be rather harsh, any consideration of possible economic diversification should certainly start by examining the traditional non-oil activities, since this indicates where the comparative advantage of the region lies.

Before the advent of the oil industry, pearling was the most valuable source of economic activity in the Gulf, especially in the late nineteenth century and the first two decades of the present one. Kuwait, then a small fortified coastal settlement of 60,000 people, had 800 boats which engaged in pearling in the major grounds of the Gulf from May to September each year, when the waters were warm and calm. Over 15,000 men were engaged in pearling, representing someone from almost every family, and by the 1920s the annual revenue from pearling exceeded $1 million.[6] Bahrain rivalled Kuwait as a pearling centre in terms of employment and revenue, while Qatar, Abu Dhabi and Dubai all had pearling fleets of over 300 vessels, and even Sharjah and Ras al Khaymah had 150 vessels each. The total revenue of the Trucial States from pearling in 1905 was estimated at $600,000, a substantial sum given the small populations of the area.[7]

The pearl merchants amassed large fortunes over the years, with buyers coming from India and Paris at the end of each season to select the best pearls for their rich clients. The rulers of the various Gulf sheikhdoms, emirates and sultanates also did well, for they levied a tax on every boat dependent upon pearling as its main source of revenue. This renenue was used by the rulers to consolidate their positions, partly through the purchase of small arms, but also by recruiting more law-enforcement officers. In contrast the divers and other crew members on the pearling boats received little for their efforts, in spite of all the dangers the work involved, and many were hopelessly in debt to the merchants.

The pearling industry did, however, have favourable effects in stimulating other local activities, boat building being the outstanding example. Kuwait was the main centre for this ancillary industry, with the sailing craft becoming increasingly sophisticated, until vessels of up to 300 tons were made. Boat building was a highly specialised activity, with skilled woodworkers and sailmakers engaged solely on their particular tasks. At first the boats were made from planks sewn together with fibre rope, but later nails started being used. Craftsmen in Kuwait specialised in nail manufacture, which came to be used for doors as well as boat construction. Today the decorative nail doors manufactured in Kuwait are found not only in the Gulf area, but throughout the coastal littoral of the Indian Ocean.[8]

Unfortunately for the Gulf states the pearling industry collapsed in the early 1930s, causing severe economic dislocation throughout the Gulf, and substantial losses of income. Boat building virtually ceased, there was a considerable amount of unemployment, and ports such as Sharjah were allowed to silt up. The collapse was partly caused by a slump in the main Western markets during the great depression, but a more important factor was the development of cultured pearls by the Japanese.[9] It was obviously considerably cheaper to produce pearls in oyster farms in shallow coastal waters rather than send boats and divers out long distances to search for natural pearls. Although there were plans for developing cultured pearls in the Gulf, nothing came of them, for by the time these had been discussed it was already too late to go into the cultured pearl business, since the Japanese had acquired complete domination of Western markets.[10]

This experience with pearling highlights the vulnerability of economies dependent on a single product. Apart from the vicissitudes of world markets, there is also the danger of competition from a new supplier. As many of the older people in the Gulf remember the slump in pearling, because they themselves were affected, there is a widespread awareness that petroleum could bring similar problems. Now, fifty years after the collapse of the pearling economy, the Gulf states are even more dependent on a single commodity than before, and as the boom resulting from the petroleum exports in the 1970s is many times the scale of the earlier one, the effect of any substantial slump would be economically catastrophic.[11]

Admittedly world demand for petroleum appears to be more inelastic than the demand for pearls, which was both highly price- and income-elastic. Nevertheless, as the experience of the mid-1970s shows, a fall in income in the West does have demand repercussions for the Gulf oil producers, and the high prices prevailing since 1974 have intensified the search for substitutes. Apart from the search for new energy forms in the West, there is also a desire to reduce dependence on Arab oil. The boycott of 1973 imposed on the United States and the Netherlands in the aftermath of the Ocober war prompted extensive oil exploration outside the Middle East. The rulers and government ministers of the Gulf oil states are of course aware of this, and, given the historical precendent of pearling, it is scarcely surprising that there is a desire to lessen dependence on oil as a source or revenue.

DIVERSIFICATION AT A PRICE

Unlike other developing countries the Gulf states have no problem in finding the funds to finance diversification. Instead, their main problem is to discover suitable projects to back, as the prospects for import substitution are unpromising given the limited extent of the local market for most consumer items.[12] In addition, as a result of the new affluence, local tastes have become so sophisticated that only the advanced industrial countries of the West can provide the consumer goods in popular demand, which require complex technology and considerable expertise. Prospects for export promotion appear equally unfavourable in most fields, for there are few lines of production in which the Gulf enjoys a comparative advantage, due to its harsh desert climate, shortages of labour and unfavourable location in relation to most of the world's major markets.

Agricultural prospects are obviously extremely poor in the Gulf as a result of the scarcity of rainfall. There are few lands suitable for farming in Kuwait, and less than 1 per cent of the state's total area is cultivated, most of it lying in the Jahrah Oasis.[13] Vegetables are the main produce, meeting about one-eighth of local market requirements, and recently cultivation has been extended using distilled sea water. This is proving more expensive, however, than the cost of importing vegetables by air freight or road from Europe, even allowing for high transport costs. Diversion of fresh water from the Shatt al-Arab in Iraq was proposed by the Baghdad government, which could prove a cheaper source of water supplies. Despite its economic attractions this scheme is unlikely to be implemented, as the Kuwait authorities have reservations on political grounds about becoming dependent on Iraq in any way.

Bahrain and Qatar each have about 4000 people engaged in agriculture. Unfortunately farming in Bahrain is declining due to a lowering of the water table and rising salinity as a result of too many wells being drilled. In Qatar, in contrast, agriculture is flourishing under centralised control from the Department of Agriculture, which prohibits competitive well drilling. Before 1960 there was no farming in Qatar, but the state has been fortunate, for hydrological surveys of the peninsula have revealed reasonable amounts of ground water. As a result of this being utilised at relatively low cost, the country has become completely self-sufficient in vegetables, with small export surpluses going to Bahrain, Kuwait and the UAE.[14] Cereals are now being produced for the first time to the north of Doha and by the 1980s Qatar may be self-sufficient in these as well. Prospects for dairying are also encouraging, with a herd of Australian Fresians providing milk for local consumption.

The most favourable environment for agriculture in the Gulf is the Emirate of Ras al Kaymah, as it receives some winter rainfall due to its proximity to the Hajar Mountains.[15] Over 15 per cent of its territorial area is cultivated, mostly fruit and vegetables, and a successful experimental farm inland at Digdogga has been running since 1955, which is now an agricultural training school. Alfalfa is grown for animal fodder, and grade cattle have been cross-bred with indigenous stock to produce animals well suited to local conditions. The most ambitious but expensive agricultural project in the UAE is on the island of Sadyat off the coast of Abu Dhabi where a market-gardening centre has been established consisting of huge plastic greenhouses which cover half the island.[16] A wide variety of vegetables are grown; but the cost is high. Undeterred by this, however, the Abu Dhabi government is financing another similar scheme at Mazaid, 125 miles south of the coast.

Historically fishing has been more important than agriculture in the Gulf, in terms of both the value of output and employment. Over 9000 people are employed today in this industry, with Kuwait being the major centre for fish and shrimps; but the industry is also of economic significance in Bahrain, Qatar and the UAE. Fish is a major item in the local diet of the Gulf, with an average *per capita* annual consumption of 30 kilos, three times the world average, although well below Japanese consumption levels.[17] Despite its high consumption the Gulf is self-sufficient in fish, and there is a surplus which is exported to East Africa and India. As fishing is carefully controlled to preserve stocks, the industry appears to have a more promising future than was apparent in the late 1960s when fish and shrimp stocks were becoming depleted. This was the result of competition between Kuwait's three major fishing companies, but in 1972 these were merged into the United Fisheries of Kuwait. As far as fishing is concerned a strong case can be argued for monopoly control over trawling rights. The United Fisheries has an annual catch of 10,000 tons, about half of which is exported, earning over $5 million annually. In collaboration with a Japanese company,

Nissho-Iwai, it has established a subsidiary venture, which is the biggest shrimping company in the world.[18]

Dwindling inshore stocks have harmed the fishing industry in Bahrain and Qatar, but in the latter a major shrimp industry has been established in collaboration with the Ross Group of the United Kingdom. Shrimps worth $3 million are exported, mainly to Japan, from a modern refrigerated storage and processing plant located in Doha. The inshore fisheries of the United Arab Emirates are better stocked than those of Bahrain and Qatar, and Spanish mackerel, sardines and tuna are caught to meet local market demand. Ras al Khaymah, Ajman and Um el Quaiwain are major centres, with over one-third of the population engaged in fishing in the latter two emirates. The fishing potential is particularly promising off the Batina coast facing the Indian Ocean, where the Emirate of Fujaira is located. Fish are more abundant in the Indian Ocean than in the Gulf, and a much wider market is available. Fujaira may well become a major fishing centre serving not only the UAE, but also more distant export markets.[19]

Compared with the relatively modest costs of building up traditional economic activities such as fishing, the costs of diversifying into modern industry are extremely high. It is only in activities related to petroleum, such as refining and petrochemicals, that the Gulf states have a comparative advantage. Needless to say all petroleum exporters want to set up refineries, since this means that there is more value added locally than is the case with crude oil exports alone. Kuwait has the world's first all-hydrogen-operated refinery at Shuaiba near the oil pipeline terminal. Major products apart from hydrogen include light and heavy diesel, sulphur and kerosene, most of which are exported. Being a capital-intensive operation, the refinery employs only 648 people, of whom a mere 81 are Kuwaitis.[20]

Bahrain's refinery is the largest in the Gulf, with 250,000 barrels of oil processed a day, compared with 135,000 barrels in Kuwait. Most of the oil processed comes from Saudi Arabia, as Bahrain's own oil production is small, and had declined to an average of only 55,000 barrels a day by 1975.[21] As a consequence the refinery has become a more important source of export earnings than crude oil itself. As refinery operations date from 1936, shortly after oil production commenced in Qatar, a considerable amount of local experience has been built up, and most of the staff employed are Bahraini. The only other refinery operating in the Gulf is located in Qatar, but this processes a limited 6000 barrels of crude oil for local consumption.[22] Two further large refineries are being built near Abu Dhabi, one with a capacity of 230,000 barrels a day, but their prospects seem doubtful given the surplus of refinery capacity worldwide.

Apart from operations such as Qatar's, refining in the Gulf makes little sense economically, for it is cheaper to export crude oil in bulk than many separate products, some of which like sulphuric acid, present major transportation difficulties because of their dangerous nature. Economically the case is overwhelming for locating refineries near centres of consumption rather than of production, and only states with enormous surplus revenues such as Kuwait could have afforded to back this type of extravagant project which yields such low returns on the capital invested. The same cannot be said, however, of the gas liquefication projects being undertaken in Kuwait, Qatar and the United Arab Emirates, as although these are even more costly than the refinery ventures, they are utilising a byproduct of crude oil extraction which would otherwise be flared off as waste.

Kuwait's $1000 million liquefied petroleum gas plant being built by Kellogg International will have the capacity to produce 5 million tons a year of butane, propane and natural gasoline.[23] Shell and the Qatar Gas Company started a similar project in 1974, worth $250 million. In addition an ethylene plant is being built for $500 million in Kuwait and a comparable, but smaller-scale, venture is being undertaken in Qatar, worth $150 million, in association with French interests. At Jebel Dhara near Abu Dhabi a huge $1,200 million gas liquefication plant is under construction, but, with Kuwait's coming into production first, prospects for marketing the gas from this additional plant seem dubious. There is little doubt that the lack of co-ordination in the Gulf over industrial projects has led to considerable wasteful duplication, and lowered the returns on investment for all parties concerned.

THE DISECONOMIES OF COMPETITION

The new dry docks provide the most outstanding example of competition amongst the Gulf states resulting in the emergence of considerable excess capacity. It is difficult to argue an economic case for even one dry dock in the Gulf, as there is excess capacity in Europe and Japan for tanker maintenance and repairs. There is in any case less chance of a malfunction occurring in a tanker in the outward unladen run to the Gulf, than in the return trip. Therefore locating dry docks in Europe or Japan seems technically best. Nevertheless in 1971 at the height of the boom in tanker traffic to the Gulf, with the Suez Canal closed, the

Organisation of Arab Petroleum Exporting Countries decided to back a dry dock project in Bahrain.[24] Once the project got past the planning stage it gathered its own momentum, and work started in 1974 before the Suez Canal was reopened. By 1977 the project was completed at a cost of $300 million, the construction work largely being carried out by migrant Korean workers. Though it is capable of handling vessels of up to 500,000 tons, its future looks extremely uncertain, and it seems unlikely that the money invested will ever be repaid.

The Bahrain project is greatly overshadowed by the eonormous Dubai dry docks scheme, which seems certain to cause ruinous competition. Work on the Dubai scheme started in 1973, and by 1980 it aims to provide one of the largest ship repair facilities in the world. Three dry docks are being built, one capable of handling tankers of up to 1 million tons, while the others can each handle 500,000-ton tankers simultaneously. In total 4000 workers will be employed, provided the labour can be found.[25] The initial costs were estimated at $185 million, but given the way the cost of the much smaller Bahrain dock has escalated, it seems the final bill could be several times that amount.

Dubai's investment in a new aluminium smelter seems as dubious as the dry docks scheme. This equally massive project was started in October 1975 at a cost of $400 million, although it is almost certain that this will rise substantially by 1981 when the plant reaches full capacity. Admittedly it is economically advisable to site aluminium smelters near a cheap energy source, as this accounts for a large proportion of the total processing cost. Once again, however, the problem is that there is already excess aluminium smelter capacity in the world, and the venture in Dubai is merely duplicating the smelter in Bahrain, started much earlier, in 1971.[26] Due to a depression in the aluminium market the western shareholders in this company decided to cut their losses and sell their shares back to the Bahrain government. The smelter in Bahrain is admittedly producing almost at its rated capacity, but this is only by cutting its prices to such an extent that only variable costs are covered. If this policy continues the fixed costs of the Dubai smelter certainly will have little chance of being recovered.

Bahrain is not the only country in the Gulf to resent Dubai's investment strategy, as the authorities in Qatar have also come to fear competition from this troublesome emirate. Qatar has embarked on the constuction of a large iron and steel complex at Umm Said, confident that it will be the only producer in the Gulf.[27] Kuwait had contemplated a similar project, but abandoned the idea, as it would have meant issuing more work permits to immigrant labour and upsetting the country's population balance. As heavy transport costs mean that imported steel is expensive in the Gulf, the Qatar authorities believed that even if their 400,000-ton plant was less efficient than Western producers', they could still sell most of their output below Western prices. Unfortunately Dubai has committed itself to building a similar 300,000-ton steel complex at Jebel Ali, using sponge iron imported from India.[28] It seems unlikely that both plants can survive economically and the construction of this second plant may spell ruin for both operations.

A large portion of the steel from both plants is intended to fulfil the local demands of the construction industry. The building boom in the Gulf has resulted in wasteful duplication in other fields, which will worsen the effects of the recession in the construction industry when it eventually occurs. Large-scale cement plants, for example, have been built in Kuwait, Qatar and the United Arab Emirates. The multiplication of plants in the Emirates alone is startling, although the first plant at Ras al Khaymah, with an annual capacity of 250,000 tons, only started operation in 1975, others are now being built at Al Ain, Dubai and Sharjah. Only Kuwait's construction industry is well placed to survive intact a building recession, since it is more diversified, producing prefabricated buildings for possible export, as well as bricks, asbestos and concrete. Paint for builder's suppliers is also manufactured in Kuwait, but nowhere else in the Gulf.[29]

Other examples of duplications in the Gulf abound, from fertiliser plants geared to exporting in Qatar, the United Arab Emirates and Kuwait, to import-substitution activities such as flour milling and soft drinks manufacture. In all these cases the problems are the same; short production runs, high fixed costs in relation to total costs and no economies of scale. Awareness of these problems has led to increasing calls for some form of economic integration in the Gulf,[30] but the various countries are unwilling to forget past differences and plan their economies on a co-ordinated basis to avoid duplication. The economic and political rivalry from the past continues up to the present day. Both Qatar and Bahrain, for example, refused to become part of the United Arab Emirates after the British withdrawal from the Gulf in 1971. Within the United Arab Emirates itself it seems impossible to get agreement for any overall economic strategy concerning which industry should be located where.

The rivalry in the Gulf embraces not only industrial activity, but is also apparent in commerce and banking. A substantial increase in banking operations was to be expected in the Gulf following the oil boom, as financial institutions were needed to handle the surplus funds, and find profitable investment outlets both internally and overseas. Traditionally the Beirut banks played a major role as financial intermediaries in the recycling of oil funds to the West, but the advent of the Lebanese civil war meant that funds either had to be placed directly in the West, or channelled through local banks in the Gulf. The five Kuwait commercial banks are the most established in the Gulf, with the National Bank of Kuwait, founded in 1952, now the largest independent bank in the Arab world. These banks for the most part handle local funds, though a major portion of their assets are in foreign holdings, estimated at $2308 million in 1976.[31]

The growth of banking has been phenomenal in the lower Gulf, with Qatar, Bahrain and the United Arab Emirates all competing as offshore banking centres. Bahrain and Qatar have been very selective in the type of banks to which licences have been granted, preferring the large American and European multinationals to smaller fringe undertakings with dubious financial records. Unfortunately similar caution was not exercised in the United Arab Emirates, which until 1975 encouraged all applicants.[32] As a consequence the Emirates have become overbanked, with the largest number of banks in the world per 1000 people, apart from notorious offshore centres like the Cayman Isles. By 1975 Dubai had 86 authorised banks, Abu Dhabi 76, Sharjah 43, Ras al Khaymah 20, and the remaining three Emirates 35 between them.[33]

The UAE Currency Board has found it extremely difficult to control banking in the Emirates. Yet controls are needed in the interest of sound finance, otherwise fringe bank operations could undermine confidence in the entire financial system. The banks frequently found that in the past they could more easily get permission for new ventures from the local rulers of the Emirates than from a centralised authority such as the Currency Board. Sheikh Rashid, for example, permitted the newly established Dubai Islamic Bank to build offices along his creek before the Currency Board gave its approval. Clearly more control is needed if the UAE are ever to prosper as a major financial centre. Competition, if unchecked and without well defined rules, can easily lead to economic ruin as far as banking is concerned.[34]

RICHES FOR SOME

The oil boom in the Gulf has brought in a flood of immigrants from all over the Arab World, and from non-Arab countries across the Indian Ocean, particularly India and Pakistan. Although the labour requirements of the oil industry itself are relatively limited, due to its capital-intensive nature, as the various Gulf states have spent their revenues on local development and diversification, an acute shortage of labour has emerged. This occurs not only in skilled occupations, but even in unskilled jobs in industries such as construction. In addition, as education, health and social services facilities are improved in the Gulf, with all the countries under consideration becoming modern welfare states, this has led to increasing demand for such personnel as teachers, doctors, dentists, nurses and administrators.

The impact of this immigration on the population structure in the Gulf has been enormous, with foreigners outnumbering local nationals throughout the area.[35] Table 5.2 shows the national origins of the immigrant population of Kuwait, which has the most reliable census data in the Gulf. Non-Kuwaitis account for over half of the state's population and this total would be much higher if there were not rigorous controls on immigration and the allocation of work permits. Amongst the non-Kuwaitis the majority are Arabs, with Palestinians forming the largest group. Most of the residents with Jordanian passports are of Palestinian origin, as well as many of those holding Lebanese nationality. Egyptians have obviously been attracted to Kuwait by the high salaries in comparison to those in their own country, especially in the 1970s, as the table indicates. The percentage of Iraqis has declined, but not the absolute numbers, although these migrants are often political refugees rather than people seeking improved financial remuneration.[36]

The immigrant population structures of the other Gulf states are not dissimilar to those of Kuwait, although in the lower Gulf the Indian and Pakistani presence is more in evidence. In Qatar over 84 per cent of the country's total active workforce are immigrants, including virtually all of those in skilled jobs. Bahrain has a slightly smaller proportion of foreign workers, but they still account for two-thirds of the active labour force according to the official returns, which are based on the number of work permits issued. Many immigrants enter illegally, of course, especially in the United Arab Emirates, where official figures for immigrants are meaningless. Prospective migrants from India and Pakistan are usually willing to pay enormous sums to owners for a passage across the Indian Ocean to some quiet beach in the Gulf which customs officials never visit. Often the owners cram into the vessel as many as possible, which makes the crossing hazardous, and it seems likely that many have perished on these voyages.

Despite the high wages there is a considerable amount of unrest amongst the immigrant population of the Gulf, although feelings are

TABLE 5.2. National origins of Kuwait's immigrant population

	1965		*1970*		*1975*	
	Number	% of total population	Number	% of total population	Number	% of total population
Jordan and Palestine	77,712	16·6	147,696	20·0	204,178	20·5
Egypt	11,021	2·4	30,421	4·1	60,534	6·1
Iraq	25,897	5·5	39,066	5·3	45,070	4·5
Syria	16,349	3·6	27,217	3·7	40,962	4·1
Iran	30,790	6·6	39,129	5·3	40,842	4·1
India	11,699	2·5	17,336	2·3	32,105	3·2
Lebanon	20,877	4·5	25,387	3·4	24,776	2·5
Pakistan	11,735	2·5	14,712	2·0	23,016	2·3
Saudi Arabia	4632	1·0	10,897	1·5	12,527	1·3
Europe and North America	4332	0·9	5672	0·7	5025	0·5
Total Arab non-Kuwait	187,923	40·2	312,849	42·4	419,187	42·1
Total non-Arab	59,357	12·7	78,417	10·6	103,562	10·4
Total non-Kuwait	247,280	52·9	391,266	53·0	522,749	52·5

Source: Kuwait Ministry of Planning, Central Statistical Office, *Annual Statistical Abstract* (1976) Appendix Tables 31–2.

seldom expressed, since all non-citizens fear being expelled. In none of the states are the immigrants allowed to own property, which means that they have to pay high rents for accommodation owned by citizens. As migrants cannot own property they are unable to benefit from programmes such as the Kuwait government's land purchase scheme whereby small plots are bought by the government at many times their market value as a means of redistributing oil income to local citizens.[37] Without being able to own property, non-citizens find it difficult to get started in their own businesses, and consequently in Kuwait over 70 per cent of non-citizen earnings is accounted for by wages and salaries, but under 54 per cent of citizen earnings.[38]

Non-citizens are entitled to some welfare benefits, such as free local phone calls in the case of Kuwait, where discrimination between users would be, of course, impossible. Medical treatment is also free, for if the immigrant population caught infectious diseases which were untreated, then these could spread to the indigenous population. Immigrants do have to pay, however, for the education of their children, which is often expensive in the Gulf. It is interesting to note that whereas Kuwaitis only spend 2·9 per cent of their total earnings on education, non-citizens spend 6·4 per cent on this item alone.[39] This figure is surprising, for many migrants leave their children behind in their home country, where school fees are generally lower or non-existent. The immigrant population are particularly resentful about this discrimination in education, as they are generally more literate than the local citizens, with under 29 per cent of non-citizens illiterate in the case of Kuwait, while over 44 per cent of citizens were still illiterate in 1975.[40]

Faced with high costs of accommodation and expensive education, migrants often decide that they cannot afford to bring their wives and families to the Gulf. This obviously creates social problems, especially for non-Moslems, who are less at home in an all-male society. Crime rates are low amongst non-citizens however, for the risk of expulsion means that migrants are keen to stay out of trouble. Nevertheless it does seem that with such large, disgruntled immigrant populations there is the possibility of widespread social unrest erupting into serious disorder eventually. As long as the oil boom lasts and wages keep rising this can be avoided, but any slowing down in the rate of growth could cause problems, even if it were restricted to one industry alone, such as construction.

The authorities in all the Gulf states are aware of the potential problems posed by large numbers of migrants. Awareness by itself does not nevertheless solve the basic dilemma, as by restricting immigration the states of the Gulf will effectively lower the absorptive capacities of their economies. In this case the opportunity for local development and diversification will be foregone, and instead the only alternatives will be either to invest in assets abroad, or else conserve petroleum resources and retain real assets rather than paper securities. Kuwait has definitely opted for the latter, by combining conservation with investment in long-term overseas holdings, which have good growth potential. The lower priority accorded to domestic development is illustrated by the decision not to proceed further with the development of heavy industries such as iron and steel. In contrast Qatar and the Emirates, particularly Dubai, are gearing their economies towards industrialisation, which implies an ever-increasing dependence on migrant labour. Given these contrasting strategies, the Gulf promises to remain a fascinating area for the outside observer, and at some future date it should be interesting to see how the upper and lower Gulf compare, economically, socially and politically.

6 Turkey: a Question of Alignment

Only the distant future can show whether Ataturk has managed successfully to graft his country's history on to that of Europe, or whether his career will be still another proof that Asiatic history is but a series of anecdotes untouched by any principles of ordered growth.

H. E. Wortham, *Mustapha Kemal of Turkey* (1930)

Until the nineteenth century Ottoman Turkey was the dominant power in the Middle East, with an empire which covered 4·7 million square kilometres, including most of the area dealt with in this present study, with the notable exception of Iran. Southward from the capital, Istanbul, the empire extended through Syria and Mesopotamia (Iraq) to the shores of the Arabian peninsula in the east, while to the south it encompassed the entire Mediterranean littoral from Palestine to Egypt. The Empire included the oldest established centres of settled agriculture in the world, the Nile Valley and the Tigris-Euphrates Valley, where the original Garden of Eden was said to be located. To the north the Ottoman territories extended through the Balkans to southern Yugoslavia, and included Greece, Turkey's ancient and modern rival.[1]

The Ottoman hold on this vast territory was seriously weakened, however, partly by internal instability, but more importantly by the growing strength of the major European industrial nations. Consequently, at the time of the outbreak of the First World War, which was to prove disastrous for Turkey, the Ottoman Empire had already been reduced to under 40 per cent of its previous size. After the war, and the subsequent conflict with Greece, more territory was lost, and today Turkey covers only 776,980 square kilometres, less than 17 per cent of the land area of the Ottoman Empire. When considering the prevailing attitudes in contemporary Turkey, it is important not to forget this Ottoman inheritance, and just how great the Empire once was before the inevitable collapse.

THE ASHES OF EMPIRE

Economic factors above all else accounted for the downfall of the Ottoman Empire. The economic structure could best be described as feudalistic, and the attempts to encourage industrial development following the 'Young Turks' revolution of 1908 proved futile. In 1913 there were only 269 factories in the whole Empire, employing less than 17,000 workers, and most of these were concerned with either food processing or textile manufacture.[2] Agriculture accounted for most economic activity. Yet the ownership of the basic means of production, land, was extremely inegalitarian. This ownership pattern undoubtedly stifled incentive, as the majority of the rural population were landless labourers, who had no hope of obtaining a stake in any agricultural progress there might have been. Incentive was further weakened by the large fluctuations in world market prices for the Empire's main export items, tobacco and cotton. Landlords saw little point in expanding production under conditions of falling prices, and even they felt themselves at the mercy of economic forces beyond their control.

Against this economic background, the new Turkish Republic which was established out of the remains of the Ottoman Empire appeared to face an extremely bleak future. Fortunately, at least it secured international recognition of its present territorial area with the Lausanne Treaty of 1923, which was much more favourable than the Treaty of Sèvres three years earlier, which ceded Istanbul and the Bosporus to League of Nations control. Under the Lausanne Treaty Turkey was, however, expected to pay the victorious Allies in the First World War a total of almost 130 million Turkish gold pounds, in yearly amounts of £8·60 million. Most Turks considered it unfair that the Turkish Republic, which comprised only part of the Ottoman Empire, should have been expected to pay off almost the entire debt burden, apart from a small amount Syria and Iraq agreed to finance. These payments, and disturbances caused by the massive exodus of Greek settlers from mainland Turkey in the 1920s, crippled the economy in the early years of the Republic.[3] Unfortunately, just when the first signs of economic recovery started to appear, the international economy was entering the Great Depression of 1929. This adversely affected the prices of Turkey's agricultural exports, which exacerbated the country's already serious foreign exchange situation.

The disappointing performance of the Turkish economy during the early years of the republic prompted the government to play a growing role in running affairs than hitherto. Kemal Ataturk, the new national leader, wanted to Westernise his country as quickly as possible, and industrialisation was seen as a key part of this strategy. The weakness of the Ottoman Empire was blamed on its feudalistic economic structure, and the reliance on agriculture. At the same time, despite government encouragement, no enterprising indigenous entrepreneural class emerged during the 1920s, although industries such as textiles and food processing which had been destroyed during the war and its aftermath were re-established. Apart from this, however, there was little industrial expansion, so Ataturk decided that the state would have to undertake industrial investment itself.

Turkey therefore became the first state in the Middle East to draw up a five-year development plan.[4] In doing this it was conscious of the progress being made by its northern neighbour, the Soviet Union, with economic planning. It was natural that the Turks should note the similarity between the two countries with regard to the meagre economic inheritance which both post-revolutionary governments had to build upon. Relations between Turkey and its northern neighbour were in fact cordial during the 1930s, and the Soviet Union made an interest-free loan of $8 million to the Ankara government in 1932 for industrial development, to be paid back over a twenty-year period. The economic philosophies of the two governments differed sharply, however, since in the Soviet Union all the basic means of production were in public ownership, whereas in Turkey private investment was encouraged as much as possible, although state institutions were established to finance ventures that promised little immediate profit. In Turkey it was the market mechanism, however, which still played a major role in the allocation of resources, a task performed by the Soviet state, as the Turkish first five-year plan, drawn up in 1933 to come into operation the following year, indicated. The government set the targets, but it had no direct powers of enforcement as far as the private sector was concerned.[5]

One of the main provisions of the plan was for the establishment of an iron and steel industry at Karabuk, where major iron ore deposits were believed to exist, and just 100 kilometres south of Zonguldak, the location of the country's richest coal deposits. Turkey's coal industry had been in production since 1848, and made a significant contribution to export earnings. During the 1930s, the industry expanded rapidly, doubling production by 1939, the year in which Turkey's first steel mill started operating and the plant for processing coke for the mill was opened. Unlike the coal industry, however, the steel industry experienced severe difficulties in meeting production targets, some of the blame for which must be attributed to Turkey's lack of experience with heavy industry. The problems were accentuated, it turned out, by the industry's location, which unfortunately proved less advantageous than originally envisaged. Local iron ore deposits proved insufficient for the industry's needs, and the country's richest iron ore deposits were discovered in distant eastern Anatolia, over 1000 kilometres away. In these circumstances the iron and steel plant came in for heavy criticism, and the image of the country's planners was tarnished, perhaps undeservedly, for they could not have envisaged the problems with iron ore supplies from the information they originally had at their disposal.[6]

Despite the problems with iron and steel production, Turkey's first five-year plan was undoubtedly a useful exercise, not least because for the first time it enabled the country's politicians to see the choice which had to be made with regard to development strategy. At the same time the constraints on development were highlighted, the most critical of which was the question of finance. The industrial investments planned proved much more expensive than originally envisaged, with expenditure on new projects soaring from 44 million Turkish lira to 100 million Turkish lira during the course of the plan. Because of its strategic position, however, Turkey was able to raise most of this money through foreign loans, and the British in particular were keen to advance credit to counter the growing influence of Nazi Germany in the area. As a result of this financial provision, Turkey's traditional industries, including cotton textiles, woollens and earthenware, were expanded considerably, and the chemical industry was diversified.[7] Encouraged by this modest success, the government drew up a second five-year plan, but unfortunately it came into operation just on the eve of the Second World War, and had to be abandoned as expenditure on security took precedence over development. By then at least the Turkish Republic was firmly established, however, and given Kemal Ataturk's tremendous achievements in transforming the country politically and socially, and the measurable, if more limited, economic successes, there were few remaining who regretted the passing of the Ottoman Empire.

BRIDGE OR DIVIDE?

Turkey's geographical position means that it is often regarded by

Europeans as the gateway to the East, while to a lesser extent it is seen by the peoples of the Middle East as the most Westernised country in their region. Only 1·3 per cent of the territorial area of the Turkish Republic lies in Europe, and in many ways the country still has more in common with its Middle Eastern neighbours than with the West. Undoubtedly modern Turkey is much more Westernised than the Ottoman Empire ever was, especially as a result of the sweeping social reforms introduced by Ataturk in the early years of the republic, including the use of Latin instead of Arabic script for writing, and the introduction of Western dress. Politically the country has a multi-party system, which few other governments in the Middle East would tolerate, and there is a degree of freedom of expression, especially in the press, which is not found elsewhere. The majority of the Turkish people retain their Moslem religion, however, and share the cultural traditions of their eastern neighbours. Politically relations with Iran, and even Syria, are much better than those with Greece, even though Turkey is a fellow member of the North Atlantic Treaty Organisation.

Although the Turkish Republic made an early start with development planning, still its standard of living and economic structure correspond much more closely with those of the less developed countries of the Middle East, than with its more prosperous European neighbours. Turkey's *per capita* income amounts to only $880 less than two-fifths of that of Greece, and less than half of that of Bulgaria, as Table 6·1 shows. Of all the countries in Europe only Albania has a lower level. In comparison to other Middle Eastern states, however, Turkey compares more favourably, as its *per capita* income is three times the Egyptian level, and well above that of Syria. To the east, Iran can boast double the Turkish figure, but this is accounted for by the country's oil wealth, for rural living standards are roughly comparable.

In terms of its occupational structure Turkey differs sharply from most of the rest of Europe, for it still has 64 per cent of its population engaged in agriculture, and less than 15 per cent in industrial employment. In comparison Greece has only 36 per cent in agriculture, and over 28 per cent in industry. Even Turkey's Middle Eastern neighbours have a lower proportion of the economically active population in agriculture: in Syria less than half are employed in this way, while in Egypt the proportion is below 55 per cent. Care must be taken, nevertheless, in interpreting these figures, for Turkey has a higher proportion of females in its enumerated workforce, most of them engaged in agriculture. Social indicators, however, also illustrate Turkey's relative backwardness, which means inadequate health and education facilities. As

TABLE 6. 1. Turkey and its neighbours: some economic comparisons

Country	*Population 1973* (thousands)	*Growth in population 1960–73* %	*Per capita GNP* (U.S$.)	*Growth rate 1960–73* %	*Proportion of agriculture in GNP* %	*Proportion of industry in GNP* %
Turkey	37,930	2·5	880	3·9	26·3	20·2
Greece	8930	0·5	2320	7·3	17·3	20·5
Bulgaria	8622	0·7	1590	4·7	20·7	52·3
Soviet Union	249,750	1·1	2030	3·6	18·4	52·7
Iran	32,136	3·2	870	6·4	11·6	51·5
Syria	6948	3·3	400	3·8	21·0	22·8

Sources: Population and GNP data from *World Bank Atlas* (Washington, 1975), except for Turkey and Greece GNP, where 1975 figures are quoted from OECD, *The Member Counties Development Indicators* (Paris, 1975). Detailed comparisons between Greece and Turkey can be made using OECD data. As the other states are non-OECD members, less comprehensive World Bank data must be used. Other data from UN, *Monthly Bulletin of Statistics*, vol. 30, no. 11 (November 1976) Table 64, pp. 205–11.

there are insufficient maternity hospitals, for example, most children are born at home, which is reflected in an infant mortality rate of 153 per 1000 live births, compared to a figure of 21 for Greece. Surprisingly Egypt, despite its poverty, has a lower infant mortality figure of 101 per 1000 live births. Illiteracy is also widespread in Turkey, with almost 40 per cent of the post-school age population unable to read or write, according to recent census statistics.[8]

It is apparent that in spite of the efforts of Ataturk and his successors to Westernise Turkey, there is still a long way to go before the gap between its living conditions, and those pertaining in Europe, can be bridged. Turkey's economic performance in the last three decades has been insufficient to raise living standards even to those prevailing in the countries of south-east Europe, although many different types of development policy have been tried. The economic history over the period provides an interesting case study of how the internationally accepted conventional wisdom with regard to development strategy breaks down when applied. When this happened the government followed new sets of guidelines, generally in line with the latest thinking on development, which in turn became the conventional wisdom, only to find these would not work either. As successive Turkish governments,and the political parties, endlessly debated different policies, all that really seemed to change rapidly was the policy itself, while the country changed much more slowly. Admittedly, however, in the absence of reliable economic indicators, it is difficult to quantify exactly what development did occur.

Rises in average *per capita* income figures do not necessarily imply that poverty is being eliminated, for instance they may merely reflect increasing incomes for the richer classes, while the majority are as impoverished as before. In Turkey income distribution remains extremely inegalitarian, both inter-personally and inter-regionally. Almost one-third of all households earn less than \$600 per annum, while three-quarters earn less than \$1500. In contrast the richest 2·5 per cent of all households earn over one fifth of the total national income. Most people in Turkey may have experienced rising living standards, but the gap between rich and poor is probably as wide as ever. Regional income disparities are equally marked, with the average *per capita* incomes in Istanbul city and Izmir almost two and a half times greater than those of eastern Anatolia. In the latter, family incomes only average \$1000,[9] although of course care must be taken when comparing declared income figures from agricultural areas with those for urban workers in enumerated employment.

During the years of the Second World War the economy marked time, as 60 per cent of government expenditure was allocated to defence: but once the conflict was over this proportion fell, and the authorities again turned their attention to development. As a result of their previous experience with planning, and the poor performance of industry under these plans, the government decided to concentrate its attention instead on agriculture, in order to improve living standards in that sector in which the majority were actually engaged. This emphasis on balanced growth was in line with the thinking of such distinguished theorists in the development field as W. Arthur Lewis, and Jan Tinbergen, and the latter actually spent a while in Turkey as an advisor. No longer was there to be any attempt at allocating resources to particular industries such as iron and steel, at the expense of other industries and sectors, as the Russians had done under Stalin, and as Turkey had done in the 1930s as already mentioned.

Agricultural output fell between 1939 and 1945 by almost one-quarter as resources were devoted to the war effort. Immediately after the conflict agrarian reform measures were announced in an attempt to boost agricultural production to former levels, as well as to ensure a more even income distribution in the rural areas. Accordingly, a ceiling of 500 hectares was introduced on private holdings, but this was never properly implemented due to the weakness of the administration at local level in rural areas. Agricultural production as a consequence rose only slowly, and it was 1950 before pre-war levels were achieved again.[10] Soon after this, nevertheless, the situation improved dramatically with the Korean War boom in world commodity prices, which resulted in Turkish agricultural output almost doubling, in response to the dramatic rise in the price of cotton, tobacco, fresh fruit and vegetables, the country's main cash products. This boom was to prove short-lived, however, for production slumped again in 1954 as prices fell, and it was only in 1959 that the output figure of six years earlier was exceeded. These fluctuations illustrate that it is prices which are the main determinant of production, and that structural charges have relatively little effect. The experience of the 1960s and 1970s bears this out, as production expanded by the modest rate of just over 3 per cent on average during this period, although there were very large annual output fluctuations due to changing market conditions and variations in weather.

With attention directed to agriculture, industry was neglected in the immediate post-war period. By the time the authorities again tried to encourage the development of manufacturing in the 1950s, deflationary measures, and the uncertain political climate until the military takeover, undermined business confidence. In the 1960s planning was again embraced as a tool of economic policy to encourage industrialisation, and this time it was to prove much more successful than the earlier attempts in the 1930s. The first five-year plan covering the 1963–7 period aimed at 7 per cent per annum growth, an ambitious target given the country's previous poor development performance. To the surprise of many the target was almost achieved, as growth over the period averaged 6·7 per cent, while in the second plan period, 1967–74, there was still a respectable growth rate of 6·5 per cent on average each year.[11] This decade witnessed major structural changes in the Turkish economy, for although agriculture remained the main source of employment, its share of gross domestic product fell from 38 per cent to below one-quarter. At the same time the growth of industry was rapid, averaging 11 per cent per annum, and progress was particularly marked in the intermediate and capital goods sectors, which by 1975 accounted for over half of the total value of industrial production.

Virtually all these new intermediate and capital goods industries are in the public sector, whose share of industrial output has risen to over 40 per cent. Industries wholly under public ownership include steel, petroleum, fertilisers, paper and petrochemicals, but there are also some state enterprises in the sugar, textile, chemical and cement industries. These industries are primarily geared to the domestic market, and are heavily protected behind infant industry tariffs. Apart from textiles and cement, unit costs in production tend to be high, largely due to the infant nature of the industries, although the state does run many at a loss so that the local industries they are supplying are not placed in an uncompetitive position as a result of high input costs. There is little doubt that but for state intervention most of these new capital and intermediate goods industries would not have been established, as the prospects for profitable investment were unfavourable, especially in this kind of technologically advanced industry where there was a complete absence of appropriate local skills.[12] Nevertheless, the industrial alternatives were equally unpromising, for the domestic market for consumer goods such as textiles was already saturated, and the prospects for exporting were poor since the EEC, the country's main market, has severely restricted quotas on textiles.[13]

Yet textiles are Turkey's most competitive industry, for the country's low wage levels keep down costs in this type of labour-intensive activity. Consumer durables such as electrical goods are more capital-intensive, but Turkey is a higher-cost producer, and therefore despite the relatively free acess into the European market that consumer durable goods enjoy, the country is unable to compete successfully. At the same time the domestic market for consumer durables is limited by low purchasing power, and the market is so restricted without export outlets that production runs are inevitably short, which means little advantage can be taken of economies of scale. Faced with these market constraints on the country's existing industry, the Turkish government realised that further industrialisation could only come about through diversification into new lines of production, rather than through the expansion of established plants.

The EEC decided to assist this diversification policy rather than grant trade concessions to Turkish exports which might hurt European industry. Aid was seen as preferable to trade, and consequently funds were made available through the European Investment Bank to help new Turkish industries, which were geared primarily to the domestic market.[14] Turkey had signed an association agreement with the EEC in 1964, which provided for its eventual accession to the community after a lengthy transition period of thirty-one years.[15] The EEC therefore felt obliged to take some action to aid Turkish economic development, so that the gap between its living standards and those of the community might be narrowed. It seems unlikely, however, that the limited amounts of low-interest loans made available through the European Investment Bank will make a major contribution in this regard. In reality these are little more than a sop to Turkey, as the EEC was less than enthusiastic about the original agreement in any case. The EEC was in fact virtually forced into making the 1964 agreement, since it did not want to be accused of discriminating in favour of Greece, with which closer economic links were sought in order to strengthen the Community's foothold in the Mediterranean.[16] As both Greece and Turkey were NATO members, the United States tried to ensure that the Europeans did nothing through discriminatory economic action which might undermine the Western alliance in a strategically important area.

The European Community's lukewarm response to Turkey's association is illustrated by the dispute over agricultural imports into the EEC. Turkey is allowed to export limited amounts of a few of its traditional crops under a quota agreement with the EEC, which covers tobacco, sultanas, hazelnuts and dried figs, and since 1976 these have entered free of duty. The market for these goods is restricted, however, and Turkey would like to capture a share of the lucrative Community market for fresh vegetables and olives. Italy strongly objects to any further concession to Turkey on these items, for it dominates the European market, and its agricultural producers do not want to see their prices eroded by competing imports from Turkey. Therefore the Turks are left with only a few concessions on specific goods, and in many respects they are in a worse position than those Third World countries who signed the Lomé convention with the EEC, which entitles them to a general system of preference on their exports, including tariff reductions on a much wider range of goods than the Turks enjoy.

THE PRODIGAL RETURNS

The greatest strains in Turkey's relations with the EEC have arisen over the question of immigrant workers.[17] During the decade 1964–74 there was a fivefold increase in the number of Turkish immigrants working in the European Community, and by 1974 there were almost 500,000 resident in West Germany alone, the main host country. Remittances to Turkey also dramatically increased, until by 1974 they were worth over \$1420 million, compared with a mere \$8 million ten years earlier, as Table 6.2 shows.[18] The value of these remittances was equivalent to 90 per cent of the total foreign exchange receipts that Turkey earned from the export of visible goods, which is an indication of their significance to the balance of payments.

As a result of the recession in European industry in 1974 following the oil price increases, unemployment in West Germany started to rise and the Turkish immigrant workers found themselves, perhaps not surprisingly, the first to be made redundant. No additional Turkish workers were taken on by European industry, and those returning to Turkey, whether voluntarily or as a result of redundancy, were not replaced. Consequently the level of remittances to Turkey fell by over \$100 million in 1975 and an even steeper fall of \$330 million occurred in 1976, instead of the expected rise. Naturally the Turkish government has become alarmed at this sudden fall in these valuable foreign exchange earnings, especially as the country is already in severe balance of payments difficulties.

Turkey's visible trade deficit in 1975 with the EEC amounted to a staggering \$1575 million, as Table 6.2 illustrates, over seventy times greater than the deficit in 1963. The country's negotiators with the EEC have pointed to this alarming trend with some justification as evidence of the discriminatory treatment they have been given by the Europeans. Since this current account deficit is no longer made up by remittances on the capital account, the Turkish lira has suffered as a result of the inevitable pressures. Between 1975 and 1976 it fell from 13·85 to the dollar to as low as 18·5 lira to the dollar. Over the same period the country's foreign currency reserves sank by almost half, to below $900 million, only sufficient to cover just over two months' imports.

Paradoxically this decline in the value of the Turkish lira makes the immigrant workers reluctant to remit to Turkey any more than the minimum necessary to keep their families back at home. The workers naturally prefer to hold their earnings in Deutschmarks or other strong European currencies, as they believe that the longer they wait before converting the further the Turkish lira will depreciate, and the more favourable the exchange rate will be for them. The Turkish authorities have of course become aware of this problem, and in 1975 introduced a convertible lira deposit scheme to attract the savings of the expatriate workers. This scheme provides interest rates three times higher than those offered by West German banks, and workers can convert deposits back to a European currency after a minimum of six months, at the same rate of exchange which prevailed when they opened their accounts. Despite this guarantee against depreciation, however, the

TABLE 6.2. Turkey's payments with the EEC (in $ million)

Year	*Visible trade deficit with the nine*[1]	*Workers' remittances to Turkey*[1]	*EIB Loans to Turkey*[2]
1964	22·2	8·1	0
1965	18·1	68·8	5·5
1966	91·2	115·3	61·0
1967	108·7	92·4	33·0
1968	181·2	107·4	22·1
1969	131·2	140·6	36·0
1970	143·1	273·0	0·6
1971	262·6	471·4	10·0
1972	424·7	740·2	0
1973	543·2	1183·3	65·0
1974	990·9	1426·3	82·9
1975	1575·5	1312·3	N/A

Sources: (1) *Middle East Economic Digest*, vol. 20, no. 42 (London, October 1976) pp. 23 and 25; (2) Data computed by the author from EIB, *Report of the Activities of the European Investment Bank in Turkey 1964–74*, (Luxemburg, 1974).

suspicious expatriate workers still prefer to keep their excess savings in West Germany, which they regard as a much safer bet for the future.[19]

If more of these emigrants workers' savings could be harnessed for development projects in Turkey instead of adding to the already swollen deposits of West German banks, there would be less need for the Ankara government to go, cap in hand, to the various international aid institutions. Turkey's position *vis-à-vis* the EEC would be strengthened, and the country would be less dependent on lending bodies such as the European Investment Bank.[20] Unfortunately only a minute portion of those earnings which are actually repatriated find their way into productive investment in the industrial sector, or even in agriculture. The funds mostly go into home improvement, as the immigrants try to bring their village houses up towards the kind of standard they have seen in Europe. Rather than invest in agricultural improvement, the immigrant workers prefer to use their earnings to purchase additional land to expand their farms, since land ownership confers prestige in rural Turkey. The migrant workers thus become absentee owners, unable to farm their new holdings themselves, and consequently land is either rented out, or else their wives undertake the farming. The wives, however, are already usually tied down by large families, and find themselves unable to farm the land properly in the limited time they have available after working in the home. The landless labourers remaining in the rural area, or peasants with small holdings, who could farm the land more intensively, seldom can, for they cannot afford to purchase additional land due to the escalating land prices resulting from the purchases by immigrant workers.[21]

Similar perverse economic trends emerge in the urban areas when immigrant workers remit their savings, as these are usually invested in apartments or other residential property, which only causes inflation of accommodation prices. Once again these remittances only result in the growth of rentier income in Turkey at the expense of productive income from domestic economic activity. The few workers who do invest in business in Turkey tend to favour service activities such as retailing, for many want to run their own small businesses when they retire from factory work in Europe. A large number of the taxis which operate in the major urban centres are owned and operated by retired immigrants. It is this kind of one-man business activity which has expanded most rapidly in recent years in Turkey.

There are few private financial institutions in Istanbul or Ankara, in any case, which could attract the savings of the migrant workers. Merchant banks have not yet developed, and there is no proper stock exchange in Turkey corresponding to those found in the major Western financial centres.[22] Financial brokers do advertise shares in the press, but there is no register of these firms, or government control, and immigrant workers are usually suspicious, probably with good reason, of such services. Most finance for Turkish industrialisation therefore comes through government channels, as has already been mentioned.

Returning migrants are just as unwilling to work in Turkish industry as they are to invest in it. Wages are low, and conditions poor in comparison to West Germany, and most expatriate Turks regard this type of employment in their own country as a demotion. This is unfortunate, for often the migrants have acquired useful industrial skills in Europe, and these are in scarce supply in Turkey. Ironically, West German firms investing in the country often find it more difficult to recruit skilled Turkish labour than they do in West Germany itself. The migrant workers often come from rural Turkey, however, and for them it does not matter whether they reside in Istanbul or Essen, because they will still be separated from their families. At least in Western Europe most companies provide the immigrants with accommodation, usually at subsidised rates, whereas in Turkish cities this can present a major problem.

The migrant workers are often the most able people of the rural areas they leave, usually those with some education, and perhaps even a skill. Their migration represents a real brain-drain from Turkey's point of view, and it is unfortunate that there is no transfer of skills back to the country again. As long as this transfer remains a one-way process, the value of migration to the Turkish economy must be open to question.[23] Against the favourable effect on the balance of payments, there must be offset the perverse effect on income distribution through the transfer from productive to rentier activity, as well as the adverse effect on the domestic labour market. In retrospect the European recession of the mid-1970s, and the halt to the inflow of migrants, may in the long-run be in Turkey's economic interest.

7 Iraq and Syria: Revolution Without Renaissance

> The ideal form of government for . . . Mesopotamia and Syria at their present stage of development is, in my opinion, a benevolent patriarchate, which consists and is to a certain extent dependent on public opinion, but which retains executive control.
>
> H. W. Young, *Memorandum on the Future of Mesopotamia* (1919)

Political factors are often observed to be of paramount importance in determining the pace of economic development, and nowhere in the Middle East is this better illustrated than in the case of Iraq and Syria. During the 1950s and 1960s both countries experienced frequent domestic political upheavals, often of an extremely violent nature, and the consequent policy changes and attendant uncertainty hardly provided favourable conditions for economic advance. The lack of continuity was demonstrated by the ambitious development plans that were being adopted by each incoming regime, only to be scrapped or changed out of all recognition by succeeding governments. Under such unstable conditions, planners found it impossible to take a five-year time horizon, when it was difficult even to be certain from one annual budget to the next.[1] Government employees found themselves always trying to fit in with the policy whims of their political bosses, and this could take up a major part of their working hours. At the same time the countrys' rulers, preoccupied with their own immediate survival, scarcely had time to deal with more than the most pressing current issues, and seldom looked far ahead.[2]

Admittedly, Syria has enjoyed a period of firm government since 1970 and the coming to power of President Assad, but unfortunately the new stability in the country's leadership is not reflected lower down, as there have not only been frequent changes of government ministers, but also of departmental personnel in the civil service. In Iraq all promotion is determined by political allegiance, not only in the civil service, but also in education, and even in the major state-owned industries. Yet there is little reason to suppose, for instance, that the politically acceptable will be the most competent industrial managers. In fact, given the large numbers of well-educated and experienced Iraqis who live in exile in the Gulf and elsewhere, it would seem that the country has lost many of its most able people, while those left are often inexperienced and incompetent.[3]

Political affiliations also play a part, of course, in determining promotion in many of the states of eastern Europe, including the Soviet Union. In Baghdad and Damascus there are those who argue that as this system of appointments has not had a detrimental effect on those communist states, why should it have adverse consequences for Arab Socialist countries? Party members, government spokesmen assert, are more in tune with the thinking of the people and share their aspirations. The problem in Iraq and Syria is not however, merely, one of party membership. In the Soviet Union the communist party is broadly based, and up and coming managers often join the party, even if they are politically apathetic, to enhance their position; but they play no part in party politics. In Iraq and Syria, in contrast, membership of the Baathist parties is far from being nominal, for members are expected to play an active role. There are also several tight cliques within the parties which constantly jostle for power and position. It is often through such jostling that positions in the state sector get allocated. There is an unfortunate mix of ideological and personality factors which all too often results in the incompetent rising rapidly into powerful positions, where they can take decisions that do real economic harm. In a period of rapid change it was inevitable, in any case, that it would take time to work out the most appropriate form of administrative organisation and determine how much power should be left with the individual decision-maker.[4]

REVOLUTIONARIES VERSUS THE OIL MONOPOLY

Iraq is in a much better economic position than Syria, as it is a major oil exporter, ranking fifth amongst the Middle Eastern producers, and accounting for around one-twelfth of the region's total production. Oil was first exploited in the late 1920s, but it had little impact on economic activity until the early 1950s, for the volume of production remained small.[5] Since then there has been an impressive rise in production, though the constant disputes with the oil companies following the revolution of 1958 have undoubtedly held down the rate of expansion. Initially prices were the main area of dispute, as the major Western oil companies had acted monopolistically to reduce prices in the 1950s, putting the interests of the consuming nations and oil sales before those of the Middle East producers. Negotiations with the Iraq Petroleum Company, which had sole exploitation rights over all oil deposits in the country, made little progress, due to resistance from its owners, BP, Royal Dutch Shell, Companie Française Petroles, Standard Oil of New Jersey, Mobil and the Gulbenkian family.[6]

The new revolutionary government of Iraq under Kassim soon realised that the country would not get a better deal for oil on their own, for if they tried unilaterally to increase prices the oil companies could merely switch production to other countries where lower prices prevailed. It was, after all, the breakdown of negotiations between the Iranians and the Western oil companies in the early 1950s, that had prompted the companies to expand operations in Iraq as an alternative source of supplies. With their revolutionary government pressing for more and more concessions, many Iraqis feared it would be their turn to lose out. To avoid this Kassim convened a meeting of major oil-exporting countries to discuss the pricing issue, and this resulted in the formation of OPEC the Organisation of Petroleum Exporting Countries in September 1960.[7]

For the first decade of its life OPEC was largely ineffective due to disagreement amongst the oil exporting countries about what kind of bargain should be struck with the oil companies. Iraq and Iran were both in agreement for once in wanting to push up prices and their own production as far as the market could bear, but the less populous countries such as Saudi Arabia and Kuwait, with lower revenue requirements, resisted all moves designed to radically alter the *status quo*. Despite the obvious danger of production switching in the absence of concerted OPEC action, the Iraqis decided to go it alone, and try to control all oil operations within their territorial jurisdiction. Accordingly Law no. 80 was passed in December 1961, restricting the Iraq Petroleum Company's concession to 0·5 per cent of its former area.[8] This measure was less radical than it appeared, however, as most of Iraq's oil production was concentrated in this limited designated area. The main consequence of these measures seems to have been that new exploration for oil was almost halted completely in Iraq, with the international oil companies concentrating their efforts in Kuwait, exactly the type of switching the

Iraqis feared.

In order to exploit other areas of the country outside the Iraq Petroleum Company's 0·5 per cent concession, the government decided in 1962 to set up a state-owned venture, the Iraq National Oil Company.[9] Western multinational oil interests were reluctant to help this new state-owned company in case it set a precedent for other countries, and the Iraqis found they were unable to undertake oil exploration and production themselves since they lacked the necessary technical expertise and experience. After the overthrow of the Kassem regime in November 1963, the new government decided to grant further exploitation concessions to the Iraq Petroleum Company in return for agreement with the Western petroleum companies to establish a new joint-venture company, the Baghdad Oil Company, of which the Iran National Oil Company would hold a one-third share, while European and American companies would hold the remainder, and thus have majority control. Not surprisingly, in view of the political climate in Iraq, this agreement could not be pushed through parliament due to opposition from those on the left, who accused the government of a sell-out to Western monopoly interests. The regime collapsed in 1967.[10] This was followed by several months of instability but in 1968, when the Baath Socialists came to power, they decided to let the Iraq National Oil Company undertake exploration and production independently of the Western companies. Consequently the joint-venture agreement was scrapped, and the Iraqis turned to the Soviet Union for technological assistance in oil production with the Iraq National Oil Company.

The Soviet Union was much less efficient in oil production than the Western companies, and in practice little new exploration and production was undertaken. Operations by the Iraq National Oil Company in the Qayyarah field in the north of the country compared unfavourably with those in the remaining Iraq Petroleum Company's concession areas, which still accounted for the bulk of the nation's oil production. As a consequence of these difficulties in dealing with the Russians, and the poor prospects for the state oil company, the government decided that some fresh action was needed. In 1972 the Revolutionary Command Council therefore passed an order nationalising the oilfields in the north of the country owned by the Iraq Petroleum Company,[11] but at the same time sought to reach an agreement under which the Western oil companies would provide the technological expertise needed by a new state company, the Iraqi Company for Oil Operations. At first the Western companies resisted, but by then the whole climate in the Middle East for their operations was changing, as nationalisation measures were being discussed and enacted even by the conservative Arab states. The oil companies finally agreed after OPEC mediation in February 1973 to purchase and market oil from the Iraqi Company for Oil Operations, in exchange for lucrative contracts for provision of management services and equipment for the country's petroleum industry. In 1975 the agreement was extended to cover the remaining oilfields at Basra in the south, including offshore exploration which only the Western companies had the expertise to carry out.

Table 7·1 shows how oil production has expanded since the 1950s, when Iraq became a major world producer.[12] The expansion in the 1960s was more modest than it might have been given the buoyant demand conditions prevailing in Western markets, and the boom in production elsewhere in the Middle East where the companies found a more favourable political climate in which to operate. The table admittedly does show a rise in the value of petroleum exports over the 1960–70 period but the figures are expressed in money terms, while in real terms, allowing for inflation, there was no rise. Even in money terms in some years, such as 1967, there was a fall in exports, but this was due to the closure of the Suez Canal as a result of the Six-Day War, as well as because of the temporary suspension of oil pumping through the Syrian pipeline.

Iraq's heavy dependence on oil is illustrated by the high proportion of export earnings accounted for by this one commodity, and this dependence has increased since the oil price rises of 1974, as the table shows. Fortunately for Iraq its oil export receipts cover all of its import requirements, and, even though there was a rise in import payments in relation to oil revenues in the early 1970s, the situation could scarcely be described as worrying, and the country has in fact stayed out of balance of payments difficulties ever since the exploitation of oil on a large scale.[13] Although the country experienced no trade gap, there was often a budget deficit, and the government did worry constantly about its own financing, which was also largely dependent on oil revenue. The government's expenditure programme had to be kept in line with the fluctuations in oil revenues, and it is interesting to note that between 1965 and 1972 there were four years out of the seven when government expenditure had to be cut back substantially, even in money terms. The worst periods were 1965/66 and 1971/72, when, as Table 7·1 shows, oil revenues fell appreciably as a proportion of government revenues, and the authorities had only a very restricted tax base to fall back on as an alternative to oil revenue.[14] It was undoubtedly these domestic financial considerations rather than the balance of payments that prompted

TABLE 7.1. Importance of oil in the economy of Iraq

	1 *Exports of crude oil* (in millions of dinar[a])	2 *Oil as a percentage of total exports*	3 *Import payments as percentage of oil receipts*	4 *Oil revenue as percentage of total government revenue*
1951	64.6	55.3	78.9	56.5
1955	182·2	87·8	66·4	64·8
1960	224·8	92·8	71·7	62·9
1965	306·9	90·5	67·6	54·6
1966	327·1	89·8	67·6	57·5
1967	285·7	89·9	64·1	60·2
1968	352·0	90·3	54·6	60·8
1969	355·0	90·2	57·8	56·2
1970	365·5	90·2	64·7	66·3
1971	487·5	91·7	64·4	62·5
1972	453·4	90·1	64·9	54·0
1973	744·6	92·0	51·4	71·4
1974	2154·8	94·9	32·5	92·6
1975	2592·1	95·1	N/A	N/A

[a] 1 Dinar = $3·38 (1977).

Sources: Columns 1–3: IMF, *International Financial Statistics* (Washington, May 1976) pp. 204–5 and 420–1. Column 4: Oil revenues: OPEC, *Annual Report* (1976); non-oil revenue: Central Bank of Iraq, *Bulletin*, no. 3 (July-September 1976) Table 14, p. 25.

successive Iraqi governments to try to get a better deal from the oil companies.

BIRDS OF A FEATHER FLOCK TOGETHER?

Iraq's northern neighbour, Syria, had as its main source of petroleum revenue until the mid-1970s the pipeline dues from Iraq and Saudi Arabia. Tapline, with an annual capacity of 24 million tons, carried Saudi Arabian crude oil to the Mediterranean port of Sidon in Lebanon through Syrian territory.[15] In addition a pipeline from northern Iraq ran to the Syrian port of Banias, with a branch going to Tripoli in Lebanon. In accordance with Syria's socialist principles, the state-owned General Petroleum Authority controls all petroleum operations, including a refinery at Homs which processed Iraqi crude oil for the country's domestic requirements.[16] The constant disputes between Iraq and Syria over royalty payments and wider political issues have, however, led to frequent closures of the pipeline, the latest being in 1977, and these have threatened the refinery.

Fortunately, Syria's own oil production has now expanded, and the refinery has been converted to handle the heavier, locally produced crude oil. After the refinery was damaged in the 1973 war by the Israelis the Syrians decided on this policy to make themselves more independent even of their supposed allies on the Arab side. This was just as well, as Iraq is no longer dependent on Syria for oil transit purposes, since it has opened a new pipeline through Turkey, and another strategic line from its northern oilfields to the Gulf coast. All these new pipelines were unnecessary, of course, as they merely duplicated existing facilities. As there has been no significant expansion either in Iraq's oil production, or in overseas demand, the pipelines must be viewed as a gross misallocation of domestic resources. They illustrate the price which Iraq and Syria pay for their constant wrangling, which seems puzzling to the outside observer, as political parties with the same name and professing the same ideology govern in both Baghdad and Damascus.

Since 1974, in Syria oil has replaced cotton as the country's main export item, with a total income amounting to over $650 million per annum.[17] This admittedly is only equivalent to Iraq's oil earnings in the 1950s, but it has nevertheless made an extremely useful contribution to Syria's hard-pressed foreign exchange position. Production for export only started in 1970, but the real breakthrough came between 1973 and

1975, when oil output doubled. The substantial OPEC price increases at that time made Syria's heavy crude oil an attractive proposition economically, although more costly to produce than other Middle Eastern petroleum. Foreign oil companies are now undertaking extensive exploration both onshore and offshore under licences provided by the state-run General Petroleum Authority.[18] Like the Iraqis the Syrians were dissatisfied with the technical advice the Soviet Union gave on drilling in the 1960s, especially at Rumailan. Now the oil exploration is carried out by Yugoslav, Romanian and French companies, and the General Petroleum Authority puts out tenders to competitive bidding, rather than relying on bilateral negotiations with a single partner as hitherto.

Syrian oil production is expected to double once again by 1980 and, with production levels reaching 210,000 barrels a day, it has become eligible for OPEC membership. The Organisation of Arab Petroleum Exporting Countries (OAPEC) has proposed Syria's accession to OPEC, though it is ironic that it is the conservative states such as Saudi Arabia and Kuwait who have supported the Damascus government the most, while Iraq, despite its similarity of political outlook, has been in opposition throughout. In OPEC itself there is also opposition from the non-Arab states, who do not wish to see an increase in Arab membership, unless perhaps there is at the same time an increase in other members. In reality they have little to fear from Arab solidarity, given the strains in inter-Arab relations as exemplified by the constant squabbling between Iraq and Syria.

ONE STEP FORWARD, TWO STEPS BACK

In both Syria and Iraq the majority of the population are engaged in agriculture. Of all the measures the revolutionary regimes in Damascus and Baghdad carried out, it was the land reforms that were therefore of potentially greatest significance as far as the ordinary people were concerned. In Syria, prior to the agrarian reform measures, half the cultivated land was farmed in large holdings of over 100 hectares, while only 12 per cent was made up of individual holdings of less than 10 hectares. Yet it was reliably estimated that 82 per cent of the rural population was either landless, or else owned the holdings of below 10 hectares.[19] The situation in Iraq was even more inegalitarian, with two-thirds of the farmers owning less than 3·3 per cent of the cultivated land, while the greatest area of land was made up of farms of over 4000 hectares of cultivable land. The five largest owners in fact possessed more than 400,000 hectares each.[20]

Despite this inegalitarian land distribution there was surprisingly little rural discontent in either country, with the farm workers on the large estates and the smallholders never thinking to question the *status quo*. This may have reflected the fact that most of the landlords lived on their properties, and fewer had moved to the cities than was the case in Egypt, for example. The landlords performed some useful services for the tenants, by providing agricultural inputs such as seeds and farm implements. In addition, in both countries the large landlords were usually tribal leaders, who provided their tenants with protection against neighbouring warlords. They ensured that water supplies for agriculture were not interfered with by outsiders, and arbitrated in disputes between tenants over irrigation. As the Ottoman Empire declined, the central authorities could no longer perform these functions and, in the case of Iraq, even when it was under British administration, the Baghdad government never succeeded in exercising effective power at the local level in the rural areas. As well as their economic and defensive functions, landlords also acted in a social capacity, by helping to arrange marriages, and gave loans for dowries, and not just for the more directly productive purposes associated with agriculture. Rural society in Iraq and Syria was therefore extremely conservative, and cut off from the outside world. Everyone was assigned a role, that of the landlord being to a large extent paternalistic.

The first attempts at land reform came at about the same time in both Syria and Iraq, but in neither country did they stem from rural agitation.[21] In Syria the first land reform measures were passed in 1958, following the union with Egypt, but these were largely due to the initiative of President Nasser rather than of the Syrians. It was felt that if there was to be a United Arab Republic in more than name only then similar statutes would have to be enacted for all its constituent parts. As Egypt had already introduced sweeping land reform measures in 1952, following its revolution, Nasser obviously could not allow feudalistic land-tenure arrangements to remain in Syria. Consequently the maximum limit on landownership was reduced to 80 hectares of irrigated land, or 300 hectares of non-irrigated land, with amounts over this to be expropriated by the state for redistribution. Landowners were compensated by non-negotiable bonds, bearing 1·5 per cent annual interest, which were to mature in forty years.[22]

In Iraq in the same year similar legislation was passed stipulating that the maximum land holding for any individual should not exceed 250 hectares of irrigated land, or 500 hectares of rain-fed land. The reform was introduced by the new revolutionary government not primarily to benefit the peasants, however, but to break the political power of the feudal landlords who backed the old regime. Kassim and his associates were from the Western-educated urban middle classes, who knew little of rural problems or agricultural organisation. Consequently they did not appreciate the adverse implications that the reform measures would have for agricultural production or the economy in general. Although over 1 million hectares were expropriated under the 1958 reform, by 1970 one-eighth of the land was still waiting to be redistributed. Many of the 66,000 beneficiaries were army officers or party officials who received land as a result of their social positions, rather than because of any farming ability or experience.[23]

Not unnaturally, agricultural output in Iraq suffered considerably as a result, especially cereal production, and consequently the country had to import a major portion of its food requirements, instead of being, as it had since Babylonian times, an agricultural surplus nation. Irrigation systems fell into disrepair, since those allowed to farm the land for the government between its expropriation and redistribution had no interest in the long term. Farmers, like other investors, will not maintain the capital stock—and certainly will not add to it—merely for someone else to derive the benefit. Unfortunately, in any case the beneficiaries often lacked the knowledge to keep the irrigation systems working, and much land became salinised, and therefore worthless, as drainage from the fields was neglected. In spite of these reversals the Iraqi government has been pressing on with further land reform measures which were introduced in 1970 providing for the redistribution of a further 1,250,000 hectares.[24] It seems that the government's desire to increase its power of patronage through being able to make land grants comes before any consideration of agricultural economics.

In Syria the 1958 land reform measures were carried out in a similar way to those in Iraq, with only 148,440 hectares redistributed by 1961 out of the 670,212 hectares expropriated. In that year the union between Syria and Egypt collapsed, and the incoming conservative government in Damascus under Manouf Dawalibi halted the reform. However, once the Baath Socialist party took control in 1963 it reinstated the 1958 act, and by 1970 over 1,500,000 hectares were expropriated, of which about half were redistributed.[25] In contrast to Iraq, much of the land redistributed went to collective settlements rather than individual families. The Syrian authorities feared that if the large estates were broken up there would be diseconomies, and production would suffer. In the event agricultural production fell, anyway, for the collective settlements were mismanaged, since there were few Syrians with the organisational abilities to run such institutions. The new farm managers boasted paper qualifications, but they were obviously not as familiar with the land they controlled as the former owners had been. Where fixed wages were paid, there was a lack of incentive for workers to put in the long hours which farming demands, yet the various incentive schemes attempted were abused, and they appeared to many as an open invitation to corruption.

Despite the problems with the collective settlements, the Syrian Baathist government's enthusiasm for socialist forms of organisation in agriculture remained unabated. By 1974 over 14 per cent of all cultivated land in Syria had been allocated to large state farms,[26] modelled on their Soviet counterparts. To any outside observer this seems strange, for the Russian experience with state farms is scarcely encouraging, as the country's dependence on the West for grain imports shows. In Syria scarce investment resources have been used to purchase expensive agricultural equipment such as combine harvesters. Such equipment admittedly raises labour productivity, but at the same time it means fewer employment opportunities in agriculture, which is unfortunate given the shortage of alternative jobs. A strong case can be argued for investment instead in innovations which raise output per hectare rather than output per farm worker, with funds used to purchase fertilisers or improve water utilisation and drainage, and where machinery is needed, to provide small tractors. This type of policy could help make Syria a major exporter of agricultural produce again, and solve the country's balance of payments problems.

SOCIALIST MYTHS

A policy of promoting state farming merely benefits a small élite of farm workers, such as the combine-harvester operators, while there is no benefit for those displaced through mechanisation. In this context the state's ownership of productive resources, including the land, in no way helps improve income distribution. As with the land reform, by overemphasising land tenure, attention is diverted from distributional questions. On paper the society appears more egalitarian when socialist organisational forms are introduced, but this may only frustrate the majority, who see themselves as no better off, and possibly even worse off, than before. This particularly applied in Syria, where before the 1958 revolution there had been a decade of rising agricultural income, due to new land being brought into productive use, an extension of pump irrigation and favourable world market conditions for grain exports after the Korean War.[27] In contrast the 1960s were a period of stagnation, not only because of the uncertainty and dislocation resulting from the land reforms, but also due to grain prices falling in world markets. A further problem was that the scope for further extension of the cropped area was limited, as the margin of cultivation with existing water resources had finally been reached.

Faced with the need to demonstrate to the rural populace that the new socialist agrarian policies could bring benefits, the Syrian government decided to embark on an ambitious irrigation project to harness the Euphrates River by constructing a massive dam.[28] Lacking the finance and expertise to undertake the project themselves, the Syrians turned to the Russians for help, as the latter had already acquired experience in dam construction in the Middle East through their work at Aswan in Egypt. The project was started in 1968, with the first stage completed on schedule in 1973, and by 1980 an additional 372,000 hectares of land will be irrigated.[29] As the Russians have been urging the Syrians to establish large-scale collectives and state farms on the newly irrigated land, it must be questioned how widely the gains from the project will be shared, however, for the reasons already discussed.

As a result of the new dam 83 per cent of the water from the Euphrates will be used for irrigation in Syria, a fact that has not unnaturally caused resentment from the Iraqis further downstream, and worsened the already strained relations between the two countries. In recent years the Government of Iraq has been making considerable efforts to improve water utilisation from the Euphrates. In 1976 a major canal project was completed to supply water from the Tigris River to the Euphrates to help increase its flow.[30] The scheme's two main objectives were to provide irrigation in the Thurthar Depression from the Tigris River, and also to increase the irrigated lands in the Euphrates Valley downstream from the canal inlet. The latter project is obviously threatened by the Syrian schemes, as are the hydro-electric barrages on the Euphrates, which depend on a plentiful and regular supply of water. The financial stakes are high for Iraq, as the cost of the 37·5-kilometre canal linking the Tigris and Euphrates has been considerable, and work is under-way on another 65-kilometre canal.[31] Returns on these capital projects will clearly be put in jeopardy unless agreement is reached between the two countries on water utilisation. Looking at Syria and Iraq from the development perspective, in external economic relations as well as internally they appear to have derived little benefit from the socialist stance of their governments. Internally, both countries have suffered economically through the elimination of competitive forces; and, externally, where co-operation between the two socialist governments and economic co-ordination could have brought mutual benefits, an opportunity has been wasted. Instead competition over the utilisation of scarce resources such as irrigation water has prevailed, and both countries have got the worst of all possible worlds.

RHETORIC AND REALITY

Despite the lip-service that the governments of Syria and Iraq pay to the need to raise living standards for the mass of the ordinary people and ensure that they share fully in the gains from development, there is little indication that this objective has been adhered to in practice. In recent years, for instance, retail food prices have been moving upward for most locally produced commodities, and in economies where most people still derive their livelihood from agriculture such a trend should help reduce rural/urban income disparities, even if it does not necessarily result in a more egalitarian personal distribution of income. However, although urban consumers find themselves paying more for food in Damascus and Baghdad and other major centres, it does not appear that the rise in retail prices is reflected in the increase the farmers actually receive.[32]

Table 7·2 illustrates the recent trends in Syria for five major commodities: wheat, barley, onions, tomatoes and potatoes. The differential between retail and farm prices appears much smaller for wheat and barley than for the other commodities, but it should be noted that few consumers purchase these grains in unprocessed form. Wheat grain will be made into flour for breadmaking, for example, and the price consumers pay for this final product will bear little relation to the payments the farmers obtain. Figures are only available for a four-year period for Syria, and no similar figures are issued in Iraq, but from this limited evidence it does appear that the gap between retail and farm prices is considerable, and shows no sign of narrowing in spite of government efforts to stamp out profiteering by merchants and middle men.

Surprisingly, retail prices and farm prices do not even appear to move in the same direction sometimes, for between 1973 and 1974 in Syria the farm prices of wheat fell, while retail prices rose. Onions present an even

TABLE 7.2. Price mark-ups in Syrian agriculture (piastres per kilo[a])

		1972	*1973*	*1974*	*1975*
Wheat	Farm price	30	48	44	49
	Retail price	29	56	55	62
	FR/RP (%)	83·3	85·7	73·3	74·2
Barley	Farm price	25	46	35	39
	Retail price	29	52	55	62
	FP/RP (%)	86·2	88·5	63·6	62·9
Onions	Farm price	12	23	18	20
	Retail price	26	46	32	90
	FP/RP (%)	46·1	50·0	56·2	22·2
Tomatoes	Farm price	15	27	30	34
	Retail price	37	65	74	75
	FP/RP (%)	40·5	41·5	40·5	45·3
Potatoes	Farm price	36	13	40	45
	Retail price	50	61	74	90
	FP/RP (%)	72·0	21·3	54·1	50·0

[a] 100 piastres=£1 Syrian, 1$ (US)=£ Syrian 3·95 (October 1977)

Source: Syrian Arab Republic, Central Bureau of Statistics, *Statistical Abstracts*: (1976) Table 4/9, p. 592; (1975) Table 4/9, p. 580; (1974) Table 7/9, p. 582; (1973) Table 7/9, p. 496.

more striking case: between 1974 and 1975 the retail price almost trebled, yet farm prices stayed virtually static. One explanation for these divergences may be the unloading of stocks by middle men, but if this is the explanation, from the data it is clear that stocks are not adjusted to smooth out retail price fluctuations. In fact retail prices appear to fluctuate to a greater extent than farm prices, which indicates that if middle men pursue a deliberate stock-adjustment policy, then it may be destabilising rather than stabilising. Thus they may withhold supplies from the market if the price is rising, rather than sell, in the expectation of further price rises from which they can profit. Shortages are therefore made worse, but the farmers themselves do not appear to derive much benefit from the misfortune of consumers.

The divergence between farm prices and retail prices in Iraq was probably as great as that in Syria, although published data is not available to confirm this. It does appear, however, that consumer prices for foodstuffs have increased more rapidly than wholesale prices, especially since 1971. Over the four-year period up to 1975 the wholesale price index for foodstuffs rose 29 points, whereas consumer prices rose 37 points.[33] These wholesale prices are, of course, well above farm prices, which probably fared much worse. Ironically, food prices in the countryside are generally higher than those in the cities, except for commodities such as tomatoes. Flour, for example, is twelve per cent cheaper in Baghdad than in the north of the country, oranges are one-seventh less, while carrots are an amazing 25 per cent cheaper.[34] This may be explained by the fact that flour mills are located near the capital, and by the competition prevailing in urban markets in comparison with the villages. Nevertheless it does highlight one further source of disparity between rural and urban incomes, by suggesting that rural purchasing power may be even lower than might be suspected.

As a consequence of the low prices prevailing for agricultural produce in Iraq and Syria, landowners have naturally been short of funds to invest in farm improvement. There have admittedly been schemes devised to provide funds to farmers through co-operative channels, but the amounts available have been pitifully small, with the agricultural Co-operative Bank in Syria advancing credits worth only one-third of those granted by other specialised banks to help commerce.[35] Peasants therefore still seek assistance from moneylenders, as they did before the revolution, and the problem of rural indebtedness remains as great as ever. Despite all the publicity given to the new agrarian organisations, such as the co-operatives, it appears in reality that there has been little affect on the ordinary agricultural worker or peasant in either Syria or

Iraq.

Income distribution has changed little under the Baathist Socialist regimes in Baghdad and Damascus, for the old rural élite of large landowners has been merely replaced by a new urban élite of managers of state sector industries, while the commercial middle men have at least maintained, if not strengthened, their positions.[36] In some cases it is the former rural landlords themselves who occupy positions of power and influence in the cities, especially in Syria, where they have been surprisingly able in adapting to changed political circumstances. All that has happened is that the rural areas no longer experience the favourable multiplier effects resulting from the landlords' expenditure on locally produced goods and services. There is an obvious contradiction between talking about a more egalitarian distribution of income, while at the same time favouring the urban areas at the expense of the rural areas where the majority live.

The Syrian authorities often point to the increases in GNP as evidence of rising living standards, for GNP doubled over the 1963–74 period. However, over the same period the population of the country rose from below 5 million to over 7 million, which meant that the increase in *per capita* GNP was much less spectacular.[37] For the majority, in fact, *per capita* incomes stagnated—or even fell—for, despite the socialist government's commitment to promoting a more equitable income distribution in principle, the gains from economic development went to the limited urban élite. In Iraq the same phenomenon occurred, although there the government could not even claim that GNP figures provided a measure of their economic success, as these merely reflected the vicissitudes of petroleum production and prices, given that sector's prominence in the national accounts. The reliability of Iraq's GNP figures is open to serious question in any case, especially in recent years, and since 1971 the International Monetary Fund has no longer quoted in its own statistics the official data provided by the Baghdad government.[38]

In both Iraq and Syria, despite the socialist ideology of the government, regional power politics appear to play a major role in determining how income is distributed. Iraq is divided on both ethnic and religious lines, although as the two divisions do not co-incide the situation is extremely complex. Just over half the total population of Iraq are Shia Moslems, but of the country's 9·6 million Arabs, around 65 per cent are Shia. The remaining Arabs, and the Kurdish population of 1·8 million, are Sunni, which is the religion of the majority of the members of the cabinet, and most of the hierarchy of the Iraqi Baathist Socialist party.[39]

Under the present regime there is little doubt that the Sunni have benefited at the expense of the Shia, as development projects have gone to the Sunni areas to the north of Baghdad, rather than to the south. The most conspicuous example of this regional preference is the Tigris-Euphrates canal project, as all the irrigated areas lie in Sunni Arab lands.

The Kurds have probably fared better under the rule of their co-religionists than they would under Shia government, but the measure of regional autonomy they have is extremely limited, since no Baghdad administration can afford to see real economic power transferred to Kurdish hands.[40] Most of the country's oil production is either in Kurdistan, or in neighbouring areas.[41] Without the revenue from this production any Iraqi government would soon be bankrupt, and all the Arabs, whether Shia or Sunni, would lose. Baghdad politics must be understood in terms of this interplay of conflicting group interests, in which the economic stakes are very high. The costs of maintaining the army to keep control in the Kurdish areas is only a fraction of the probable loss to the country if the Kurds seceded and established their own state. At least, however, the Baghdad government has succeeded in maintaining relative peace in the area in recent years, and thus minimised the cost of the conflict for the country as a whole. It has done this partly by improving its previously troubled relations with Iran, which is the main source of supplies for the Kurdish rebels.

Syria's internal conflicts of interest are not as dramatic as those of Iraq, for they represent the more usual interplay of social classes rather than that of religious and ethnic groups. Nevertheless the same tools of economic analysis can be used to ascertain their effect on development. Fortunately in Syria's case if modern oligopolistic theory is used the net effect will probably be a zero sum game, but, in Iraq, where the conflict means an opportunity cost in terms of resources deployed into largely unproductive military activities, the result is undoubtedly negative in terms of game theory. In both societies the ruling groups, and those with vested economic interests, go to considerable lengths to prevent their monopolistic control over resources being threatened. This perhaps partly explains why these groups embrace socialism, not because of its emphasis on equity, but because of its ideological opposition to competition. It is this aspect of socialism which is most often stressed by the Baathist hierarchies, who realise that the emergence of free competitive forces would help undermine their positions.[42] Socialist ideals in these respects happen to be convenient, as they mean a quieter life than would otherwise be the case. The apparent contradiction between rhetoric and reality in both Syria and Iraq becomes less once the blanket revolutionary socialist terms which the rulers use are broken down, and their more limited meaning understood. As always in the Middle East, appearances can be deceptive.

8 The Yemens and Oman: Far Away but Not Forgotten

> At a certain stage . . . the conditions under which feudal society produced and exchanged, the feudal organisation of agriculture and manufacturing . . . became so many fetters. They had to be burst asunder; they were burst asunder
>
> K. Marx and F. Engels, *Manifesto of the Communist Party* (1848)

Situated on the southern fringes of the Arabian Peninsula, the Yemens and Oman are the most remote part of the Middle East for the European, American, or indeed even the Arab traveller. Apart from the port of Aden, which flourished as a trading and entrepôt centre on the Suez-Red Sea route to the Orient, the other regions were cut off from major trade routes or markets. A growing number of tankers and other shipping plying between the oil sheikhdoms of the Gulf and Europe passed the shores of Oman and North Yemen from the 1950s onwards, but neither country had adequate port facilities. There was in any case little reason for these ships to break their journeys to call on such inhospitable lands. The closure of the Suez Canal in 1967 resulting from the Arab-Israeli War meant that Aden was no longer significant as a transit port. In consequence the isolation of these corners of Arabia from the outside world became almost total, and although the canal has reopened again, Aden had not been able to regain its former role. In a period when the rest of the Middle East was becoming increasingly opened up to the outside world, the reverse seemed to be happening in these particular areas.

The recent economic isolation contrasts sharply with the historical role the Yemens and Oman played as major centres of trade, commerce, manufacturing and even agriculture. Omani Dhow owners traded throughout the Gulf and the Indian Ocean littoral for hundreds of years until the mid-nineteenth century, with the greatest period for trade occurring from 1650 onwards following the expulsion of the Portuguese.[1] Omanis colonised Zanzibar off the East African coast, and their influence extended to Madagascar and across to the Indian subcontinent. Small ports along the Gulf coast from Sohar to Salalah prospered as a result, with increasing commerce, shipbuilding, and the manufacture of craft goods for export.

Yemeni civilisation is much older than that of Oman, as the area flourished under the Minaeans from the thirteenth until the seventh centuries B.C., and later under the Sabaeans and the Himyarities.[2] The latter coincided with the height of the Roman Empire, but although the region had economic links with Rome, it maintained the territorial independence it had enjoyed from the time of the Queen of Sheba. As North Yemen was well-watered in comparison to the rest of Arabia, it became known to the Romans as '*Arabia Felix*', or 'Fortunate Arabia'. The cool highlands between 1500 and 3600 metres high constituted the only large area of settled agriculture in the Arabian Peninsula, and one of the main sources of grain in the Middle East.

Summer rainfall in North Yemen can reach up to 90 cm., while the winters are cool, with even occasional frost and snow in the highest regions.[3] The main crops grown today include coffee, fruit, vegetables and cereals, as well as a shrub called qat, which has a leaf which produces a mildly narcotic effect when chewed. Agriculture remains the mainstay of the North Yemen's economy, accounting for 70 per cent of gross national product and 90 per cent of export earnings. In addition, over nine-tenths of the country's large resident population of 5·5 million are engaged in farming activities, mostly on small terraced plots in the mountainous interior which have been built up over the centuries.

In comparison to North Yemen, the agricultural potential of South Yemen and Oman is severely limited, with only 100,000 hectares cultivated in the former, and a mere 36,000 hectares farmed in the latter,[4] representing less than 1 per cent of the total land area of both countries. As in North Yemen agriculture remains the main traditional economic activity, accounting for more than 70 per cent of employment opportunities, though the absolute numbers employed in both countries are of course much less than in North Yemen, as the population of South Yemen is only 1·7 million, while that of Oman is probably around 600,000. The share of agriculture in gross national product amounts to only 19 per cent in South Yemen, and 18 per cent in Oman, a mere fraction of that of North Yemen.[5] In the case of South Yemen this probably reflects the importance of commerce in relation to gross national product, and the major contribution made by the oil sector in Oman. The figures nevertheless are probably an understatement of the share of agriculture in national product, as most of the farming in South Yemen and Oman is geared to subsistence needs, and is therefore not counted in official income estimates, unlike the marketed output of North Yemen.

From this brief survey of agriculture, it is obvious that the relative population sizes of North Yemen, South Yemen and Oman reflect to a large extent the varying resource endowments of the countries. Within the countries themselves this is also the case, for although South Yemen and Oman are sparsely populated in comparison to North Yemen, the population density in the cultivated areas is remarkably similar. Densities exceed 730 people per square kilometre on arable lands in South Yemen and 600 per square kilometre in Oman, compared with 500 per square kilometre in North Yemen.[6] These densities are comparable to those of the suburbs of major Western cities such as London or Paris, yet these city dwellers use the land only for their places of residence, and, unlike the peasants of the Yemens and Oman, are not of course dependent on it for their livelihood.

GLORIOUS PAST AND IGNOMINIOUS PRESENT

It is a testimony to the ingenuity of the civilisations of Southern Arabia that rural communities have been able to sustain populations comparable to those of the urban conglomerations of the industrial world. Some of the irrigation systems in these areas are of similar age to those of the Nile and Tigris-Euphrates Valleys, but given the mountainous nature of the terrain in Southern Arabia, they represent a much more impressive technological achievement. Bridges were constructed to carry the irrigation water across valleys, while hydrologists carefully calculated the speed of flow to decide the optimal pattern for the canals, and determine the rate of erosion so that banks could be strengthened where necessary. The Marib Dam in North Yemen represented the first large dam project undertaken anywhere in the world and it enabled the summer rainfall to be stored for utilisation in the early spring before the next season's wet period.[7] Rainfall has always been a problem in North Yemen, but with the dam the times for planting and harvesting were no longer dependent on the start of the rainy season.

Over the last 500 years the civilisations of Southern Arabia based on cultivated settlements have gradually decayed, partly as a result of conflicts with the nomadic pastoralists of the desert fringes, but also because of inter-tribal conflicts amongst the settlers themselves. As a consequence the irrigation systems have either been alowed to fall into disrepair as civilian activities have been sacrificed to military priorities, or else they have been physically destroyed as obvious military targets during the actual conflicts. Even the famous Marib Dam was destroyed, and as a consequence agriculture went into a period of steady decline. Production was at its lowest during the Yemeni civil war, which raged from 1963 until 1970, causing enormous destruction.[8] Until 1962 the country was known as the Mutawakkilite Kingdom of Yemen, but at the end of that year a military coup brought into being the Yemen Arab Republic. The royalists resisted, however, and a violent conflict followed, with the Egyptians and the Soviet Union supporting the Republicans, while the Saudi Arabians supported their fellow royalists. Nasser sent over 40,000 Egyptian troops to support the Republicans, which gives some indication of the scale of the fighting.

This was not the first time that Yemen had suffered as a result of becoming a pawn on the international political scene, rather than a largely self-sufficient economic entity, able to decide on its own external relationships and internal policies. Over a century earlier, in 1839, the country was divided in two when the British occupied the South, and established a major military base in Aden to safeguard their interests in the Indian Ocean. With the opening of the Suez Canal, Aden assumed an even greater significance for the British by safeguarding the route to Queen Victoria's Empire in the east, and India in particular. Apart from developing the port of Aden as a transit centre, the British made no attempt to encourage economic growth in the territories under their control. They showed little interest in the hinterland of Aden, except through the appointment of political agents to try to keep the peace between the warring tribes, and hence ensure the safety of the British base.

Growing disquiet with the way the British were handling the affairs of the territory led to the outbreak of a guerilla war in 1963 in Aden, which ultimately prompted a total British withdrawal from the area four years later.[9] It is ironic that it was the urban proletariat of Aden who were in the vanguard of the resistance to continued colonial rule, for these were the people who did gain economically from the British occupation through being employed on the military base in a civilian capacity, or as employees in the port itself.[10] Initially the rebels received Egyptian backing, largely through North Yemen, but Nasser soon became wary of their Marxist stance and radical economic philosophy, which was well to the left of the ideas of Egypt's Arab Socialist party. Meanwhile Aden's prosperous traders and merchants, alarmed by the success of the radicals, and seeing the inevitability of British withdrawal, decided in 1965 to form a liberation organisation of their own, which they hoped would assume power eventually and safeguard their interests. Heartened by this development, the Egyptians promptly shifted their allegiance to the new organisation, the Front for the Liberation of Occupied South Yemen (FLOSY)[11] By then it was too late, however, and although FLOSY made a spirited attempt at seizing power just before Britain's withdrawal in 1967, it was the Marxist National Liberation Front which formed the first government of the country after independence. Aden thus became the People's Democratic Republic of Yemen, the only Marxist state in the Middle East.

Although Oman did not suffer like South Yemen through direct colonial intervention, it nevertheless has been a victim of international power-politics in recent years. Sultan Said Bin Teymour, the father of the present ruler, tried to exclude all foreign influence on his people, for he feared that this might threaten Omani society, which was organised on ultra-conservative Islamic lines.[12] The British, who acted as Teymour's advisers, were prepared to support these policies so long as the Sultan did nothing to threaten their interests in the Gulf, especially the vital oil routes. Not surprisingly under Teymour's rule the country's economy stagnated and this period was viewed as a dark age in contrast to the past. As already mentioned, then it had prospered through its seafaring traders, but as the Sultan curtailed their activities, the economy reverted to a subsistence basis. The importation of foreign material goods was seen as a threat to the spiritual values of Islam, while items such as transistor radios were regarded with extreme suspicion, since the Sultan believed they could undermine the social attitudes of the people by informing them of alien ideas. There was no education system apart from Moslem schools where the Koran was taught, and these only provided primary schooling in any case. Any Omani who wanted an education had to slip out of the country and reside abroad, although this presented problems, as the Sultan did not permit parents to send funds abroad to support their relatives. Internally the spread of ideas was equally limited, as few propple travelled far beyond their own villages due to poor communications, there being no surfaced roads in the country.

STRUGGLE ON THE ARABIAN FRINGES

The attempt to cut Oman off from the outside world had a paradoxical effect, for it led to widespread unrest, especially in the south-western province of Dhofar, and the emergence of a guerilla movement, the Popular Front for the Liberation of Oman (PFLO). This organisation was initially backed by Saudi Arabia, Egypt and Iraq, as well as the National Liberation Front of Occupied South Yemen. Like the latter however, because of the PFLO's Marxist ideals, it soon lost the support of other established Arab governments, but it gained in strength after the withdrawal of the British from Aden, and the formation of a leftist government there which shared its aspirations.[13] Seeing the gains of the PFLO, and the inability of Teymour to curb its activities, Qaboos Bin Saud, the Sultan's son, decided in 1970 to oust his father and take control himself before it became too late.

After consolidating his position as Sultan, Qaboos immediately started to modernise the country by building up basic infrastructure, especially roads and airports, believing that this would help both strategically against the guerrillas and economically as well, by demonstrating that the PFLO was not the only force to bring about change. At the same time the defence budget was steadily increased, and the army strengthened, partly by recruiting additional British officers, most of whom had served previously in Aden, and were attracted to Oman by the offer of attractive salaries. Despite rapidly increasing oil revenues, worth $210 million by 1971, Qaboos found it impossible to finance both a substantial development budget and military commitments at the same time, even although the country was in a much more fortunate position than the Yemens, which had no oil. Official defence spending amounted to almost 40 per cent of the total budget,[14] yet by 1972 there was still little sign that this was producing results, for the PFLO remained as strong as ever. Meanwhile Oman was running a deficit on both its budget and its balance of payments account. Clearly Qaboos, in an increasingly desperate position, had to take some action to retain his position, and in the event he decided to call on the Iranians for help.

The Iranians, who had always wanted to replace Britain in the Gulf as the major military power, were only too willing to give military assistance of a direct nature to Sultan Qaboos. The Shah also welcomed the opportunity of being able to intervene officially on the Arab side of the Gulf, as events there were of vital importance to Iran because of its oil-based economy.[15] Naturally the Shah was well aware of the strategic importance of Oman, given its situation near the mouth of the Gulf and the sea routes which still carry a major proportion of Iran's oil to the outside world. Clearly the emergence of any left-wing revolutionary government in Oman would scarcely be a welcome political development when viewed from Tehran, especially if other regimes were threatened further up the Gulf. Apart from these longer-term policy issues, the Shah also believed that there might be a more immediate economic gain, for if his forces were in the area this would be another means of applying subtle pressure on the major Arab oil producers over the question of prices.

In 1973 over 15,000 Iranian troops were sent to Oman, together with modern military equipment, including helicopters, which the rebel forces could not hope to match. This soon changed the course of the war, as by the following year a large area of Dhofar had been captured, and the rebel forces were cut off from their supply lines to South Yemen. In December 1975 Sultan Qaboos was able to announce that victory had been achieved in Dhofar, and in the next few months the main leaders of the Popular Front for the Liberation of Oman surrendered, although a few pockets of resistance continued to hold out in the mountains in the east of the province. Having secured a military victory, the next stage of the struggle was to win the hearts and minds of the people of Dhofar, by pursuing a large-scale programme of economic development.[16] Initially, as in the rest of the country, the emphasis was on building up infrastructure, and a coastal road has been built from Salalah, the regional capital, to the port of Rakhyut, and a new surfaced highway now runs for 80 kilometres across the mountains from Salalah to Thamarit. Eventually it is hoped to link the road system of Dhofar to that of the Batina by building an 800 kilometre road to Nizwa to connect up with Muscat itself. This will help ensure the economic integration of Dhofar with the rest of Oman, thus reducing the likelihood of any future secessionist movements developing.

It is interesting to note that Oman, despite its oil resources, received in 1975 more financial assistance from the rich Arab oil producers to carry out this modernisation than the two Yemens put together. This in itself reflects the importance which the Arab oil producers attach to keeping Oman as an ally.

In North and South Yemen, as in Oman, the virtual ending of military hostilities has been followed by an economic campaign to win the allegiance of the population; or, in cruder terms, to buy off potential discontent. The military struggle has been replaced by an economic contest, with the West, Saudi Arabia and the Gulf states supplying substantial aid to North Yemen, while the communist states, particularly the Soviet Union and China, back the South Yemeni government. By the early 1970s it was apparent that a type of race had developed between the two Yemens, with the winner being judged in terms of its economic growth performance.[17] As a consequence of the considerable amount of outside interest in both countries, the stakes are much higher than the size of the economies might suggest. What happens on the Yemeni testing grounds will undoubtedly have economic and political implications throughout Arabia as well as in the rest of the Middle East.

A TEMPTING DEPENDENCE

Details of financial assistance to North and South Yemen are given in Table 8.1. From the data presented it is clear that North Yemen receives considerably more aid than the South in absolute terms, as might be

TABLE 8.1. Foreign assistance to the Yemens

North Yemen	*1971*	*1972*	*1973/74*	*1974/75*
Total aid ($ million)	33·9	41·8	67·4	128·5
Percentage of government spending financed by aid	75·0	43·0	77·1	100·0
Percentage of imports covered by aid	17·9	14·6	17·3	12·5

South Yemen	*1969*	*1973*	*1974*	*1975*
Total aid aid ($ million)	5	38	92	57
Percentage of government spending financed by aid	14·5	25·5	34·9	55·1
Percentage of imports covered by aid	5·8	32·2	52·0	32·2

Source: Calculated from World Bank data.

expected given its much larger population and greater absorptive capacity. The cost of providing basic infrastructure such as roads is particularly high in North Yemen because of the mountainous nature of the terrain, but this limits benefits in relation to aid given for these purposes. Only 700 kilometres of road are surfaced in North Yemen, and much of this was carried out in the early 1960s when the Chinese aided the republican forces by asphalting the strategic route linking Sanaa with the port of Hodeida. In South Yemen only 330 kilometres of road are asphalted, almost half of which were constructed by the British around Aden township itself during their occupation.[18] Clearly the recent aid for infrastructure improvements has yet to have a marked impact in terms of extending the road systems beyond the meagre inheritance from the past.

North Yemen's main aid donors were Eastern bloc countries—the USSR, China, East Germany and North Korea—but since the end of the civil war these have been replaced in importance by the Arab states, West Germany and the USA. Communist hopes of Yemeni republican ideas spreading to Saudi Arabia have been dashed, and as early as 1967 China and the Soviet Union became disillusioned as they saw rightist forces becoming more powerful, even amongst the republican leadership. Not surprisingly Saudi Arabia is the main aid donor, especially since the 1974 coup for Colonel Ibraham Hamdi and his successors after the 1977 assassinations have been in general pro-Riyadh. In contrast Abdul Rahman Iriani, who ruled until 1974, tolerated the leftist anti-Riyadh parties within the country, and tried to improve relations with South Yemen.[19] In 1975 Saudi Arabia agreed to provide aid worth \$272·6 million, of which \$146 million was for road construction to link North Yemen's highway system to that of the rest of Arabia, by surfacing the road from Sanaa to Sadah, and across the border to Medina.

Most of the aid to South Yemen still comes from Eastern bloc countries, especially the Soviet Union, which is providing finance for a fisheries project that includes a processing plant. Other major areas for assistance include electric power, hospitals, irrigation schemes and help in establishing state farming ventures modelled on their Soviet counterparts. The Chinese, not to be outdone by the Russians, are helping to construct a new surfaced highway from Aden to the interior, and have a textile factory similar to those they have successfully brought into production elsewhere in the Third World, including Tanzania. Other communist aid donors include East Germany, Czechoslovakia and Bulgaria, who are providing project-tied assistance similar to that given by the Soviet Union and China.[20]

Recently the South Yemeni authorities have decided to seek general budgetary support for current expenditure as well as project-tied aid. From Table 8.1 it is apparent that until recently only a minor proportion of the spending of the Aden government was financed from aid, in contrast to North Yemen where the proportion was much higher. In South Yemen levels of taxation are much greater than in the

North, particularly the level of personal income taxes, as might be expected in a country professing a socialist ideology. As a consequence of its draconian taxation policies, current government revenue as a proportion of GNP has risen from 12 per cent in 1969/70 to 17 per cent in 1974/75, an extremely high figure for a country with a *per capita* income of a mere $240, the lowest in the Middle East apart from North Yemen.[21] In addition government employees, who comprise the majority of the workforce in paid employment, have been further squeezed financially by having their salaries cut twice, in 1968/69 and 1972/73. Needless to say these efforts on the part of the Aden government to finance internally as much of its expenditure as possible did not help its popularity, particularly as far as its own employees were concerned.

Considering the circumstances it was scarcely surprising that when Saudi Arabia and the oil-rich Gulf states offered general budgetary support to South Yemen, the government found the offer too tempting to resist in spite of its Marxist ideology.[22] South Yemen had been unable to obtain this type of unconditional assistance from its communist allies, partly because project-tied aid suited the Eastern Europeans better, since they could supply most of the equipment necessary for the various projects on a bilateral basis, without harming their own foreign exchange positions. In addition the communist states were dubious about providing finance to the South Yemeni authorities to spend as they wished, for the Russians in particular were wary of corruption in the Arab world after their experiences in Egypt, and they preferred to back projects which the populace of the recipient countries could see and readily identify.

By the financial year July 1974/June 1975, North Yemen had become completely dependent on funds from Saudi Arabia and the Gulf to finance all its expenditure, as Table 8.1 shows, while over half of state expenditure in South Yemen was financed in the same way. In North Yemen, in fact, the government found itself in the unusual position of being able to spend only three-quarters of the funds allocated to it by Saudi Arabia, while the rest was put aside as a budgetary surplus.[23] This situation was not new in North Yemen, however, as during the first two years of the 1973–6 development plan actual expenditure amounted to less than 17 per cent of the total anticipated. In such a situation there is likely to be more pressure to reduce even the limited taxes which do exist in North Yemen, particularly import duties, which still account for 60 per cent of fiscal revenue. If a similar state of affairs emerges in South Yemen as a result of aid from the Arab oil-exporting states, there will be enormous pressure on the authorities to relax their tough fiscal measures.

The dependence of both North and South Yemen on aid for import finance would be much greater than indicated by Table 8.1 were it not for the large amounts each country receives through remittances from nationals working abroad. In 1975 the first national census of North Yemen revealed that over 1,234,000 people were working abroad, representing almost one-fifth of the total population.[24] It appears that nearly every family in North Yemen has at least one member resident outside the country, mostly in Saudi Arabia and the Gulf. Detailed estimates of the number of South Yemeni migrant workers are not available, but it seems likely that the proportion of migrants relative to the total population may be even higher than in the North, possibly around one-third, judging by the amounts of remittances repatriated.[25] Although this figure is the highest in the world for migrants proportionally, it may however still represent a substantial underestimate, as South Yemeni migrants are reluctant to repatriate funds because they fear the Marxist government in Aden could freeze any bank deposits made there.

Table 8.2 provides details concerning workers' remittances to North and South Yemen over an eight-year period. In 1969 the amount of remittances sent to the South was well in excess of that going to the North, but by 1972 this had been reversed, partly because of the migrants' fears regarding funds repatriated to South Yemen, as just mentioned, which meant that the value of remittances was only half of its earlier level. At the same time there were few investment opportunities in South Yemen, for the state sector encompassed virtually the entire economy and private enterprise was discouraged. As a consequence the migrants often brought back consumer durables from Saudi Arabia, such as portable radios and television sets, rather than sending cash, but even these were subject to heavy import duties. Nevertheless the practice became widespread, particularly as so few imported goods were available in Aden itself, compared to earlier, under the British occupation, when it had been a duty-free port.

While South Yemen was becoming a less favourable environment for the repatriation of earnings, the North in contrast was becoming more attractive. With the civil war over, the country had returned to relative stability, and the government, although republican, favoured a mixed economy and consequently introduced a generous investment code for private capital.[26] The parties of the left, particularly the Baathist Socialists, appeared to be losing support domestically, and the threat of possible government seizure of private assets had receded. As a result

TABLE 8.2. Significance of workers' remittances for the balance of payments of the Yemens.

North Yemen	*1969*	*1970*	*1971*	*1972*	*1973*	*1973/74*	*1974/75*
Total remittances ($ million)	42·0	45·0	47·2	81·0	108·5	130·8	220·5
Imports ($ million)	65·6	58·4	72·3	102·4	155·0	194·2	258·5
Remittances as a percentage of import payments	64·0	50·9	65·3	78·9	70·0	67·4	85·5
South Yemen	*1969*	*1970*	*1971*	*1972*	*1973*	*1974*	*1975*
Total remittances ($ million)	56·6	57·1	47·8	27·1	32·9	41·0	56·0
Imports ($ million)	86·5	92·8	85·0	88·1	118·2	175·2	176·7
Remittances as a percentage of import payments	65·4	61·5	56·2	30·8	26·9	23·4	31·7

Source: Calculated from World Bank data.

North Yemen was able to import an increasing amount, although most of this comprised foodstuffs and consumer goods for the immigrants' families rather than capital or intermediate goods for industry. The largest increase in the value of remittances came after the petroleum price rises, and the consequent wages rises in Saudi Arabia, which benefited the Yemeni workers considerably, as the 1974/75 figure for remittances in Table 8.2 indicates.

Faced with an increasingly worrying balance of payments situation, the South Yemen government realised by 1973 that it would have to sacrifice some of its Marxist principles and follow North Yemen's example in encouraging the flow of remittances. Interest rates were raised on non-resident bank accounts, but the government was reluctant to take any measures to liberate foreign payments, since this would reduce its overall control of the economy.[27] The South Yemeni authorities remain dubious about the benefits of such large-scale migration, but as it started long before the country became independent, they are powerless to halt it, especially given the shortage of similar income-earning opportunities internally.

Unfortunately the beneficial effects of migration from the point of view of the balance of payments of both North and South Yemen are to a large extent offset by detrimental effects on the domestic economies. The substantial migration has led to manpower shortages in many fields, especially in North Yemen, where this is undoubtedly one of the main factors responsible for the decline in agriculture. Over half of North Yemen's imports consist of foodstuffs,[28] yet the country remains primarily agrarian, and historically it was a major centre of food production, as already noted. North Yemen's agriculture was extremely labour-intensive, especially the maintenance of the irrigation channels and the terraces, and the loss of the youngest and ablest people to Saudi Arabia and beyond has severely disrupted this work. This parallels the situation which emerged in Oman during the earlier part of this century when a similar migration caused agricultural decline which could not easily be rectified. Irrigation works that take years to establish can be destroyed in a few months if not properly maintained.

There is little doubt that the large-scale migration has appreciably lowered the absorptive capacity of the two Yemens. Profitable investment in industry, for instance, would be extremely unlikely, for prevailing wage levels, especially in North Yemen, correspond to those in Saudi Arabia, which makes them extremely high by Third World standards. Many of the skilled craftsmen, who would be the most adaptable to modern industry, are no longer resident, while those few with secondary education who could perform managerial functions already do this kind of work elsewhere.[29] In the case of South Yemen many of the more educated are political exiles anyway. Ironically this was also what occurred in Oman under Sultan Teymoor, when commerce and trading declined as those with the most experience and expertise became political exiles, although of course they were on the opposite side of the ideological spectrum.

Apart from political considerations dependence on migrant earnings may in the long-run prove undesirable. At present the Yemens can easily gain access to outside capital for diversification, but they now lack the workforce to implement such ventures. Yet if eventually the boom in Saudi Arabia and the Gulf states comes to an end, and the migrants return, by that time Arab sources of aid will probably no longer exist. Only then are there likely to be conditions from which a new social order could emerge. It appears that in present circumstances even those migrants employed in the lowest positions are too concerned with immediate material gain to press for social and economic reform. The Marxist movement on the Arabian fringes which appeared to be gaining adherents so quickly in the 1960s now seems to be in retreat on all fronts.

MARXISM AND THE WORLD OF ISLAM

Although a sizable proportion of the intelligencia of all three countries under review have become adherents of Marxism, it is only in South Yemen that they have succeeded in occupying positions in central government. In North Yemen during the civil war some of the republican leadership were keen to put Marxist ideas into practice in the territory they controlled, by reforming the local feudal structures, especially with regard to landholding, but their grip was neither firm enough nor sufficiently long-lasting to implement such changes on a large scale. The same applied in Oman, as despite the fact that the rebels were in virtual control of the province of Dhofar for a number of years, they were too preoccupied with the war to embark on a programme of socialist reconstruction.[30] With Sultan Qaboos now firmly in control of Oman, and North Yemen increasingly under the sphere of influence of Saudi Arabia, the few socialist measures that were introduced over questions such as landownership and the rights of women have been reversed in most cases.

South Yemen is the only country in the Middle East where a socialist economy run along Marxist-Leninist lines has been firmly established. As such it is interesting to consider its experience in the decade following the 1967 British withdrawal in some detail, as this should indicate if Marxist ideas can be applied in a Moslem country, or whether those critics are correct who assert that the materialist basis of a communist society is incompatible with Islam. If the Marxist revolution succeeds in South Yemen, then the prospects for communist infiltration elsewhere in the Middle East would appear more promising; but if it fails this may well preclude a communist economic system as a possible option for other Islamic states.

From the point of view of Islamic law there appear to be several conflicts with the practices prevailing in most communist states. The ban on usury is admittedly less of a problem under a Marxist administration than under a capitalist system, where the private banking system plays a major role in providing finance for development. Even if communist ministries use a rate of return analysis for project appraisal, for instance, this can scarcely be considered comparable to interest returns. Islamic law also stipulates that remuneration cannot be made conditional on performance over a fixed time period, and instead wages and salaries should either be based on an hourly or weekly rate regardless of product, or else on a piece rate per unit of output.[31] This stipulation is more likely to preclude the incentive bonus systems found in capitalist societies than the type of wage or salary structures prevailing under communism.

The greatest legal constraints to the transformation of Arab societies along communist lines are undoubtedly the Moslem laws on inheritance, which stipulate how property should be divided amongst sons and daughters. First, male relatives are treated more generously than females, in direct contradiction of socialist ideals of sexual equality. Second, there is no provision for the state to obtain a share in property bequeathed, yet in communist countries estate duties are usually extremely high in order to promote a more egalitarian distribution of wealth.[32] In the past in Islamic societies, which were largely static from the development point of view, it has however been through the inheritance factor above all else that income disparities have been perpetuated, for family fortunes have accumulated over many generations. It is interesting to note that the South Yemeni government has still not enacted new legislation dealing with the thorny question of inheritance, probably because it is well aware of the problems such a legal change could bring in a country where Islam remains the state religion, and still enjoys widespread support.

Despite these legislative shortcomings, in terms of the austerity of South Yemen's economic policies in recent years the country corresponds quite closely to the Stalinist ideal. The government was of course unfortunate in the meagre inheritance it received from the British, especially when they cut their budgeting support grant from a pre-independence offer of £60 million to a mere £3 million.[33] In addition the loss of transit trade revenue from the port of Aden after the Suez Canal closure was a serious economic blow. As a consequence the new government had little choice but to cut its current expenditure, and raise taxes, as already mentioned. Income tax rates went up to 47·5 per cent for the more affluent earning over £250 a month, but the less well off earning less than £23·50 per month were not affected.[34] The military budget was cut back, despite the risks of confrontation with neighbouring hostile states, in order to divert the limited funds available to civilian development projects.

The government's main economic objective in South Yemen was to establish a strong and effective public sector, and hence nationalisation measures were enacted in 1969 bringing the majority of foreign-owned companies under state control. This included manufacturing establishments such as the soft drinks plant in Aden, as well as most of the modern service sector, which comprised banking, insurance, shipping and trading. The largest foreign-owned enterprise in the country, the BP refinery, was not however nationalised, since it had been running well below capacity since the 1967 Suez Canal closure. There seemed little point in taking on such a burden, and with no local oil suppliers in any case, South Yemen would have had difficulty in obtaining oil for refining had it ousted BP completely.[35] After the nationalisation measures the locally owned private sector was confined to small trading establishments and handicraft activities.

Despite South Yemen's shortages of funds, a considerable amount of investment has already been carried out, and several new state sector light industries have been established. These include a medium-sized textile plant, a shoe factory, a tomato paste plant, as well as factories for cigarettes, matches, fishmeal and plastic ware. Under the 1974–9 five-year plan a flour mill has been built, a cottonseed oil plant, a date-processing plant and an animal fodder factory.[36] Many of these new factories are export-orientated, as the restricted size of the domestic market limits the scope for import substitution. The most promising exporting industry would appear to be fishing, which has already surpassed cotton in terms of foreign exchange earnings. The fishmeal plant is being extended under the auspices of the Public Corporation for

Fish Wealth and a canning factory is being built at Mukalla, as well as cold stores and a freezing plant. Fishermen's co-operatives have been established, and credit given through them for the purchase of new fishing vessels, as well as outboard motors for the older craft.[37]

As a consequence of South Yemen's foreign exchange problems the government has tried to make the country as self-sufficient as possible in food production. Agriculture has been reorganised into state farms and co-operatives, and the feudal systems of land holding abolished. High production targets have been set for wheat and other grains, and output has risen 70 per cent over the 1969–75 period, but to some extent this has been at the expense of cotton, which has declined substantially. The state farms and co-operatives have suffered from many teething problems, and as it has been difficult to find farm managers of a suitable calibre, their contribution to agricultural production is well below what was expected. There is no doubt that agricultural production could have been increased further if more fertilisers had been used, but South Yemen has no fertiliser plant of its own, and imported agricultural inputs of this type have become very expensive in recent years.

In order to finance the purchase of items such as fertilisers the South Yemeni government can of course ask for external assistance, but the project-tied aid from the communist states has often taken time to negotiate. The Eastern bloc countries have usually been more keen to provide finance for items such as agricultural machinery, rather than fertilisers, partly because of their belief that progress can only come about through mechanisation, but also no doubt due to the fact that they could readily supply such equipment themselves. In a country such as South Yemen it is certainly inappropriate to treat farming as a branch of industry, since for those in the rural areas, who comprise the majority of the country's population, it is a way of life rather than just a means of earning a living.[38] If Marxist ideas concerning capital accumulation are applied blindly, without taking any account of local conditions, then the results will inevitably be disappointing. Religion is not the only obstacle to the creation of a communist society in South Yemen.

The same applied to the emphasis on the development of industry, for although prospects for the expansion of traditional activities such as fishing are excellent,[39] the limited extent of the local market and shortages of skilled labour rule out large-scale expansion. If Marxist planners merely emphasise industrialisation for its own sake, without taking account of where the produce can be marketed, or the availability of factor inputs, the results can be disastrous. Yet in Aden the planners have often been so preoccupied with production targets that they have ignored the costs involved in achieving them. South Yemen, in any case, as a small country, cannot hope to develop a diversified industrial economy unless it improves its trade relations with neighbouring Arab countries, for its overseas communist allies are not prepared to offer market outlets.[40] The authorities are faced with a dilemma, however, as the closer the country moves economically to North Yemen or Saudi Arabia, the greater the risk of the revolution being undermined. This is already so in the case of workers' remittances which, as described, have prompted the government to pursue more capitalistic banking practices in order to attract the funds involved. South Yemen's situation is not like Cuba's, and eventually the increasing interdependence developing on the Arabian peninsula may spell the end for Marxism there. Communism cannot exist on the Arabian fringes in isolation, and as it missed its chance of spreading further because of the chain of events in Oman and North Yemen, it may well become just another legacy from the past rather than a hope for the future.

9 Libya and the Sudan: Rich Man, Poor Man

> Whoever possesses the house you dwell in, the vehicle you ride or the income you live on, takes hold of your freedom, or part of your freedom, and freedom is indivisible. For man to be happy, he must be free, and to be free, man must possess his own needs.
>
> M. Gaddafi, *The Green Book: Part II: The Solution of the Economic Problem* (1977)

At first sight it may seem strange to examine Libya and the Sudan together, as the differences between the two states are more readily apparent than the similarities. Libya, blessed by its new oil wealth, enjoys a *per capita* GNP of $4275, the highest in Africa, whilst the Sudan, with a *per capita* income of $290, must be counted amongst the poorer countries of the continent.[1] What the Sudan lacks in financial resources it makes up for in manpower, however, as it is the second most populous Arab-ruled state, with almost 18 million inhabitants, although one-third of these are non-Arabs.[2] Libya's population, in contrast, is under two and a half million, most of whom are still nomadic pastoralists, rather than being settled cultivators as in the Sudanese case. The Nile Valley is in fact one of the oldest areas of settled agriculture in the world, and Sudan's economic links with the outside world, like Egypt's, date back to the development of cotton production for export in the nineteenth century. Libya's commercial links with the outside world are much more recent, for although it was colonised by Italy, domestic agriculture was relatively unimportant, and it is only in the last twenty years since the growth of the oil economy that the country has emerged as a significant trading nation.

Despite the differences in factor endowments and historical experiences, there are nevertheless many ways in which distinct parallels can be drawn between the two countries, especially from the economic point of view. First, the gap in living standards is much narrower than might be imagined from the *per capita* income figures, as that for Libya merely reflects the value of its oil production, and though the country is now developing a comprehensive welfare state, the conditions under which the majority of its population live are not noticeably different from those prevailing in other Third World countries, including the Sudan. The second similarity is the dependence of each country on a single commodity: cotton in the case of the Sudan, and oil in Libya. In the latter oil and natural gas accounted for over 97 per cent of export receipts in 1975, and, although during the course of the latest five-year plan it is hoped to reduce this dependence, the most optimistic forecast the planners in Tripoli can make is that by 1980 non-oil exports should account for 11 per cent of overseas earnings.[3] In the Sudan cotton accounted for almost 55 per cent of export proceeds in 1975/76, while exports of groundnuts made up another one-fifth of overseas earnings, and arabic gum and sesame a further one-eighth of the total.[4]

As a consequence of their dependence on single commodities, both countries find themselves in an extremely vulnerable situation economically. The prices paid for Sudan's cotton, as well as its other primary product exports, are determined in world markets, over which the Khartoum government has little control, and any attempt to regulate prices by controlling production would only have marginal effects, since there are so many other producers. Thus the Sudan has been powerless in recent years to stop prices falling, and in 1975 alone the world recession caused a loss of revenue of 30 per cent as demand for cotton slumped.[5] Oil differs from cotton in that the producing nations do determine prices to a large extent, independent of free market supply and demand considerations, through the OPEC cartel. Libya, however, has little say in pricing policy despite its membership of OPEC, for although its production amounts to 1·7 million barrels a day, this is small in comparison to that of Saudi Arabia and Iran, who tend to dominate OPEC proceedings. Therefore Libya, like the Sudan, is largely a price taker as far as its main export commodity is concerned, rather than a price maker.

The Sudan's problems as a result of this export dependence are much greater than Libya's, for the latter enjoys a much greater margin of latitude because its export receipts are almost twice its level of imports. Since the revolution of 1969 Libya has therefore been able to take a tough line with the Western oil companies, initially by demanding the participation of its own state company, the Libyan National Oil Company, in all domestic production undertaken by the multinationals, and later by nationalisation measures such as those taken against British Petroleum in December 1971.[6] Therefore the Tripoli government was not unduly worried when the multinational companies reduced their purchases of Libyan oil after the state intervention, even though by 1974 total production was only half of the 1970 level, and it has risen only slightly since.[7] The decline in the quantity sold has been more than compensated for by price increases, especially since the quadrupling of prices in 1974 following OPEC pressure on the Western consumers.

Cotton producers are not in this fortunate position, for fluctuations in output due to variable harvests have not been compensated for by higher prices, basically because the cycles of production do not coincide in all the exporting ountries. It has been impossible for cotton producers to act together like the oil producers, as quotas on production would be difficult to supervise in all the vast growing areas. In any case the United States is a major producer, and, since its policies favour consumers, it could increase supplies to counter any production cuts elsewhere. The problems for the Sudan, as with the other producers, are accentuated by the fact that the cotton industry is the largest single employer in the country, and hence any curtailment of production would lead to widespread unemployment and economic dislocation. In contrast the petroleum industry employs few people because of its capital-intensive nature, and in the Libyan case as there were few local nationals engaged in the industry before the revolution, the government has not needed to worry on this account. Hence the Sudanese have much less freedom of manoeuvre economically than their Libyan neighbours, and this no doubt helps explain the more venturesome stance of the Revolutionary Command Council in Tripoli compared to that adopted by the authorities in Khartoum.

ARABS IN AFRICA

The contrast between the venturesome stance of the Libyans and the more conservative policies of the Sudanese, is perhaps best illustrated in the pan-African relations of the two countries. Libya as a financially rich aid donor is courted by many of the poorer countries of Sub-Saharan Africa, while few bother about trying to find favour with the poorer Sudanese, who have nothing to give. So keen have the governments of Sub-Saharan Africa been to get financial assistance from Libya, that they have often been willing to change their policies with respect to the Middle East conflict, and support the Arab cause, especially in United Nations debates, and in their voting at the General Assembly in New York. Due largely to Colonel Gaddafi's determination to use Libyan funds to win African support, Israel now finds itself with few friends in Africa, and the efforts which the Jerusalem government made to aid the poorer countries of the continent by assisting with agricultural projects have yielded few political dividends.

Uganda provides a classic example of this turnabout in policy, for there the Israelis granted military as well as civilian assistance to the Obote government; but after the 1970 coup which brought a Moslem, General Amin, to power, the Libyans stepped in with aid, and the Israelis were blamed for many of the shortcomings of the previous regime. Although President Amin has seriously mismanaged the economic affairs of Uganda, the country has been saved from international bankruptcy, and the government from internal collapse, largely thanks to considerable assistance from Libya. In return Amin has himself tried to promote the Arab cause with his African neighbours, in particular by using his position when he was head of the Organisation of African Unity.

The Sudan's links with non-Arab African states date back much longer than those of Libya, largely on account of the country's geographical position, since it shares common frontiers with Ethiopia, Kenya, Uganda, Zaire, the Central African Empire and Chad. Sudan has only two Arab neighbours, Egypt and Libya, and communications with these northern states are poor. There are no roads overland linking Libya and the Sudan, and the route north along the Nile Valley to Upper Egypt usually involves a slow boat journey across Lake Nasser (or Lake Nubia, as the Sudanese prefer to call it) to Aswan, near the High Dam. Communications across the Red Sea to Saudi Arabia are also poor, but these will be improved when the highway from Khartoum to Port Sudan is asphalted in 1979, and the modernisation programme gets under way at the port.[8] Libya, in contrast, enjoys better communications with its Arab neighbours as its centres of settlement are mainly along the Mediterranean littoral, and this sea acts as a major communications artery for the countries around it. An overland highway links Tripoli and Tunis, while to the east Benghazi is connected by road with Alexandria, although strained political relations between Gaddafi and his Arab neighbours have resulted in frequent border closures. These disputes result from close contacts, however, and while Libya's southern frontiers with Chad and Niger remain quiet, for the most part, although Gaddafi supports the Moslem rebels in Chad who challenge the French-backed government. Libya's economic links with the south, however, are slight, in contrast to the movement across Sudan's southern border which is considerable. A new 150-mile asphalted road is planned to link Juba, the main commercial centre of the South, with Lodwar in the Turkana District of Kenya, under a £4 million aid scheme being financed by the Norwegian government.[9]

The greatest difference between the two countries being examined here as far as their African dimensions are concerned, is that, while all Libyans are Arabs, over one-third of the inhabitants of the Sudan are non-Arab Africans, as already mentioned, and the majority of these are Christians rather than Moslems. The provinces of Equatoria and the Upper Nile, where most of these non-Arabs live, have more in common with the surrounding African states economically, socially and culturally than they do with the Arab regions further north, even within the Sudan itself. In 1955, one year before independence, an armed conflict broke out in the south, for the African population there did not want to be part of an Arab ruled country. After independence the struggle intensified and by 1964 it had developed into a full-scale civil war with 20,000 northern troops deployed in the Juba area. As a consequence of these bitter hostilities the people on Sudan's borders tend to view Arabs as oppressors rather than as allies, and until recently the Third World solidarity that President Gaddafi espouses has been notably absent in relations between the Khartoum government and its Sub-Saharan African neighbours.

The 1972 Addis Ababa agreement which ended the civil war in the Sudan has helped the country's economy appreciably.[10] During the 1960s almost one-quarter of all public expenditure was devoted to maintaining the army in the south, but since the ending of open hostilities it has been possible to scale down military expenditure, and devote more resources to civilian projects. The defence cut-backs could have been even larger, however, had it not been for the provision in the Addis Ababa agreement whereby 6000 former Anya-nya guerrillas under General Joseph Lagu were absorbed into the regular army, and paid generous salaries. Apart from this continuing injection of defence funds, which at least now go to southerners for the first time, there has been little expenditure by the central government in the south, but to a large extent the southerners have only themselves to blame. When a new joint Sudanese-Egyptian scheme was announced for the construction of a canal between Malakal and Juba to drain the Sudd swamps and reclaim the land for agriculture, this met with violent local opposition, which arose because of a rumour that 50,000 Sudanese Arabs and Egyptians would be brought into the area to farm the reclaimed land.[11]

The greatest constraint on development in the south of the Sudan is the lack of infrastructure. Agricultural projects which aim to increase output cannot be viable unless the additional produce can be marketed, and at present this presents enormous difficulties as there is no rail link to Equatorià or the Upper Nile regions from Khartoum. Meanwhile the 700-mile road to the north remains unsurfaced, and many of the unsurfaced feeder roads in the south deteriorated considerably during the civil war. Yet the south contains over half of all the country's livestock, which could be profitably exported to the rich markets across the Red Sea. With this in mind the Kuwait-based Arab Fund for Economic and Social Development plan to invest over $1,000 million in the region, in order to promote a greater degree of self sufficiency in foodstuffs in the Arab world as a whole. The World Bank has also lent funds, though on a much smaller scale, for livestock development, together with West Germany and Qatar.

Although this development finance for the south has not involved Sudanese government funds, there are many in the north who resent any money being spent in the non-Arab areas, from whatever source. The northern regions themselves have pressing needs for finance, yet they have to act through the Khartoum government; while the south, because of its new autonomous status, can negotiate directly with outside aid agencies. The Khartoum government is unlikely to veto economic proposals for which there is strong support in the Juba parliament, for the ending of the civil war is regarded as President Nimeiri's greatest achievement, and the central administration wants to avoid at all costs any action which might undermine this. Sudan is the largest country territorially in Africa, and also the largest in the Middle East, so it is perhaps inevitable that it should have regional problems. President Nimairi has staged a delicate balancing act to ensure that the country is kept intact by peaceful means, but it is impossible to satisfy all regional interests at the same time. In any discussion of Sudan's future, the question of inter-regional income will inevitably loom large.[12]

The Sudanese government, because of the ethnic and geographical composition of its own country, has far more knowledge of African problems than other Arab governments. In their external policies the Khartoum authorities have been trying hard to try to bring Arabs and Africans together, as they have succeeded in some measure in doing domestically. As Sudan is often viewed as a bridge between the Moslem world and the rest of Africa, it seemed only natural that when it was decided to establish an institution for channelling funds from the Arab oil-rich states into Africa, it should be located in Khartoum. The Arab Bank for Economic Development in Africa (BADEA) was first founded in 1973 with an authorised capital of $231 million, but this has subsequently been increased to $886·5 million.[13] Shares in the bank are held by eighteen Arab states, with Saudi Arabia, the largest subscriber, contributing $285 million, while Libya and Kuwait, the second largest shareholders, have shares worth $120 million each. In 1977 BADEA absorbed the Special Arab Fund for Africa (SAFA), which was designed to help poor Sub-Saharan African states with their oil payments following the 1974 price increases, and this accounts for most of the lending. BADEA, however, is increasingly becoming concerned with long-term development projects rather than with granting short-term balance of payments assistance, and by the fourth year of its operations project loans worth $208 million had been advanced to a large number of African countries, including Rwanda, Guinea, Tanzania, Mozambique and Botswana.[14]

LANDS OF THIRST AND PLENTY

As well as acting as an intermediary to channel Arab funds to the rest of Africa, it seems that during the next few years, the Sudan itself will be a major recipient of loans from the oil-producing nations. Reference has already been made to the assistance being given by the Arab Fund for Economic Development to the south of the country. This only accounts for less than one-quarter of the foreign exchange being made available by the Arab Fund for projects throughout the country, as Table 9.1 shows. In recent years Sudan has been the second largest recipient of Arab loans after Egypt, but this reflects the country's development potential, especially with respect to agriculture, which is probably greater than that of any other Arab state. Most of the Finance being provided by the Arab Fund under its 1976-85 plan is for agricultural projects, around two-thirds of which are seen as commercially viable, as the table indicates.

There is little doubt that it makes sense economically to direct funds into development in the Sudan rather than trying to start ambitious agricultural projects in the arid oil-rich Arab states themselves, for as the Sudan has a much more favourable resource endowment for farming, the costs per unit of output are likely to be consequently considerably lower. The commercially viable projects are either being financed by

TABLE 9.1. Arab Fund projects in the Sudan

		Cost £m[a] Sudanese			Finance £m Sudanese		
	Number of projects	Total	Local currency	Foreign exchange	Investment in equity	Commercial loans	Soft loans and grants
Commercially viable projects							
Crops	9	385	190	195	194	191	—
Livestock	9	240	93	147	124	116	—
Agro-industry	11	355	117	238	180	175	—
Transport	2	63	11	52	32	31	—
Sub-total	31	1043	411	632	530	513	—
Non-commercial projects							
Crops	9	376	124	252	—	30	346
Livestock	10	169	86	83	—	—	169
Agro-Industries	6	28	7	21	—	11	17
Sub-total	25	573	217	356	—	41	532
Infastructure							
Transport	23	411	105	306	—	—	411
Water resources	6	122	35	87	—	—	122
Supporting services	5	78	21	57	—	14	64
Sub-total	34	611	161	450	—	14	597
Institutional supports	10	60	12	48	10	—	50
Total	100	2287	801	1486	540	568	1179

[a] \$ = £ Sud. 0·35, £ Sterling = £ Sud. 0·60 (October 1977).
Source: Arab Fund for Economic and Social Development, *Basic Programme for Agricultural Development in the Democratic Republic of the Sudan 1976–1985* (Kuwait, October 1976) Appendix 3, pp. 16–17.

investment in equity or by commercial loans on terms similar to finance made available to the oil importing nations of the west. Soft loans and grants only have to be provided for the non-commercial projects and infrastructure development, as Table 9.1 shows, so that the more directly productive projects are certain of paying their way. Overall the Arab Fund programme for the Sudan represents the most ambitious joint Arab project undertaken to date, and one of the largest development schemes undertaken anywhere in the Third World. It is encouraging to see that despite their political differences economic reason is prevailing amongst the Arab states, and if succesfully implemented the $7,000 million programme may represent the most useful outcome from the Middle East oil bonanza.[15]

Although the prospects for agricultural projects in the oil-rich states appear to be unfavourable in terms of any short-term gains in crop production on a large scale, the funds being devoted to arid land research may contribute to a long-term scientific breakthrough in agricultural methods. The Sudanese projects use known technology, and the problems encountered are largely organisational, whereas in states such as Libya researchers are dealing with the technologically unknown. The Libyans are nevertheless spending over $2000 million before 1983 on land reclamation, in an attempt to convert over 1,500,000 acres of arid land into agricultural production. The first priority has been to fix the ever-shifting sand dunes, and to achieve this over 28 million seedling trees were planted in 1974 alone as part of a continuing programme.[16]

The greatest constraint on Libyan agriculture is, of course, water supplies, and desalinisation of water from the Mediterranean for agricultural purposes is not economically feasible. A cheaper water purification scheme involves the recycling of Tripoli's sewerage water for irrigation, but this will only provide supplies for 100 farms occupying 1500 acres.[17] Most of the new water being harnessed for agriculture will come from artesian sources located in areas such as the Kufra depression, over 600 miles south of Tripoli in the desert, where 24,000 acres have already been reclaimed.[18] Through the use of artesian water here and elsewhere Libya's planners hope that by 1980 the country's irrigated areas will have increased by over 250,000 acres to almost 750,000 acres.[19] At the same time dry land farming in the coastal region will cover four times this amount. Despite this expansion it seems that the best Libya can hope for in regard to self-sufficiency in foodstuffs is that one-fifth of its domestic needs can be met from local production by 1980, compared with 14 per cent in 1975. This modest target is dependent on supplies of artesian water being up to expectations, and not becoming salinised, as they have elsewhere when utilised intensively. In these circumstances returns on spending on water development schemes seem at best extremely limited, and possibly rather uncertain.

The Sudan has experienced few of the difficulties of Libya in the implementation of its own agricultural projects, since the main constraints on its rural development have been the supplies of man-made productive factors, rather than physical factors such as arable land and water resources. In particular the lack of infrastructure services, especially adequate communications, has proved a major problem, as already indicated, while manpower with appropriate skills has also been a constraint. These difficulties are perhaps best illustrated by referring to the case of the massive Kenana sugar project, in which the London-based multinational company Lonrho had an important stake. This venture represented the largest sugar scheme in the world, and was scheduled initially to produce 350,000 tons of refined white sugar a year, rising eventually to over 1 million tons.[20]

The Lonrho-managed project provides a classic illustration of how short-term constraints can harm the long-term prospects of what was regarded by most experts as an economically promising scheme. When the initial feasibility study was conducted for the Kenana project in 1973, the cost was estimated at $150 million. By 1975, however, even the most optimistic estimate put forward by the Sudanese Ministry of Industry suggested a figure of $250 million, while the Arab Investment Company, which was providing a large part of the finance, believed that $290 million was a closer estimate. By the following year, however, costs had increased to over $475 million, over three times the original estimate, and the Arab backers of the project were beginning to have second thoughts concerning their investment.[21] For the most part this cost escalation was due to the difficulties of transporting plant and equipment to the site of the project through congested Port Sudan, where surcharges on freight had been introduced because of shipping delays.

Lonrho, as the project managers, were held responsible for the difficulties that had arisen in implementation, since it was they who had drawn up the work schedule for the scheme in the first place. If a longer time-period had been allowed for implementation, much of the congestion at Port Sudan would have been cleared. The company was paying a high price for trying to do too much too quickly.[22] In addition Lonrho were accused of not hiring the most experienced subcontractors. Lonrho itself was partly Kuwaiti-owned, and as a result of this connection it engaged the little-known International Contracting Company of Kuwait to undertake the construction work on the irrigation canals.[23] This company had difficulties from the start in coping with a project as large as Kenana. But this was not the first time that the dealings of Lonrho had been criticised, for the activities of its managing-director, Mr Tiny Rowland, in the United Kingdom in the early 1970s, had already been described as the 'unacceptable face of capitalism' by the Prime Minister of the time, Edward Heath, which was a surprising statement from a conservative leader.[24] It seemed that by May 1977 the shareholders in the Kenana project were starting to share Heath's view, and Lonrho was ousted from its management role. Apparently even Lonrho's part-Kuwaiti ownership was insufficient to ensure its survival in the managerial role. Where finance is concerned, profit and loss considerations matter more than maintaining business connections.

NEO-COLONIALISM IN REVERSE

At the time of the 1969 revolutions in Libya and the Sudan both governments adopted a hostile stance towards the capitalist West, and multinational companies in particular. The Libyans denounced the exploitation of their resources by the Western petroleum companies, and demanded a larger share in royalty payments, while the Sudanese complained about the low prices for their cotton exports in international markets, although the situation regarding fluctuations in prices and export volume has not improved in recent years, as Table 9.2 shows. There was resentment that private funds had not been forthcoming for downstream investments to help diversify the economies of both countries out of primary production through the development of new industries. Most Libyan oil was refined abroad in the consuming nations rather than domestically, while Sudanese cotton was also exported in its raw state, since there were no local textile factories. Thus Libya had to import many of the refined petroleum products required domestically, and Sudan imported virtually all of its cloth and cotton clothing. In these circumstances it was hardly surprising that the new revolutionary regimes believed that the multinational enterprises acted against the economic interests of primary producing nations.

Following their 1969 revolutions both Gaddaff and Nimeiri encouraged closer commercial and economic relations with the communist world in order to reduce the dependence of their respective countries on

TABLE 9.2. Recent trends in Sudanese cotton exports

		1970	*1971*	*1972*	*1973*	*1974*	*1975*
Cotton price (Piastres per 100 lbs of lint)		1651	1810	1043	2049	2790	1600
Total exports	(thousand bales)	1197	1239	1287	1203	498	762
Exports of Western Europe	(thousand bales)	384	258	393	377	188	250
Exports to the USSR	(thousand bales)	311	317	8	0	7	22
Exports to China	(thousand bales)	94	188	205	288	85	119

Note: Prices are for cotton grade XG_3VS, which is representative of average prices.
Source: Bank of Sudan *Sixteenth Annual Report* (Khartoum, 1975) Appendix 6, p. 107, and Appendix 7, p. 108.

the capitalist West. At the same time the two governments tried to exercise more control over domestic economic activity, and drew up plans for establishing strong state sectors, as an alternative to the private businesses which had hitherto dominated both economies. In this the Libyans enjoyed more success than the Sudanese, for the former were able to provide the necessary capital themselves from their oil revenues, whereas the aid the Khartoum government requested from the Eastern bloc countries never came. The new Libyan industries launched during the first five years of the young republic included two dairy factories, four cereal mills, four fish canneries, a shoe factory, a cotton textile complex, a tyre factory, a pipe-making plant, and an electric wire and cable industry, as well as many other manufacturing establishments.[25]

In spite of this Libyan success in the development of import substitute industries, often with Russian technical assistance, relations with the communist world cooled considerably as time progressed. To a large extent this reflected political factors, for the Russians resented President Gaddafi's enthusiastic support for revolutionary movements throughout the world, which often conflicted with their own interests. The Russians were also disturbed by the attacks Gaddafi made, as a devout Moslem, on the materialism of the communist world. In trade relations the Libyans found their Eastern European connections almost worthless, since there was no possibility of exporting oil in volume to communist markets as an alternative to exporting to the West. As consequence of these factors, economic relations between Libya and Western Europe have once more been restored, while relations with the Eastern bloc have become steadily more strained. Prospects seem promising for continued economic co-operation, for now that the Libyans have agreed on compensation with the Western companies whose oil interests they nationalised, the one major issue outstanding between Libya and the West has finally been resolved.

In the Sudan the return to closer economic alignment with the West was much more sudden than the gradual turn-around that Libya made. It was the 1971 attempted coup against Nimeiri that marked the turning point, for then the Sudanese communists, who had obtained many of the key positions in central and local government, attempted to overthrow the regime and seize power.[26] Nimeiri believed that outside communist intervention had supported this almost successful coup, and relations between the Sudan and the Eastern bloc have never been the same since. Although these events were essentially political, they inevitably had widespread economic ramifications—first externally, for trade and financial relations, especially aid, tend to reflect political alignments, and these were immediately affected. Table 9.2 shows how cotton exports to the USSR virtually ceased and the Sudanese tried to direct more exports towards Western Europe and China instead. Second, there were major internal repercussions as, in the aftermath of the coup, communists were purged from their positions of power and influence in central and local government, and economic decision-making once again fell into the hands of those more favourably disposed to private enterprise and competitive markets.

The turn-around in Sudanese policy helps explain how, while the government remains revolutionary in name, it takes a very liberal stance regarding foreign investment and private economic activity in general. All foreign investment in new industry is exempted from tax for a five-year period, although this exemption only runs to three years in the case of investments in transport, warehousing and agricultural projects.[27] After that a profits tax is levied at a rate of 60 per cent,[28] but as depreciation allowances are calculated on a generous basis, once these allowances are taken into account, the rate is not as punitive as it at first appears. Exemption from customs duties is permitted for imported components and other inputs for use in new projects which are not made locally. Best of all from the point of view of the foreign investor are the provisions of the law for free repatriation of profit and investment funds. As an added incentive a 15 per cent exchange rate bonus is granted on incoming funds, although this is deducted from all exported capital, but not profits.[29]

In the case of Libya there is obviously less interest in attracting direct foreign investment, for there is plenty of finance locally available. The Libyan authorities would like to see local private investors playing a more active role in industrial activity, and the most recent development plan states that 'private investors are still deficient in the spirit of risk taking and initiative which are necessary if the profit motive of businessmen is to be economically valuable.'[30] These would appear to be remarkably pro-business sentiments for a regime which is supposedly revolutionary. Foreign businessmen visiting Libya find that it is the quality of their goods and the prices that determine what can be sold, not the country of origin, though of course the Arab boycott of Israel is strictly observed. Large contracts, however, are only awarded to companies who have appointed an agent in Libya, and any local subsidiaries of foreign companies must by law have 70 per cent of their employees as Libyan nationals.[31] Under profit-sharing laws, one-quarter of all profits must be distributed to employees.[32]

Instead of being antagonistic towards capitalist companies, the Libyan authorities have in recent years been keen to enter into joint ventures with Western private interests. In a deal announced in November 1976, for instance, the Libyan government agreed to set up a factory near Tripoli in co-operation with Massey Ferguson, the United Kingdom tractor producers. Massey Ferguson is investing $2,250,000 in the project over a period of five to six years, and the Libyans are investing a larger sum. When completed the factory will have the capacity to produce 3000 tractors a year, and will provide employment for 300 workers.[33] The Libyans are also willing to establish joint ventures with Western partners in other Third World countries. In June 1977 Libya took a major shareholding in a new company, Medelec, set up with British and Maltese interests, to manufacture transformers and electrical switchgear. This Malta-based company will be able to sell its products on an exclusive basis in ten countries—Algeria, Chad, China, Cuba, Ethiopia, Libya, Malta, Morocco, Tunisia and North Yemen. Components for the transformers will be provided by the British General Electrical Company (GEC), which itself has a minority shareholding in the Maltese venture.[34]

As a result of this kind of overseas involvement with major multinational companies, the Libyans are already being regarded by radicals in the Third World as willing participants in the international capitalist system. This is certainly a sign of the *volte-face* which Gaddafi's Revolutionary Command Council appears to have made as far as its international economic relations and policies are concerned. The most striking instance of Libya's involvement with Western multinational companies has been the Fiat participation deal, under which the Libyan Arab Foreign Bank invested $415 million in the Italian company, and took a 9·6 per cent stake in the shareholdings.[35] Libya's ownership share may be raised to 13 per cent by 1982 if the bank converts the bonds it has bought from Fiat. As well as providing a profitable outlet for oil revenue surpluses, the deal also gives Libya a stake in one of the most technologically sophisticated Western companies, whose worldwide interests include Arab states. Within Libya itself, Fiat are building a lorry and bus assembly plant at Tajoura near Tripoli to produce 4000 vehicles a year.[36] Although this will provide employment for local citizens, it is nevertheless ironic that the Libyan 'revolutionaries' should be directing funds into the country which formerly colonised them. Instead of hearing accusations of exploitation on the part of the colonised, it seems that soon it will be the citizens of the former colonial power who may be taking up the call.

10 Lebanon and Jordan: Enclaves of Capitalism

> I have never known much good done by those who affected to trade for the public good. It is an affectation, indeed not very common among merchants, and very few words need be employed in dissuading them from it.
>
> Adam Smith, *Wealth of Nations* (1776)

These two small countries have been left to the end of this study of the economies of the Middle East. This is not because their limited size makes them any less significant, but rather is due to the fact that both their economies are very dependent on the economic health of the other countries already covered. Lebanese commerce and banking served the whole Middle East, and only a small portion of its business was generated internally. Similarly the Hashemite Kingdom of Jordan was, and is, dependent on financial support from the oil-rich monarchies and shiekhdoms to the south, to cover both its budget deficit and its balance of payments. A knowledge of the Middle Eastern neighbours of both states therefore helps the reader understand the forces underlying Lebanese and Jordanian development, as well as the economic constraints.

In addition, because of the cosmopolitan nature of both countries, especially the Lebanon, their economic and social problems represent in a microcosm the problems of the whole Middle East region. It is, of course, well known that both countries militarily have been to some extent a testing ground for the region's opposing forces, comparable in many ways to the situation of Spain in relation to Europe during the inter-war period. On the economic plane as well, however, the debate about economic systems and philosophy has been much wider than the exchanges elsewhere in the Middle East. This partially reflects the greater freedom of expression that both countries enjoy, as well as the high educational attainments of many of their residents. If any distinct Arab, Moslem or Middle Eastern economic philosophy ever emerges, then it seems highly likely that either Lebanon or Jordan will be its birthplace.

Lebanon's total residents number only 2·8 million,[1] while Jordan has only 1·8 million inhabitants, excluding the Israeli-occupied West Bank, lost in the 1967 war.[2] This makes both countries the smallest included in the study, apart from the sheikhdoms and emirates of the Gulf, which can scarcely be considered as nation states in the usually accepted sense of the term. Such small populations imply limited domestic markets, which mean that producers cannot take advantage of any economies of scale unless they are primarily export-orientated. This size factor therefore dictates to a large degree what type of economic development is possible, and means that, in the absence of any regional economic integration, heavy industry for example would never be a viable proposition. Instead light industries, with low overhead costs, would appear to be a more appropriate alternative for both countries, as the least cost unit of output can be manufactured on a small production run.

A major feature of the population structures of both Lebanon and Jordan is the high proportion of immigrants. This is of course the direct consequence of the emergence of Israel as an independent Jewish state, for the largest single immigrant group in the two countries is of Palestinian origin. More than half of the population of Jordan are Palestinian refugees, for it has been the state in the Middle East most affected by the Arab-Israeli conflict. Many of these Palestinians hold Jordanian passports, however, especially those from the West Bank of the Jordan, which used to be part of the Hashemite Kingdom. There are still 750,000 Arabs holding Jordanian passports residing on the Israeli-occupied West Bank, but for most practical purposes they are now part of the Israeli economy, so they are excluded from the discussion in this chapter, and omitted from the population figure cited earlier for Jordan.[3] Those Palestinians who hold Jordanian passports of course owe allegiance to King Hussein, or at least acquiesce to his rule, but the King's most loyal subjects are the Bedouin minority from the eastern desert, whom many regard as the true Jordanians, rather than the Palestinian urban dwellers of Amman or the settled cultivators down in the Jordan Valley. It is the descendants of the nomadic Bedouin who form the backbone of the King's army, which played a major part in preventing a Palestinian take-over of the country during the civil war of 1971. Needless to say many Palestinians remain violently opposed to King Hussein, and will never forget the 'Black September' of 1971 when Palestinian resistance to Hashemite rule was ruthlessly crushed.[4]

The Palestinians also form the largest single minority in the Lebanon, as there are 212,800 resident in refugee camps, and 95,000 living outside the camps.[5] In contrast to the situation in Jordan, however, few of these Palestinians hold Lebanese passports, apart from a minority of Christians from the Haifa area and the north of Israel, who sought refuge with their fellow co-religionists in Lebanon rather than in neighbouring Moslem states following the Israeli war of independence in 1948. The feeling of being left out led to considerable discontent, especially as most of these Palestinians were unable to acquire any citizen's rights in the country in which most of them had resided for over twenty-five years, and into which the majority of the younger generation had been born. As a result of these frustrations, some outbreak of hostility was inevitable, as it had been in Jordan, although the severity of the Lebanese civil war in 1975 and 1976 was graver than even the most pessimistic had predicted.[6]

Like Jordan, over half of the population of Lebanon are immigrants or their first generation descendants. Apart from the Palestinians already discussed, there are 250,000 Syrians resident in Lebanon, which makes them the second largest minority group. Many of these had migrated to Beirut for economic reasons, although some were political dissidents who chose to live in exile. The presence of this minority was a major factor determining Syrian intervention in the Lebanese civil war, although historical and strategic factors also undoubtedly played a part. By 1975, in addition to Syrian residents, there were a further 31,500 Syrians in Lebanon, many of them military personnel, but also some civilian administrators in the two-thirds of the country occupied by Syrian forces from the spring of that year. This new influx probably more than offset the departures of other immigrant groups resulting from the civil war. According to a private census undertaken in 1974, before the hostilities these included 75,000 Egyptians, 78,000 other North Africans, 30,000 French, 15,000 Americans and 14,000 British.[7] These groups have made Lebanon the most ethnically mixed country in the Middle East, and Beirut the most cosmopolitan city of the region.

THE FIXER

The physical resource bases of Lebanon and Jordan are extremely limited, which precludes any substantial development of primary economic activity, even if the constraints imposed by the size of their domestic markets could be overcome. In these circumstances both countries have relied more on their human resources rather than their physical ones, and have emerged as major service centres, with tertiary activities the most developed. Lebanon does of course boast some agriculture because of its winter rainfall, especially in the Bekaa valley behind the coastal mountains, but the country's limited territorial area, only 10,170 square kilometres, just over half the size of Wales, means that it can never be a major agricultural producer. Similarly, although the territorial area of the East Bank of Jordan is almost nine times greater than that of Lebanon, most of this is desert or arid scrub, and apart from the irrigated lands of the Jordan Valley there is little agriculture. Jordan however, unlike Lebanon, can boast some mineral resources, and phosphate extraction has become the country's leading industry in terms of value of output. Phosphate production alone accounted for almost one-tenth of GDP in 1975, and has become Jordan's largest single source of export earnings.

The significance of phosphates for the Jordanian economy can easily be exaggerated, however, and, in the 1976–80 development plan in particular, too much emphasis is given to extractive industry.[8] Only a small number of people are engaged in phosphate extraction and, even if the $75 million allocated to the industry is actually invested, it seems unlikely that the proportion of the active workforce engaged in the phosphate industry will amount to more than 1 per cent. This is a poor return on investment in terms of job creation, and it seems likely that if the funds were used for alternative projects the impact on employment in Jordan would be much greater. The usefulness of phosphates as a source of export earnings can also be exaggerated, although exports were worth $65 million in 1974, making it the largest single foreign exchange earner, it seems unlikely that the earnings projection of $300 million by 1980 will ever be realised. The record earnings in 1974 were a result of a fourfold increase in the price of phosphates on world markets. During 1975 and 1976 the price started to fall again as the United States and the Soviet Union started to expand their own phosphate production. Due to this vulnerability to world market conditions, the future for phosphates in Jordan remains uncertain, despite the territory's vast reserves, estimated at around 3000 million tons, of which only 15 million tons has been extracted. They will probably continue to provide valuable foreign exchange, but the country's planners would be unwise to rely on a steady stream of earnings, for Third World producers do not dominate phosphate markets as is the case with oil, and no OPEC for phosphates seems probable.[9]

The impact of commerce and services on the Jordanian economy is already much greater than that of either agriculture or manufacturing, since service activities account for over 63 per cent of total employment,

TABLE 10.1. Employment by sector in Jordan and Lebanon (%)

	Jordan		Lebanon
	1961	1975	1970
Agriculture	35	18	19
Industry and construction	21	19	25
Services	44	63	56

Sources: Hashemite Kingdom of Jordan, *Five-Year Plan 1976–80* (National Planning Council, Amman, 1976) p. 25; *Recueil de statistiques Libanaises*, (Ministère du Plan, Direction Centrale de la Statistique, Beirut, 1972) no. 8, p. 91.

as Table 10.1 shows, including wholesale and retail trade, transport services and financial institutions. This represents a substantial increase over the 1961 figure, when the share of services in total employment was 44 per cent. In contrast, over the 1961–75 period, the share of agriculture in employment has declined from 35 per cent to 18 per cent. In Lebanon services also account for most employment, though unfortunately no figures are available to illustrate the change in employment over time. It seems likely, however, that the trends are comparable to those in Jordan. Care must be taken, of course, with employment data, as many of those in agriculture are not registered employees. The data in Table 10.1 however includes the self-employed, as well as employees and employers, but not seasonal or part-time workers.

The service sector in Lebanon was geared to the needs of the entire Middle East region, and not merely to the domestic economy, as is primarily the case in Jordan. Since the Lebanese civil war, admittedly, Amman has vied with other Middle East capitals to acquire Beirut's role as the region's main financial centre, but although it has probably attracted more business than any other single centre in the region, apart from Bahrain, it cannot really be considered as a serious alternative to Beirut. Amman does offer the usual offshore banking incentives, including free convertibility of deposits held in non-resident accounts, exemptions of foreign companies and their expatriate employees from local taxes, freedom from import duties for goods in transit or imported components to be used in export industries, etc.[10] However, Amman is not an entrepôt centre in the sense that the port of Beirut was, nor does it have the office space, telecommunications facilities and other commercial infrastructure which the Lebanese capital once had. Nevertheless these have been improved in recent years, and a growing number of international banks have started operating in Amman.[11]

Major financial centres are usually located in countries with strong and stable currencies, and in this respect Jordan is well placed. The stability of the Jordanian dinar is perhaps surprising given the country's large and growing foreign trade deficit, with imports over four times greater than exports in recent years. In addition there is a high rate of domestic inflation, with the cost-of-living index for Amman almost doubling over the 1970–6 period, and prices rising by over 20 per cent in 1976 alone. Despite this domestic inflation the dinar has actually appreciated slightly against the United States dollar during the 1970s, and rose substantially against the Israeli pound on the unofficial West Bank currency markets. It is foreign aid, however, that helps Jordan maintain adequate reserve holdings to support its currency. Aid from the United States and Western Europe has been disappointingly small in spite of King Hussein's pro-Western stance, but since 1974 the shortfall in Western aid has been more than made up by finance from the Arab oil producers. This is mostly in the form of government bilateral grants and loans, as fellow monarchs such as King Kalid are concerned that King Hussein should survive and Jordan prosper. In contrast, most of the finance that went into Lebanon before the civil war was private funds, deployed to make a profit, rather than because of political factors. These private funds helped maintain the value of the Lebanese pound, and the authorities tried to retain international confidence, even during the first few months of the civil war, by continuing to have the currency 90 per cent backed by gold holdings.

As well as having a strong and freely convertible currency, several other factors helped Beirut to keep its position as the commercial and banking centre of the Arab world for over two decades, not least of which was its entrepreneural tradition.[12] Financial growth was admittedly aided by the passing of the Bank Secrecy Law in 1956, modelled on the Swiss practice, which meant the amounts and ownership of bank deposits did not have to be disclosed. This liberal banking approach contrasted strongly with the restrictionist policies adopted in many of the leading Arab revolutionary states during the 1950s and early 1960s, when commercial activity was increasingly taken over by the state, and the banking systems nationalised.[13] As a consequence money flowed into the Lebanese banking system from all over the Middle East, and the ratio of bank deposits to total national income rose from 20 per cent to 90 per cent over the twenty-year period up to 1973, At the same time the number of banking institutions proliferated, until there were over seventy different banks operating in Beirut alone.[14] However, after the collapse of the Intra Bank in 1966, banking regulations were tightened, no new licences were granted, and minimum reserve requirements were raised. In this way it was hoped that confidence in the Lebanese banking system would be maintained, and the steady growth of deposits over the 1967–75 period showed that these hopes were realised.[15]

The Jordanian authorities would have been well advised to study this Lebanese experience before enacting their own legislation in 1975 to liberalise banking procedures, so as to attract some of Beirut's business. Then they made registration of new banks simpler and faster, and in addition removed the 12 per cent legal reserve requirement on non-resident deposits. These provisions may well attract numerous fringe banks, but they run the risk of undermining confidence in Amman as a financial centre. Liberal legislation is only one prerequisite for the establishment of a banking centre; another is financial caution.

Although Jordanians lack the commercial expertise and experience of the Lebanese, the Kingdom's main economic attraction is undoubtedly its stability of government and political institutions. King Hussein has managed to survive longer than any other ruler in the Arab world, and his country enjoys the continuity of rule that so many of the other states in the region lack. Admittedly the Lebanese constitutional arrangements did help to ensure political stability for a long period, which in turn fostered economic confidence, but in the end they proved too rigid, and could not adapt easily to the changed situation of the mid-1970s. King Hussein, in contrast, has managed to display tremendous flexibility, and to guide his country, from his position as absolute monarch, out of the chaos of the 1970 civil war towards economic recovery. It remains to be seen whether President Elias Sarkis will be able to do the same from his much weaker political and constitutional position.

To a large extent the contrasts between Lebanon and Jordan today reflect their different historical circumstances. Both countries were strongly influenced by European colonial powers, Lebanon falling under the French sphere of influence, and Jordan under the British. In the Lebanon many of the Christians are bilingual, and often even discuss business between themselves in French, conducting their affairs in a similar manner to businessmen from Paris or Lyon. Like the French they are excessively preoccupied with legalistic formulae, and perhaps lack the pragmatism that King Hussein and his advisors have acquired through their British connections. The Lebanese are conscious, however, of being part of a much older trading tradition, which dates back to the time of the Phoenicians, who traded throughout the eastern Mediterranean and beyond. It is this that gives them their reputation as merchants, able to negotiate involved business deals. Unfortunately, the Jordanians lack such traditions—the Bedouin nomads acted as carriers rather than 'fixers'. In view of this it seems unlikely that Amman will ever rival Beirut as a major trading centre for regional and international transactions.

SMALL IS BEAUTIFUL

Prior to the Lebanese civil war, the emphasis on the development of the service sector restricted interest in manufacturing. Yet the country has a strong tradition of industry and craft, dating back to the time of the Phoenicians, who not only traded in foreign goods, but also dealt with domestically produced articles. Many of the gold and silver *objets d'art* which the Phoenicians traded were made locally by highly skilled craftsmen, and these craft activities still thrive. So do glass blowing, spinning, weaving and dyeing, furniture manufacture and metal work.[16] All these industries are on a small scale, with furniture manufacture and metal work usually being carried out in workshops employing fewer than ten people.[17] Often the owner himself works alongside his family in the workshop, teaching his sons the skills that were previously passed on to him. As the tools used are simple, and little machinery is needed, the capital requirements of such businesses are limited, and most of the profits made from retailing the produce accrue directly to the owner himself, and the skilled craftsmen employed. Often the workshops retail direct to the customers, which eliminates the need for any middle men, who so often take a substantial portion of the profits of modern manufacturing.

Most spinning and weaving in Lebanon by the mid-1970s was carried out on modern mechanised looms, rather than the traditional hand looms, and as a result of this innovation cottage industry no longer existed in this field of manufacturing. Spinning and weaving, together with food-processing, accounted for over half of the total number of Lebanese engaged in manufacturing, which in 1974 amounted to 120,000 workers. All the new plants concerned had been developed since the 1950s, and until the civil war the Lebanon had more privately owned light industries than any other Arab country in the Middle East. The country's liberal economic policy had encouraged the growth of this private industry, while the well-developed banking sector meant that ample funds were available to finance investment in plant.[18] All the industries were light, however, orientated to the production of consumer goods. This was a result of its being in private hands, with the profit motive paramount, for investors went into those areas of production where the country had its most obvious advantage.

Private investors were unwilling to invest in the heavy industries such as iron and steel, which have been developed within the state sectors of other Middle Eastern states. Lebanon has few raw materials, and no iron ore, which means the economic viability of heavy industry is extremely doubtful. Instead, private entrepreneurs have invested in activities such as fruit canning and jam manufacture, where local agricultural produce is used. Local clothing manufacture have also expanded, using domestically produced fabrics, and many of the garments are attractively styled, with the French influence still apparent. The leather goods industry is another expanding activity, using both Lebanese and Syrian hides and skins to make shoes, jackets, bags and other products.

Some Lebanese light industries owe their establishment to events in the late 1960s when, after the crash of the Intra Bank and the war with Israel, there was a major loss of confidence in the service sector, even though Lebanon itself was not involved in the conflict. At that time leading figures in the country began to realise that an excessive dependence on services rendered the economy vulnerable, and that the only remedy was to diversify into manufacturing. The government, however, was reluctant to intervene itself in the economy, and instead encouraged the commercial banks to lend out more funds to help private ventures. In 1973 the government decided to take more direct action, and established the National Bank for the Development of Industry and Tourism, with an initial capital of £20 million. This was a joint venture, with the state subscribing 51 per cent of the paid-up capital, and a consortium of 46 private Lebanese and foreign banks providing the rest. Between 1973 and 1975 the bank aided 14 major industrial projects, and provided two-thirds of its funds for industry.[19] This promising start was unfortunately halted prematurely, as were so many new Lebanese ventures, by the outbreak of the civil war.

Jordanian manufacturing industry, like that of Lebanon, is mostly on a small scale, catering primarily for the domestic market. The government favours import substitution, for this reduces the country's heavy dependence on external supplies and saves valuable foreign exchange. As a result of generous tariff protection industrial diversification is gathering momentum, and almost 30,000 people are now employed in manufacturing. The tariff protection given to Jordan's new industry ranges from 15 per cent on chemicals to 77 per cent on textiles and food processing. Between 1973 and 1975, 184 new factories were licensed, and 720 new workshops registered. As in Lebanon, most factories are small, however, and only 78 establishments employ more than 100 people, while over 1000 firms employ between 5 and 99 people. The remaining establishments, estimated at 6000, employ under 4 people.[20]

Table 10.2 indicates the size distribution of industrial firms in

TABLE 10.2. Size of industrial firms in Lebanon and Jordan

	Lebanon		*Jordan*	
No. of employees	*No. of firms %*	*No. of employees %*	*No. of firms %*	*No. of employees %*
5–9	51·4	12·9	57·2	5·5
10–24	33·0	20·9	23·5	6·6
25–49	8·9	15·0	8·5	5·7
50+	6·7	51·2	10·7	82·3
Total	2099	41093	1149	60949

Sources: Recueil de statistiques libanaises, (Ministère du Plan, Direction Centrale de la Statistique, Beirut, 1972) no. 18, p. 156.
Hashemite Kingdom of Jordan, *Statistical Yearbook* (Department of Statistics, Amman, 1972) no. 25, Table 148, p. 198.

Lebanon and Jordan. Further indication of the neglect of industry in Lebanon is provided by the statistics themselves, as those cited in the 1972 official publication refer to 1964, the last year when an employment survey was undertaken of the country's firms. In comparison to the 1972 figures for Jordan, the Lebanese data obviously provide an underestimate of the size of its manufacturing sector, although it is probably a reasonably accurate portrayal, as industrial progress was slow in the eight intervening years compared to the expansion of services in Beirut. It is interesting to note from the table similarities in both countries between firm size and employment structure. In Lebanon workshops employing under ten people are of relatively greater importance, and this picture would be reinforced if workshops employing under five were included. Larger firms would appear to be of greater significance in Jordan, although much of this is accounted for by a few modern plants in the Amman area, such as the Jordan Spinning and Weaving Company. The expansion of the latter has to some extent merely served to drive small spinning and weaving establishments of the cottage-industry type out of business, so it may not have contributed much to employment overall.

Protection for local modern textile plants in Jordan has produced a boom in the industry. One share issue by the Jordan Spinning and Weaving Company was thrice over-subscribed. The cement industry has recently been in the same happy situation, due to a local construction boom, but it is protected by the high cost of importing cement rather than through deliberate government tariff policy. The Jordanian Cement Company is planning to build a new plant costing £7 million, which will have a daily output capacity of 2000 tons. A new ceramics industry has been established, with its products marketed locally for the first time in 1976, and the quality is so good that there would appear to be considerable export market potential within the Middle East, if not in the outside world. In recent years confidence in the Jordanian economy has been such that over fifty companies, formerly resident in Beirut, chose to move to Amman in preference to other Middle East centres, including Cairo and the Gulf capitals.[21]

Despite all these encouraging developments, there has been to some extent a misallocation of investment resources in the Jordanian economy, with small workshops and agriculture suffering at the expense of the larger-scale establishments. Yet these small workshops still account for many of the jobs in manufacturing, as Table 10.2 shows, and provide training in skills, at no cost to the government, which larger concerns usually fail to undertake themselves. In addition they are especially well suited to the small Jordanian market. It has already been mentioned how substantial investment funds have been channelled into phosphates, despite doubtful market prospects and uncertainty over prices in world markets. As well as this, it is noticeable that only forty industrial establishments have benefited from loans granted by the Industrial Development Bank, which provides low interest credit, and most of these beneficiaries have received two loans or more. In contrast the owner of a small workshop, or a peasant in the Jordan Valley, usually borrows from a moneylender at exorbitant rates of interest. This discriminatory treatment in favour of larger modern plants only adds to that which they enjoy already through tariff protection and the high exchange value of the Jordanian dinar.

GOODBYE MR CHIPS

In an attempt to widen the market to help the expansion of Jordanian manufacturing industry on a larger scale, King Hussein has since 1975 been seeking closer economic links with Syria, corresponding to the political turn-about in relations between the two countries. Political tensions were extremely high between Jordan and Syria in the early 1970s, when King Hussein was crushing the Palestinians, with whom Syria then sided; but since Syria has itself been fighting against the Palestinians in Lebanon, an unusual alliance has emerged between Damascus and Amman. Tariff restrictions have been removed on goods traded between the two countries, under the Arab Common Market agreement, to which both countries adhere. More significantly, quota restrictions have been relaxed, making Jordan and Syria the first two members of the Arab Common Market to do this. As a consequence, since 1975 there have been few delays on the Jordanian-Syrian border, in contrast to the situation a few years earlier when vehicles carrying goods could wait several days for clearance in either direction.

During 1976 even more ambitious plans for economic co-operation were announced, involving the establishment of an industrial free zone on the Jordanian-Syrian border.[22] This project is being handled by a company which is registered in both Jordan and Syria, with a six-man board of directors, three drawn from each country. The initial funds allocated to the company amount to $15 million, much of which will be used to provide basic infrastructure on the 600-hectare site on which the free zone is to be situated, south-east of Dera in Syria, and north of Mafraq in Jordan. This is near to the existing railway between Jordan and Syria and the Damascus–Amman highway. The financial provision excludes the amount previously paid in compensation to the landowners who farmed the area. It is hoped that this free zone, with its favourable location, and ready access to the Syrian and Lebanese markets, will attract a wide range of new import-substitute industries. It seems probably that light rather than heavy manufacturing plants will be established, however, despite the free market access, for there are few raw materials or energy supplies near the site, although power transmission lines for electricity are being installed.[23]

Lebanon's links with Syria have of course been increased in the aftermath of the civil war, especially since the direct Syrian military intervention to halt the conflict. Unlike Jordan, however, which entered a special relationship with Syria of its own volition, this can hardly be considered to be the case with Lebanon. Nevertheless, many Lebanese did welcome Syrian intervention in the first instance, as it was the only power in the area which was both willing to and capable of bringing the fighting to an end. It remains to be seen however, whether the two countries will become more closely integrated economically. Even while the civil war still raged there was free trade between the two-thirds of Lebanon occupied by the Syrian army and Syria itself. With Bekaa Valley virtually cut off from Beirut, whose port lay in ruins in any case, all of eastern Lebanon was supplied through Syria.

There is no doubt that both Lebanon and Syria could derive considerable benefit from having a wider integrated market, and the two economies do complement each other rather well. Syria has a range of heavy industries, such as iron and steel, which could easily supply Lebanon's light industries. (Such external linkages are an important prerequisite for development, according to some economists.) At the same time Lebanese consumer-orientated industry could find Syria a useful market outlet, and could invest in new plant to take advantage of economies of scale. In addition the increased trade links could help reduce transport costs for Syria, as Beirut is the nearest Mediterranean port to Damascus, and historically the major proportion of Syrian imports came through Lebanon from abroad. The re-establishment of this trade would mean that Beirut's status as an entrepôt would be further enhanced. It also seems likely that Beirut would emerge as the financial centre for the two countries, as its reputation and accumulated expertise would help guarantee its success in this role. If the Beirut financial institutions were able to attract once again substantial funds from abroad, upon which Syria could draw, this would obviously be an attractive proposition for the Damascus government. Syria in the past has experienced great difficulty in financing new development projects, and its balance of payments is frequently in deficit, as it has few mineral resources to exploit to ensure a steady flow of export earnings.[24]

In spite of these advantages, for Lebanon there are considerable dangers in the increasing links with Syria, especially as its status has become in many respects that of an occupied country. Many Syrians believe that Lebanon was an artificial creation, in any case, and would not have emerged as an independent nation state but for Western collusion with the Lebanese Christians to ensure that they had sovereignty over the Mediterranean littoral of what should have been part of the Greater Syria. There was general regret in Damascus when the economic union between the two countries was dissolved in 1950, since Damascus was left as a desert oasis, cut off from the rich Bekaa Valley to the west, which was a natural part of its agricultural hinterland. Now that the Damascus government has gained dominance over what it always wanted, a Greater Syria, many Lebanese fear that it will be reluctant to withdraw, and at the same time any government in Beirut will be left with little freedom of manoeuvre, whether political or economic.

It seems unlikely that the socialist government in Damascus will allow the old capitalist order, with its free-enterprise climate, to establish itself again in Beirut. The Syrians may allow Beirut to become a free zone for financial purposes, if they can draw on some of the funds deposited there, as already mentioned, but this type of conditional freedom seems the most the Lebanese can hope for.[25] Many Lebanese, however, especially those on the left of the political spectrum, do not mourn the passing of the old economic establishment, and may ultimately be thankful for a strong Syrian presence. Although before the civil war Beirut was superficially prosperous, it was only a small élite that benefited from the city's status as a financial centre. Most of these were expatriates from the West, Lebanese Christians, and a small number of rich Moslem families. Income distribution was extremely skewed, and for those Lebanese Moslems living in poor conditions, and the majority of Palestinians resident in refugee camps, life was a continual struggle merely to subsist.[26]

The old regime in Lebanon to a large extent brought about its own downfall and must bear most of the responsibility for the civil war which erupted so violently. Corruption was widespread, and it was impossible to get any new projects started unless some government minister or administrator was bribed, and there were those who took a percentage cut from all expenditure on development schemes. Agriculture was neglected, and the so-called 'Green Plan' existed on paper only,[27] while major irrigation schemes, such as that proposed for the Litani River, never were undertaken, even though vast sums of money were available, in contrast to the meagre financial resources of neighbouring Arab states which did implement new projects. As a consequence people drifted out of agriculture into the urban areas, to join the discontented masses.

The economic boom of the early 1970s in Lebanon paradoxically had the effect of making conditions worse for many of the poorer classes. House and apartment rentals soared in Beirut to levels that were well above the wages and salaries of most workers, even including those of employees holding clerical jobs in the buoyant service sector. Food costs also rose rapidly, which contributed to an accelerating rate of increase in wholesale prices, resulting in a 16 per cent increase between 1973 and 1974.[28] This undoubtedly squeezed the living standards of the urban workers, and lead to further dissatisfaction with the whole economic system. The general feeling of resentment was probably heightened by the presence of large numbers of rich visitors in the city of

Beirut, who, together with the wealthy classes of Lebanese, indulged in extremely lavish consumption, which was visible for all to see.

Given these stark economic contrasts as well as the growing social and political tensions, the outbreak of fighting in Lebanon came as no surprise to those who were in touch with working-class feeling in Beirut; indeed the only surprise was that it took so long to erupt.[29] In Jordan, where the economic and social pressures are in many ways similar to those in Lebanon, there is little doubt that if it were not for the commanding presence of King Hussein, and the ability of his army to control internal disorder, the country could well follow the Lebanese path towards disaster.

After considering the experiences of these two remaining enclaves of capitalism in the Middle East, an outside observer must ask whether a private enterprise economic system has any place in the region. Does the operation of free market mechanisms ultimately unleash forces that must lead to the inevitable collapse of the whole system, and consequential widespread social disruption? It does appear that, with urban wages kept down through continual immigration into the cities, while at the same time the cost of living soars, only very firm rule can keep the economic pot from boiling over. Historically the colonial powers that were involved in the area provided sufficiently strong rule to profit from the situation, but it seems improbable that any government within the Middle East can resist such tremendous economic forces for an indefinite period.

11 Conclusions

When first surveying the economies of the Middle East it is easy to be so dazzled by the wealth of economic experience that the common aspects of development are overlooked. The variety of economic systems is enormous, ranging from economies relying largely on private initiative and market forces, such as Jordan and the Lebanon, to state-controlled economies organised on Marxist lines, such as South Yemen. Even the mixed economies functioning between these two extremes vary considerably, as the role of the state in economic management is entirely different in Baathist Socialist states such as Iraq and Syria, from its role in Libya, where for instance, the individual enterprise enjoys a much greater measure of local autonomy in determining its own production level and prices. Although many Arab countries profess to be trying to adopt a middle path between capitalism and communism, and like to refer to themselves as Arab Socialist states, this does not imply that there is any common set of guidelines for economic organisation. Thus while centralised planning has been fairly rigidly adhered to in Iraq and Syria, in Nasser's Egypt only one plan was ever adopted, and this was never properly implemented because of the conflict with Israel. In Sadat's Egypt, despite the country's remaining nominally Arab Socialist, the encouragement given to foreign private investment through the 'Open Door' policy clearly marks a deviation from the direction in which the Damascus and Baghdad governments are aiming.

In the oil-rich states of Saudi Arabia, Iran and the Gulf, the governments are playing a much more significant role in economic activity than might be expected from their political ideology. Most of the new heavy industries are not only financed by the state, but are being run as nationalised concerns. Private business is admittedly flourishing in these oil-exporting states, especially trading and service activities, but much of this prosperity is dependent on state management of oil revenues, and multiplier effects from government spending. Through their overall control at the macro-level, governments like that of Iran want to ensure that the gains from development are more widely distributed, and the ownership of productive assets is dispersed. Accordingly, a profit-sharing scheme and a share-participation scheme are being enforced. In Israel there is also a measure of popular participation in economic activity, but this is a result of trade union ownership of many of the country's main industries, rather than because of any specific legislation.

POLES APART

Unfortunately the one characteristic feature of virtually all of the countries of the Middle East covered in this study seems to be economic inequality. The gap between the living standards of rich and poor in the region is becoming steadily wider, despite the lip-service that most of the regimes pay to promoting a more egalitarian distribution of income, and despite the policies that even the more conservative governments have adopted, on paper, to ensure a greater degree of social harmony. Interestingly there is little indication that income inequalities are less pronounced in supposedly socialist states than in those adhering to a rightist ideology. In Iraq, Syria and South Yemen, for instance, although the former feudal landlords have been displaced, it is the urban middle classes who have benefited most from development. The living standards of the managers of the state-owned factories or the top government bureaucrats do not differ significantly from those of their counterparts in the developed countries of the West. In contrast the welfare of the rural workforce remains near subsistence levels, while the prices which the peasants receive for their farm produce steadily decline *vis-à-vis* the prices of the manufactured goods they purchase from the urban areas.

The living standards of the professional middle classes, such as medical doctors, teachers and lawyers, are in fact appreciably lower in the less radical states of Egypt, Israel or Turkey than they are in Syria or Iraq. To some extent the high middle-class earnings in Iraq reflect the country's oil wealth, but the same cannot be said of Syria. In general in the Middle East it appears that supply and demand factors in labour markets affect relative earnings more than any deliberate acts of government policy. Thus in Egypt, Israel and Turkey in skilled occupations there are more qualified people available in relation to the numbers required, which tends to lower the rates of remuneration.

Government intervention, in so far as it has any influence on earnings, tends to work through the labour market, with most of the effect being felt through the creation of market imperfections. The condition that only personnel with certain paper qualifications can fill a particular job, for instance, even if these qualifications do not mean much in practice, obviously restricts the supply of labour, and raises wage rates. Specifying that people with different levels of qualifications will be paid different rates for the same job is another means of affecting relative earnings. Throughout the Arab world and in Iran there is one level of earnings in the civil service and nationalised industries for those with B.A. degrees, and automatically higher levels for those with M.A.s and Ph.D.s, regardless of merit.

The income inequalities in the Middle East are undoubtedly accentuated by the marked lack of social mobility, which restricts the entry into many of the higher job categories. Admittedly, there are more people than ever before with secondary, and even higher, education in the region, but most of these are the sons and daughters of the old wealthy classes comprising landowners, merchants and to a lesser extent skilled artisans. To talk of a new élite can be misleading when what has happened is that the descendants of the old privileged classes have adapted themselves to a new situation in which a Western academic system of education has become all-important. The old élite, even if they are uneducated themselves, have gone to considerable efforts to send their children to the best schools and colleges, for they realise that this is the only way their families can maintain powerful social and economic positions. In contrast, the chances of the son or daughter of a rural peasant, or unskilled urban worker rising up the social hierarchy to obtain a top position in government or industry are negligible in the Middle East. Indeed, most of those who call themselves revolutionary leaders or radicals come from bourgeois family backgrounds.

Apart from interpersonal wealth and income inequalities, within the countries of the Middle East there are also considerable regional imbalances. These to some extent reflect urban-rural differences, but there are in addition great geographical income variations, even in quite small areas. Within the United Arab Emirates, for example, although the country as a whole boasts the world's highest *per capita* income, much of this is concentrated in the oil emirates of Abu Dhabi and Dubai, and to a lesser degree Sharjah, while living conditions in the non-oil emirates of Ajman, Fujaira, and Umm Al Qaiwain are not very different from those found elsewhere in the Third World. In neighbouring Oman regional imbalances are almost as pronounced, for most development has been concentrated around the capital, Muscat, while the more remote areas, such as Dhofar, have been comparatively neglected until recently. The enormous territorial area of some Middle Eastern states inevitably results in marked regional disparities in the level of development. In Turkey, for instance, since the time of the Ottomans there have been great differences between the north-west of the country and the south-east. The Istanbul area has income levels much closer to those of the neighbouring European states than to those of eastern Anatolia where conditions correspond closely to what is found in northern Syria.

The greatest income disparities are still between the countries of the Middle East, however, rather than between the regions of any single state. *Per capita* income levels range from the highest in the world, as in the case already mentioned of the United Arab Emirates, to some of the lowest found in underdeveloped countries anywhere. North Yemen's *per capita* national income, for example, was only \$240 in 1975, while that of near-by Saudi Arabia was \$3060. Egypt's was only \$310 in 1975, in contrast to \$4270 in neighbouring Libya. Of course, *per capita* income as a measure of development is far from sufficient, and structural indicators such as the relative shares of industry and agriculture in gross national product presented in Appendix Table B4, are generally accepted as more indicative. Nevertheless *per capita* incomes do provide a guide to the financial resources that countries have at their disposal for investment purposes.

It is unfortunate in the Middle East that apart from Iran, and to a lesser extent Iraq, there are no states with both adequate finances for investment and a substantial range of fields where productive investment is possible. Egypt has a large industrial structure which is functioning very inefficiently partly as a result of lack of finance, while Saudi Arabia has abundant finances, but few citizens who are prepared to enter local industrial employment. There has admittedly been some recycling of surplus petro-funds within the Middle East to countries in need, both on a bilateral government-to-government basis, and through the many regional aid organisations such as the Kuwait Fund for Arab Economic Development. However, in relation to the size of oil revenue earnings, and the enormous financial requirements of countries like Egypt, the amounts recycled have been pitifully meagre.

INEQUALITY OR INDEPENDENCE?

The income inequalities on the personal, regional and international levels within the Middle East have influenced considerably the pattern of development which the area has experienced in recent years. There is, for example, a growing rather than a lessening dependence on the outside world, as increasing quantities of luxury goods are imported from the West to satisfy the demands of the newly affluent classes. This applies not only in the conservative oil-rich states of the Arabian peninsula, but also in supposedly radical states like Iraq and Libya. Of course the oil-exporting states have the foreign exchange to pay for these imports, but countries such as Syria or Egypt are falling into greater than ever balance of payments difficulties through legal, and illegal, imports of Western comsumer goods. In contrast to the high marginal propensities to import of the richer classes, the less wealthy in the Middle East require fewer foreign goods, apart from foodstuffs where there are local deficiencies. Some redistribution of income could therefore result in substantial balance of payments savings.

To lessen external dependence, import-substitution policies have been adopted throughout the Middle East in recent years, as the country studies in this volume show: yet the marked degree of income inequality has to a large extent determined the type of industry which has been promoted, while at the same time the resultant pattern of economic activity has further accentuated inequalities. The goods produced in the new import substitution industries are primarily designed to meet the demands of the middle classes, who want consumer durables such as cars, television sets, refrigerators, etc. These goods can only be produced using highly mechanised processes, which increases the need for imports of capital goods, and uses up valuable foreign exchange earnings. Often the new industries merely assemble imported components, resulting in the degree of value added domestically being minimal. In terms of job creation such industries do little to solve problems of unemployment and underemployment, for, being capital-intensive, few workers are required. Moreover frequently, and at least initially, expensive expatriate labour from the West has to be employed to service the machines.

It is apparent that there is a direct relationship between income inequality in the Middle East and the region's economic dependence on the outside world. One means of reducing this dependence would be through progressive taxation, or other fiscal means, which would decrease the consumer spending of the wealthier classes on luxury imports, while at the same time using the fiscal revenue to promote projects which would benefit a wider section of the population. Another means of reducing dependence would be to redistribute income from urban areas to poorer rural areas by raising the prices of farm produce *vis-à-vis* manufactured goods. The lower income groups who would benefit from such policies are more likely to spend their extra earnings on modest household improvements, locally produced textiles for clothing, or basic consumer durables such as bicycles which could be produced domestically. This type of spending would widen the market for locally produced, labour-intensive goods, thereby augmenting domestic employment opportunities in manufacturing industry. Benefit would also accrue to low-cost service activities, especially public transport, as the poorer classes would have more money for travel, which would in turn further increase employment. Even the investments undertaken could help to augment employment opportunities; if farmers, for instance, decided to embark upon simple agricultural improvements such as better boundary fences to prevent the spread of disease amongst farm animals, or improvement of irrigation and drainage ditches to ensure more efficient water utilisation.

In the Middle East, as in other parts of the Third World, frequent accusations are made that the advanced industrial countries of the West are using their economic power to prevent the region from becoming more self-reliant. The West is charged with neo-colonialism, for it is argued that the huge multinational corporations, which dominate much of the world economy, do not want to see rivals emerging to threaten their global monopoly of markets. The eighteen sovereign states covered in this survey nevertheless all have the power to assert their economic independence, and have set out on different paths of development from those taken by either the capitalist or communist world. As all the countries of the Middle East have enjoyed at least two decades of political independence, there is little point in blaming the outside world for the region's economic ills. The cure lies within, yet governments appear to lack the political will to take economic decisions which act against powerful vested interests, even if they are in the interests of the majority. It is only when there is the self-confidence to take such decisions, however, that the countries of the Middle East can hope to achieve a greater measure of economic self-reliance.

Appendix A: Periodic Publications on the Economies of the Middle East

In recent years an increasing number of magazines and journals have appeared dealing in whole or in part with Middle Eastern economic affairs. Many readers will of course be acquainted with the well-established and authoritative *Middle East Economic Digest*, published weekly in London, which covers all of the region apart from Israel. The *Middle East Economic Survey*, published weekly in Beirut, is perhaps less well-known, but is particularly useful for developments in the oil sector. An alternative is the more recently established *Arab Report and Memo*, published in Paris, which provides a weekly analysis of economic and political news from the Middle East. *Telex Mediterranean*, a Brussels-based fortnightly paper, contains economic information on the countries of the Mediterranean, including the Arab World, Turkey and Israel. Its coverage of trade developments is especially good. Two current affairs periodicals serving the area also provide business news sections, the monthly magazine *The Middle East*, and the fortnightly *Events*, both published in London. The Beirut-based monthly *The Arab Economist* also contains articles of interest to the business reader, but better coverage is provided by *Near East Business*, published in Nicosia.

There is at least one periodical in English dealing with economic affairs published in most of the countries of the region. Many of these are official government publications, issued by the Embassies or Ministries of Information, and are more in the nature of propaganda sheets, the Libyan-sponsored *Arab Dawn, Flash of Damascus* and *Iraq Today* being notable examples. Others, however, are more independent, and two particularly worthy of note are *Sudannow*, which is extremely well-written, with a critical approach on a par with the best investigative journalism, and *Israel Economist*, which, though less critical, covers in considerable detail developments in Israel. Rather different in nature are the *Economist* Intelligence Unit's *Quarterly Economic Reviews*, with Egypt, Israel, Iran, Turkey, Sudan and Iraq in separate volumes, and the other countries of the region jointly in four further volumes. A quarterly compendium is produced by the *Economist* Intelligence Unit on *Oil in the Middle East*, while in addition annual supplements are provided for this and for each of the country surveys.

Several useful reference books appear annually, providing summaries of Middle Eastern economic development. Foremost amongst these is the *Europa Survey of the Middle East and North Africa*, which contains brief but reliable surveys of all the countries of the region, including their histories, economies and statistics. Also published in London is the *Middle East Yearbook*, sponsored by *The Middle East* magazine, which provides general articles and country surveys written by staff members of Durham University. Most of the contributors are geographers, which is reflected in the style and presentation. The *Middle East Annual Review*, distributed by Macmillan, has better coverage of political developments in each country, as it is written by journalists and academics concerned with current affairs, but the economic material is sketchy, despite its being supplied by the *Economist* Intelligence Unit. A similar annual guide to the Middle East in French is *Afrique et Moyen-Orient*, published by *Jeune Afrique* in Paris.

The Gulf Handbook, published annually by *Middle East Economic Digest*, contains detailed economic information, and a useful diary of the main economic events in each country, but, as its title implies, the coverage is restricted to the Gulf, though this is taken to include Iraq and Iran. A more specialised *Middle East Economic Digest* publication is the *Middle East Financial Directory*, which gives information on banking activities on a country-by-country basis. This information is also provided in Graham and Trotman's *Arab Business Yearbook*, but in less detail, although there are useful sections on taxation, investment regulations and customs duties. The only specifically economic publication appearing annually is the *Arab Economic Report*, published in Beirut by the General Union of Chambers of Commerce, Industries and Agriculture for the Arab Countries. This contains country surveys, but its scope is of course restricted to the Arab states of the Middle East and North Africa.

Academic journals devoted to the study of Middle Eastern affairs include the *International Journal of Middle Eastern Studies*, published in Cambridge, and *Middle Eastern Studies*, published in London and the oldest-established. Both these quarterly journals contain articles on economic topics written by university scholars, but generally with the non-specialist reader in mind. An American counterpart is the *Middle Eastern Journal*, published quarterly in Washington. Details of most of the new books appearing on the Middle East, including economics studies, can be found in the *Gazelle Review of the Literature on the Middle East*, published at least once a year in London. Also in London, the monthly current affairs magazine *Middle East International* occasionally contains reviews of new economics literature, but most of the articles deal with political affairs.

Appendix B: Selected Statistical Indicators

1. Demographic variables
2. Educational indicators
3. Sectoral shares of Gross Domestic Product
4. Expenditure of Gross Domestic Product
5. Earnings and taxation from national income
6. Oil production

TABLE B.1. Demographic variables

	Population size 1975 (thousands)	*Rate of population increase 1970–5* (%)	*Surface area* (1000 km²)	*Density of population 1975* (per km²)
Turkey	39,180	2·4	780·6	50
Egypt	37,233	2·2	1001·4	37
Iran	33,019	2·9	1648·0	20
Sudan	17,757	2·5	2505·8	7
Iraq	11,124	3·3	434·9	26
Saudi Arabia	8966	3·0	2149·7	4
Syria	7355	3·3	185·2	40
North Yemen[a]	6668	2·9	195·0	34
Israel	3371	3·1	20·8	162
Lebanon[a]	2869	3·0	10·4	276
Jordon	2702	3·3	97·7	28
Libya	2444	4·2	1759·5	1
South Yemen	1690	N/A	333·0	5
Kuwait	996	6·0	17·8	56
Oman[a]	766	3·1	212·4	4
Bahrain	256	3·5	0·6	411
U.A.E.	222	3·2	83·6	3
Qatar	92	3·1	11·0	8

[a] UN estimates only, no reliable population censuses undertaken.
Source: UN, *Demographic Yearbook* (1975) Table 3, pp. 142–5.

TABLE B.2. Educational indicators (1974)

	Thousands enrolling Primary school	Secondary school	Higher Education	*Percentage in secondary education relative to those in primary school*	*Percentage in higher education locally relative to those in secondary school*	*Student-staff ratio in education overall*	*Expenditure on education as a percentage of GNP*	*Expenditure on education as a percentage of total public spending*
Turkey	5355	1517	218·9	28·3	14·4	30·8	5·6	N/A
Egypt	4145	1983	408·2	47·8	20·6	34·0	5·8	17·6
Iran	4119	1990	135·4	48·3	6·8	28·8	3·8	12·2
Iraq	1524	480	78·8	31·5	16·4	26·2	4·3	11·5
Syria	1212	461	64·1	38·0	13·9	36·2[a]	N/A	7·5
Sudan	1131	256	4·8	22·6	1·9	34·0	8·0	14·8
Saudi Arabia	626	179	19·8	28·6	11·0	18·6	N/A	8·2
Israel	523	168	75·3	32·0	44·9	N/A	6·7	7·4
Libya	522	130	12·0	24·8	9·2	19·8	N/A	12·2
Lebanon	498	175	44·3	35·1	25·3	N/A	2·7	18·6
Jordan	372	143	9·3	38·6	6·4	29·6	3·6	8·3
North Yeman	233	18	0·9	7·7	5·3	36·7	N/A	6·3
South Yemen	196	40	0·9	20·2	2·3	28·7	3·5	N/A
Kuwait	102	98	5·8	95·9	5·9	13·8	2·6	14·7
U.A.E.	53	12	0	22·6	0	30·2	N/A	N/A
Oman	49	0·7	0	1·5	0	23·0	2·1	N/A
Bahrain	40	17	0·7	41·7	4·0	N/A	5·6	20·3
Qatar	22	8	0	35·0	0	17·4	3·8	N/A

[a] Excludes secondary education.

Source: UN, *Statistical Yearbook* (1976) Table 207, pp. 838–59 and Table 208 pp. 862–6.

TABLE B.3. Sectoral shares of Gross Domestic Product

	Year	*Agri-culture*	*Extractive Industry* (mainly oil)		*Manufactur-ing Industry*	*Electricity*		*Con-struction*	*Whole-sale and retail Trade*	*Transport and Commun-ications*	*Others* (including defence)
Egypt	1974	31·0	2·2		17·4	1·2		3·4	9·1	4·2	31·5
Iran	1975	9·1	—	46·4	—	0·8		7·6	5·4	3·6	27·0
Iraq	1971	14·5	35·0		8·1	0·8		3·0	6·4	5·4	26·7
Israel	1973	4·6	—	18·4	—	—	10·3	—	8·1	6·4	52·2
Jordan	1974	15·9	3·4		10·9	1·1		5·0	16·5	7·4	40·0
Kuwait	1973	0·2	68·6		3·5	2·0		1·0	5·3	3·1	16·2
Lebanon	1972	9·9	—	13·9	—	2·0		4·6	31·5	7·5	30·6
Libya	1974	1·6	58·4		1·8	0·3		9·8	4·5	4·7	18·9
Oman	1971	11·6	65·0		0·1	0·1		14·5	1·8	0·7	6·1
Saudi Arabia	1975	1·0	71·0		4·6	0·2		7·4	3·0	3·7	9·0
Sudan	1974	38·7	0·3		9·2	1·4		4·3	16·2	5·9	24·0
Syria	1976	22·1	11·0		10·6	0·7		7·0	19·7	5·0	24·0
Turkey	1975	26·3	1·2		19·0	1·6		4·9	13·4	7·6	25·9
North Yemen	1974	63·4	0·5		2·1	0·2		3·0	14·6	1·8	14·3
South Yemen	1970	19·4	0		25·2	1·7		0·7	12·7	5·4	35·0

Source: UN, *Monthly Bulletin of Statistics* (December 1977) vol. XXXI, no. 12, Table 65, pp. 207–13.

TABLE B.4. Expenditure of Gross Domestic Product

	Year	*Government Expenditure as percentage of GDP*	*Private consumption Expenditure as percentage of GDP*	*Increase in stocks as percentage of GDP*	*Gross capital formation as percentage of GDP*	*Exports in relation to GDP (%)*	*Imports in relation to GDP (%)*
Egypt	1974	27·7	65·4	2·3	16·2	21·8	33·5
Iran	1975	21·1	42·0	— 30·1	—	— 6·8[a]	—
Iraq	1975	— 56·3	—	10·1	18·9	57·9	43·3
Israel	1975	41·5	54·2	4·0	26·4	27·1	53·1
Jordan	1975	33·3	78·6	3·7	26·9	27·6	70·1
Kuwait	1975	15·8	18·0	0·3	7·5	80·8	22·4
Lebanon	1972	9·0	87·1	0·5	19·9	— 16·4[b]	—
Libya[c]	1974	21·4	29·3	0·4	24·8	61·6	37·6
Saudi Arabia	1975	18·2	12·2	1·3	21·8	77·6	31·1
Sudan	1974	13·7	77·5	3·3	14·2	12·1	20·9
Syria	1976	20·5	60·1	— 35·3	—	23·4	39·2
Turkey	1973	14·4	70·1	0·8	17·9	8·4	11·6
North Yemen	1973	0·0	96·7	1·8	10·4	3·1	22·0

[a] Surplus of exports over imports.
[b] Deficit, with imports exceeding exports.
[c] GDP, excluding statistical discrepancies.
Source: UN, *Monthly Bulletin of Statistics* (December 1977) vol. XXXI, no 2, Table 63, pp. 193–9.

TABLE B.5. Earnings and taxation from national income

	Year	*Employee remuneration*[a] *as percentage of national income*		*Operating surplus*[b] *as percentage of national income*	*Earnings from the rest*[c] *of the world in relation to national income*	*Indirect taxes net of subsidies as percentage of national income*
Egypt	1973	43·3		45·3	(—) 0·8	12·3
Iraq	1971	31·0		79·5	(—) 18·3	7·8
Israel[d]	1973	50·9		36·1	(—) 3·2	16·2
Jordan	1974	34·5		47·5	8·8	9·2
Lebanon	1972	—	88·6	—	3·7	7·8
Libya[d]	1974	28·0		83·0	(—) 13·8	2·8
Saudi Arabia	1975	15·5		91·4	(—) 6·6	(—) 0·3
Sudan	1974	51·3		37·6	(—) 1·1	12·2
Turkey	1973	—	84·9	—	4·9	10·2
North Yemen	1973	13·1		81·7	0·5	4·7

[a] Wages, salaries, etc.
[b] Profits, depreciation allowances, etc.
[c] Income from property, profits, etc., from investments overseas. Negative sign indicates net outflow of earnings.
[d] National income excluding statistical discrepancies.

Source: UN, *Monthly Bulletin of Statistics* (December 1977) vol. XXXI, no. 2, Table 64, pp. 200–6.

TABLE B.6. Oil production (in million metric tons)

	1950	*1960*	*1975*	*1977*	*Percentage share of Middle East Production in 1977*
Saudi Arabia	26·6	61·1	352·0	453·2	41·0
Iran	32·2	52·1	266·7	276·4	25·0
Iraq	6·6	47·5	110·1	110·9	10·0
UAE	0	0	81·9	96·6	8·7
Kuwait	17·3	89·1	104·8	94·3	8·5
Egypt	0	0	11·7	22·0	2·0
Qatar	1·6	8·2	20·8	21·4	1·9
Oman	0	0	16·8	16·9	1·5
Syria	0	0	9·6	8·9	0·8
Bahrain	1·6	2·2	3·0	2·8	0·3
Turkey	0·03	0·3	3·1	2·6	0·2
Total Middle East	86·0	260·7	980·6	1106·0	
Total world	538·5	1090·7	2706·9	3025·1	

Sources: 1950, 1960 Institute of Petroleum Information Service, *World Statistics* (London 1977) p. 2; 1975, 1977: *Petroleum Economist*, vol. XLV no. 1, January 1978) p. 6.

Notes

CHAPTER 1

1 Calculated from data in *The Budget 2536 (1977-78): A Summary* (Plan and Budget Organisation, Tehran, 1977) Part III, Table 3, p. 9. Conversions from riyals are at current exchange rates for the years 1975, 1976 and 1977.
2 A standard source on Iranian history is Percy Sykes, *A History of Persia*, vol. 1 (Macmillan, 1915). Chapters XIII and XIV give an account of the Persian Empire at its zenith, on p. 148 ff. For an account of its links with China over 1500 years ago see Chapter XXXIX, p. 483 ff.
3 Julian Bharier, *Economic Development in Iran 1900–1970*, (Oxford University Press, 1971) p. 171.
4 Ibid., p. 172.
5 The first regional censuses in Iran were undertaken between 1939 and 1941. The 14 million figure cited which is based on these limited censuses must therefore be treated as approximate, as the first comprehensive census of Iran's population was not carried out until 1956. See *Iran Almanac* published in Tehran for details. For example, in the 1975 edition population details are given on pp. 373–80.
6 Julian Bharier has compiled a price index for the whole 1900–69 period. See op. cit., pp. 46–7.
7 Ibid., p. 159.
8 Table originally cited in my article 'Iran's Economy and Development Plans', *Focus Research* Report on Iran (London, 1977) p. 7.
9 For details of Iran's development during this period see Charles Issawi, 'Iran's Economic Upsurge', *Middle East Journal*, vol. 21, no. 4 (Autumn 1967) pp. 447–62. Also his chapter on 'The Economy: An Assessment of Performance' in Ehsan Yar-Shater (ed.), *Iran Faces the Seventies* (New York: Praeger, 1971) Chapter 2, p. 44 ff.
10 See IMDBI, *Functions and Policies* (Tehran, 1972) p. 6 ff, especially. The bank also produces detailed annual financial reports.
11 Nicholas Cumming-Bruce, 'Developments in Petrochemicals', *Financial Times* Survey of Iran (25 July 1977) pp. 14–15.
12 For a less critical, purely factual account of the Aryamehr steel industry see Iran Trade and Industry, *Iran 1973* (Tehran, 1973) pp. 28–33.
13 Robert Graham, 'Steel Industry', *Financial Times* Survey of Iran (21 June, 1976) p. 18.
14 Ibid.

15 *Iran Almanac* (1975) p. 377.
16 Walter Elkan, 'Employment, Education, Training and Skilled Labour in Iran', *Middle Eastern Journal*, vol. 31, no. 3, (spring 1977) p. 176 ff.
17 Rodney Wilson, *Trade and Investment in the Middle East* (Macmillan, 1977) p. 75.
18 The Ministry of Art and Culture does assist on average one handicraft establishment in each major region, in order to prevent particular Iranian fine arts from disappearing completely, but this affects less than 1 per cent of all workshops.
19 Plan and Budget Organization, *Statistical Yearbook 1392* (March 1973–March 1974) p. 42.
20 Though that is not to say that they should not try to develop new product lines as market tastes change. There should be a living craft tradition, not one that merely reproduces what has been made in the past. Innovations can be introduced, however, without having to use new machinery or techniques.
21 The average annual earnings of Iranian workers in 1977 was $2570 (*Bank Markazi Bulletin*, no. 82 (lst Quarter 1977) pp. 70–1), while managers' salaries often exceeded $25,000 annually.
22 The official outline of the principles governing *The Revolution of the Shah and the People* has been published in 10 short volumes in English by Transorient (London, 1967).
23 'The New Industrial Revolution', Volume 5 of *The Revolution of the Shah and the People*, p. 5.
24 Ibid., p. 7.
25 Deutsche Bank, *Report on Iran* (Frankfurt, 1976) p. 50.
26 Survey of Iran, *The Economist* (28 August, 1976) p. 31.
27 Details of dealings on the Tehran Stock Exchange are given in *Bank Markazi Bulletins*. See, for example, no. 82, pp. 76–102.
28 Robert Graham, 'Share Stakes', *Financial Times* Survey of Iran (21 June, 1976) p. 14.
29 'Survey of Iran', *The Economist*, p. 32.
30 Robert Graham, 'State a Barrier to Investment', *Financial Times* Survey of Iran, (25 July, 1977) p. 17.
31 Wilson, 'Iran's Economy and Development Plans, p. 11.
32 For brief details of this organisation see 'Special Report on Iran', *Middle East Economic Digest* (February 1977) p. 14.
33 See Volume 3, 'Land to the People', and Volume 4, 'Financing Land Reform', of *The Revolution of the Shah and the People*.
34 The reform measures are dealt with in detail by Ann Lampton, *The Persian Land Reform 1962–66* (Oxford University Press, 1969) Chapter 3, p. 63 ff, espcecially. For an alternative rather uncritical account see D. R. Denman, *The Kings Vista: A Land Reform which has Changed the Face of Persia* (Geographical Publications Ltd., Berkhamsted, 1973) Chapters 5, 11 and 12 especially, p. 159 ff.
35 Keith McLachlan, 'Land Reform in Iran', in W. B. Fisher (ed), *Cambridge History of Iran* (Cambridge University Press, 1968), vol. 1, p. 687.
36 Julian Bharier, 'The Growth of Towns and Villages in Iran, 1900–66', *Middle Eastern Studies*, vol. 8, no. 1 (January 1972) p. 51–62.

37 Bharier, *Economic Development in Iran 1900–1970*, p. 138. For a more recent evaluation of the reform measures see Ismail Ajami, 'Agrarian Reform, Modernization of Peasants and Agricultural Development in Iran', in Jane W. Jacqz (ed.), *Iran: Past, Present, Future*, (New York: Aspen Institute for Humanistic Studies, 1976) p. 131 ff.

38 N. R. Keddie, 'The Iranian Village Before and After Land Reform', *Journal of Contemporary History*, vol. 3, no. 3, (July 1968) p. 87. For a critical account of the official data on land reform see M. A. Katouzian, 'Land Reform in Iran: A Case Study in the Political Economy of Social Engineering', *Journal of Peasant Studies*, vol. 1, no. 2 (1974) pp. 220–39.

39 An even higher figure of 12 per cent is cited in 'Special Report on Iran', *Middle East Economic Digest*, p. 17.

40 Bharier, *Economic Development in Iran 1900–1970*, For further details of the Agro-businesses and farm corporations see R. Doroudian, 'Modernization of Rural Economy in Iran', in Jacqz (ed.), *Iran: Past, Present and Future*, p. 159 ff.

41 Liz Thurgood, 'Agriculture', *Financial Times* Survey of Iran (21 June 1976) p. 16.

42 Ibid.

43 'Special Report on Iran', *Middle East Economic Digest*, p. 20.

44 'Survey of Iran', *The Economist*, p. 40.

45 Ibid.

46 'Special Report on Iran', *Middle East Economic Digest*, p. 20.

47 *Financial Times* Survey of Iran (25 July, 1977) p. 19.

48 Ibid.

CHAPTER 2

1 For a comprehensive survey of Egypt's industrial development see Robert Mabro and Samir Radwan, *The Industrialisation of Egypt 1939–1973* (Oxford University Press, 1976) Part 2, Chapters 5 and 6 especially, p. 79 ff.

2 Figures from OECD, *Development Co-operation* (Paris, 1976) Statistical Annex, Table 46, p. 270.

3 These issues have been studied in detail by Mahmoud Abdel Fadil. See his study of development, *Income Distribution and Social Change in Rural Egypt 1952–1970* (Cambridge University Press, 1975) Chapter 3, pp. 51–70 and Chapter 5, pp. 82–108 especially.

4 Figures from Central Agency for Public Mobilisation and Statistics, *Statistical Yearbook of the Arab Republic of Egypt* (Cairo, October 1975) page 4.

5 *Ibid*, p. 14.

6 See Robert Mabro, 'Employment and Wages in Dual Agriculture', *Oxford Economic Papers*, vol. 23, no. 3 (1971) pp. 401–17. The survey results are reported by the International Labour Organisation in their *Rural Employment Problems in the U.A.R.* (Geneva, 1969).

7 Robert Mabro, *The Egyptian Economy 1952–1972* (Oxford University Press, 1974) p. 183.

8 Ibid, p. 159.

9 The weights assigned to the four main commodities in the author's index are: wheat 0·31, maize 0·37, millet 0·12, rice 0·2.

10 The basket of commodities used in the consumer price index is valued at the prices charged in state-run shops, yet most food is retailed through private channels.

11 Although the latter course of action may in turn save foreign exchange. See my earlier study on *Trade and Investment in the Middle East* (Macmillan, 1977) Chapter 2, pp. 35–6.

12 A convenient list of the ministries is provided in the *Statistical Yearbooks*. See for example the 1975 yearbook, pp. 243–5.

13 See Rodney Wilson, 'Industrialisation and Foreign Capital', *Focus Research* Report on Egypt (London, 1976) p. 14 ff.

14 Ibid. Appendix B lists the foreign investment regulations.

15 For a useful background study see Monroe Berger, *Bureaucracy and Society in Modern Egypt* (New York: Russell & Russell, 1957) Chapter 1, p. 3 ff, and Chapter 8, p. 176 ff. especially.

16 See D. C. Mead, *Growth and Structural Change in the Egyptian Economy* (Homewood, Illinois: Irwin, 1967) p. 132. He quotes figures for the size of the civil service in 1937, 1947 and 1960.

17 *Statistical Yearbook* (1975), p. 206.

18 The General Organisations established under Nasser to supervise whole industries further complicated matters by introducing another tier of bureaucracy. See Patrick O'Brien, *The Revolution in Egypt's Economic System* (Oxford University Press, 1966) p. 247 ff. These organisations were subsequently abolished by Sadat.

19 See Wilson, *Focus Research* Report on Egypt (1976) pp. 18–19.

20 Samir Radwin estimates that less than 30 per cent of the foreign investment carried out under the Open Door Policy has gone into industry and agriculture. See 'The Egyptian Economy in the 1970s: A Brief Outline' in *Focus Research* Report on Egypt, p. 27.

21 *Statistical Yearbook* (1975), p. 158.

22 As punctuality is rare amongst Egypt's bureaucrats, the day in practice seldom starts before 8.30 or 9.0 a.m.

23 Estimate given by the International Institute for Strategic Studies in London in an unpublished 1977 paper by Paul Rivlin on the '*Economic Costs and Choices for Defence in Israel and Egypt*', p. 6. (1975/76 figure).

24 For details of the plan see Bent Hansen and G. Marzouk, *Development and Economic Policy in the U.A.R. (Egypt)*, (Amsterdam: North Holland Publishing, 1965) Chapters 11, p. 295 ff. Also Magdi M. El Kammash, *Economic Development and Planning in Egypt* (New York: Praeger, 1968), where Chapter 10, p. 297 ff., gives a broader perspective of planning efforts in the 1960s.

25 The plan envisaged that £7 billion would have to be spent on reconstruction alone, yet by January 1977 less than £450 million had been invested through the Open Door Policy. See Wilson in *Focus Research* Report on Egypt (1976), p. 14.

26 For details of military spending during this earlier period see N. Safran, *From War to War* (New York: Pegasus, 1969) Appendix A, Table A, p. 433.

27 Peter Mansfield, 'The Egypt/Israel Stalemate', *Focus Research* Report on

Egypt (London, 1974) p. 10.

28 For full assessment of the effect on the Egyptian economy of he 1967 war see Eliyahu Kanovsky, *The Economic Impact of the Six Day War* (New York: Praeger, 1970) Chapter 15, p. 279 ff.

29 Rodney Wilson, 'Industrialisation and Foreign Capital' in *Focus Research Report on Egypt* (1974), p. 18.

30 Rodney Wilson, 'Revival of Canal Traffic is Key to Success', *The Times* Special Report on Cairo (7 October, 1976) p. 27.

31 Figure from International Institute of Strategic Studies, *The Military Balance 1974–75* (London, 1974) pp. 32–3.

32 Michael Tingay, 'A.O.I. Aims at Arms Self Sufficiency', *Financial Times* Survey of Arab Cooperation and Development (26 September, 1977) p. 26.

33 Rodney Wilson, 'Caught in Trap over Soviet Debt', *The Times* Special Report on Egypt (5 November, 1975) p. 5.

34 Interest payments already amount to £1800 million. See John Bullock, 'After Sadat, the Deluge', *Daily Telegraph* (23 February 1977) p. 16.

35 Tingay, art, cit.

36 Michael Tingay, 'Egypt', in Michael Field (ed.), *Middle East Annual Review*, (London, 1977) p. 162.

37 For brief details of the subsidies given during the Nasser era see Hansen and Marzouk, op. cit., pp. 153–5.

38 See Tingay, in Michael Field (ed.), op. cit., p. 161.

39 Ibid., p. 162.

40 For the first detailed evaluation of this policy see Yusuf J. Ahmed, *Absorptive Capacity of the Egyptian Economy*, (Paris: OECD, 1976) Chapter 5, p. 98 ff.

CHAPTER 3

1 The most comprehensive account of the Saudi Arabian economy to date is Ramon Knaverhase, *The Saudi Arabian Economy* (New York: Praeger, 1975).

2 According to the official statistics 40 per cent were engaged in agriculture in 1970, and this had declined to 28 per cent in 1975. These figures refer to enumerated employment, however, while the majority of rural population are not accounted for in the official employment statistics. See *Saudi Arabian Development Plan 1975–80*, English edn. (Riyadh, 1975) p. 11.

3 For information on oil pricing see Raki Rifai, *The Pricing of Crude Oil* (New York: Praeger, 1974).

4 A highly critical account of recent developments in Saudi Arabia is presented by Fred Halliday, *Arabia Without Sultans* (Harmondsworth: Penguin, 1974).

5 Naturally, a very different picture of ARAMCO's role in the Saudi economy is presented in *ARAMCO World*, the official company magazine, but this has a notable lack of statistical material.

6 See Arab World File (*Fiche du monde arabe*) (Beirut, 23 October 1974) no. 108. This gives a brief, factual account of Saudi's agricultural development projects.

7 Despite this experience, further similar fertiliser deals are being worked out with Western companies. See *Middle East Economic Survey*, vol. 18, no. 30 (May 1975) p. 3 ff.

8 Rodney Wilson, 'Big Importer', *Financial Times* Survey of Saudi Arabia (12 January 1975) p. 20 For details of recent construction work see Saudi Arabian Monetary Agency, *Annual Reports*, issued in Riyadh. Information on foreign companies operating in Saudi Arabia is given by Anthony Purdy (ed.), *The Businessmans Guide to Saudi Arabia* (Arlington, 1976) p. 77 ff.

9 *Middle East Economic Digest*, vol. 19, no. 6 (7 February 1975) p. 19.

10 *Middle East Economic Digest*, vol. 19, no. 3 (17 January 1975) p. 19.

11 For analysis of the projections in the 1975–80 development plan see Richard Lawless, 'Education Expansion', *Financial Times* Survey of Saudi Arabia (12 January, 1975) pp. 26–7.

12 Saudi Arabian Monetary Agency, *Annual Report 1392–93* (Riyadh, 1973) p. 67.

13 11,500 new beds are to be provided by 1980. See *Middle East Economic Survey*, vol. 18, no. 32 (30 May 1975) p. 4.

14 For a discussion of some of the issues involved in the latter course see *Middle East Economic Survey*, vol. 18, no. 22, (21 March 1975) pp. 1–3.

15 Jan Tulir, 'Oil Payments and Oil Debt in the World Economy', *Lloyds Bank Review* (June 1974).

16 Minos Zombanakis, 'Arab Funds and the Markets', *The Banker* (July 1974).

17 Some of the more recent exchange rate dilemmas facing Saudi Arabia and other OPEC producers are discussed in *Arab Economist*, vol. 18, no. 30 (May 1975) p. 18 ff.

18 See *Middle East Economic Survey*, vol. 18, no. 22 (21 March 1975) p. 13.

19 Mostly on a bilateral government-to-government basis or through the Saudi Arabian Development Fund.

CHAPTER 4

1 Calculated from national income figures given in U.N., *Monthly Bulletin of Statistics*, vol. XXXI, no. 2 (February 1977) Table 61, pp. 186–8, using population figures for *per capita* estimate used in same volume, Table 1, pp. 1–4. Exchange rate conversion figures are from I.M.F., *International Financial Statistics*, vol. XXX, no. 2 (February 1977) pp. 196–7 and pp. 366–7.

2 As even Israeli geographers admit. See Yehuda Karmon, *Israel: A Regional Geography* (Wiley, 1971) Chapters 3 and 4, pp. 36–60.

3 M. W. Wilmington, *The Middle East Supply Centre* (State University of New York Press, 1972) Chapter 8, p. 103 ff.; E. M. H. Lloyd, *Food and Inflation in the Middle East 1940–45* (Standford University Press, 1956) pp. 267–8 and 299–301.

4 For a useful account of the events leading up to 1948 war see Christopher Sykes, *Cross Roads to Israel* (Collins, 1965) Chapters 13 and 14, p. 375 ff; also Noah Lucas, *The Modern History of Israel* (Weidenfeld & Nicolson, 1974) Chapters 10 and 11, p. 203 ff. An analysis of the war from the Israeli

perspective is given by Netanel Lorch, *The Edge of the Sword* (Jerusalem: Massada Press, 1961) p. 161 ff. especially.

5 Vivian Bull, *The West Bank: Is it Viable?* (Massachusetts: Lexington, 1975) Chapter 4, p. 63 ff.

6 Details of pre-independence industrial development are given by Nadav Halevi and Ruth Klinov-Malul, *The Economic Development of Israel* (New York: Praeger, 1968) pp. 23–9.

7 David Horowitz, *The Enigma of Economic Growth: A Case Study of Israel* (New York: Praeger, 1972) pp. 24–5; Arthur H. Doerr, Jerome F. Coling and William S. Kerr, 'Agricultural Evolution in Israel in the Two Decades Since Independence', *Middle East Journal*, vol. 24, no. 3 (1970) pp. 319–37.

8 *Israel Economist*, vol. XXXII, no. 6 (June 1976) p. 24.

9 *Israel Economist*, vol. XXXII, no. 7 (July 1976) p. 17.

10 Several studies have been made covering Israel's contribution to rural development in developing countries. See Leopold Laufer, *Israel and the Developing Countries* (New York: Twentieth Century Fund, 1967) Chapter 6, p. 83 ff.; Mordechai E. Kreinin, *Israel and Africa* (New York: Praeger, 1964) Chapters 5 and 6 especially, p. 71 ff.; Shimeon Amir, *Israel's Development Co-operation with Africa, Asia and Latin America* (New York: Praeger, 1974) Chapter 4, p. 12 ff.

11 Eliyahu Kanovsky, *The Ecomony of the Israeli Kibbutz*, (Harvard Middle Eastern Monographs no. 8, 1966) Chapters 2 and 3, p. 16 ff.; Martin Pallmann, *Der Kibbuz* (Basle: Kyklos-Verlag, 1966) Chapter 4, p. 118 ff.; Yonina Talmon, *Family and Community in the Kibbutz* (Harvard University Press, 1972) Chapter 1, pp. 1–14.

12 Maxwell I. Klayman, *The Moshav in Israel* (New York: Praeger, 1970) Chapter 5, p. 89 ff.; Maurice Konopnicki, *La Co-operation en milieu rural Israelian* (Faculté de droit de Liège, 1968) Chapter 7, p. 211 f.; Harry Viteles, *A History of the Co-operative Movement in Israel* (Vallentine Mitchell, 1966), vol. 1, p. 32, and vol. 2, p. 21 ff.

13 *Israel Economist*, vol. XXXII, nos. 2–3 (February–March 1976) p. 248.

14 Ibid.

15 *Israel Economist*, vol. XXXII, nos. 4–5 (April–May 1976) p. 9.

16 Bank of Israel Research Department, *The Economy of the Administered Territories 1971* (Jerusalem 1972) pp. 22–3.

17 Abdul-Ilah Abu-Ayyash, 'Israeli Regional Planning Policy in the Occupied Territories', *Journal of Palestine Studies*, vol. 5, nos 3 and 4 (Spring/Summer 1976) p. 96. See also *The Arabs under Israeli Occupation*, Palestine Research Centre Monograph no. 55 (Beirut 1969) p. 91 ff.

18 Ministry of Defence, *Four Years of Military Administration*, (Jerusalem, 1972) p. 39.

19 *Israel Economist*, vol XXIX, no. 3 (March 1973) p. 84.

20 Israeli Central Bureau of Statistics, *Administered Territories Statistics Quarterly*, vol. VI, no. 3 (1976) Table D3, pp. 30–1.

21 A detailed study of the Palestinian population has been undertaken by Edward Hagopian and A. B. Zahlan, 'Palestine's Arab Population: The Demography of the Palestinians', *Journal of Palestine Studies*, vol. III, no. 4 (Summer 1974) pp.32–73.

22 Tawfig Zayyad, 'The Fate of the Arabs in Israel', *Journal of Palestine Studies*, vol. VI, no. 1 (Autumn 1976) pp. 92–103; Sabri Jiryis, *The Arabs in Israel*, (Beirut: Institute for Palestine Studies, 1969) Chapter 4, p. 119 ff.

23 Details of Israel's exports are given by Michael Michaely *Foreign Trade Regimes and Economic Development: Israel*, (Columbia University Press, 1975) p. 17. Diamonds have increased their share of exports since this book was published.

24 Howard Pack, *Structural Change and Economic Policy in Israel* (Yale University Press, 1971) p. 82.

25 Michael Szenberg, *The Economics of the Israeli Diamond Industry* (New York: Basic Books, 1973) p. 21.

26 Ibid., p. 4. The $600 figure is low even in comparison with other sectors in Israel in the 1950s. See A. L. Gaathon, *Capital Stock, Employment and Output in Israel*, Bank of Israel Research Department Special Studies no. 1 (Jerusalem, 1961) Table 2, p. 5; also A. L. Gaathon, *Economic Productivity in Israel* (New York: Praeger, 1971) Table 30, p. 101.

27 *Israel Economist*, vol. XXX, nos 9–10, (September–October 1974) p. 197.

28 For recent developments in the diamond industry see the *Israel Yearbooks*. For example on pp. 189–202 of the 1977 *Yearbook* there are two articles by Azriel Ben-Moshe, the director of the diamonds division of the Ministry of Commerce and Industry.

29 Meir Heth, *The Flow of Funds in Israel* (New York: Praeger, 1970) Chapter 4, p. 73 ff.

30 The favourable investment climate has undoubtedly helped attract these funds. See Meir Heth, *The Legal Framework of Economic Activity in Israel* (New York: Praeger, 1967) Chapter 17, p. 228 ff.

31 Nicholas Balabkins, *West German Repatriations to Israel* (Rutgers University Press, 1971), Chapter 8, p. 155 ff., especially; Inge Deutschkron, *Bonn and Jerusalem: The Strange Coalition* (Philadelphia: Chilton, 1970) p. 28 ff.; Kenneth Lewan 'How West Germany Helped to Build Israel', *Journal of Palestine Studies*, vol. IV, no. 4 (Summer 1975) pp. 41–64.

32 *Israel Economist*, vol. XXXII, no. 4–5 (April–May 1976) p. 35.

33 For an account of the Histadrut's structure see Alex Rubner, *The Economy of Israel* (Cass, 1960) Chapter VI, p. 40 ff.; also Haim Hanegli 'The Histadrut: Union and Boss', in Arie Bober (ed.), *The Other Israel* (New York: Anchor, 1972) Chapter 7, pp. 123–33.

34 *Israel Economist*, vol. XXXII, nos 2–3 (February–March 1976) p. 261.

35 The factors determing comparative advantage and their relevance to Israel are discussed by Seev Hirsh, *The Export Performance of Six Manufacturing Industries* (New York: Praeger, 1971) Chapter 3, p. 35 ff.

36 Shlomo Sitton, *L'Économie d'Israel* (Paris: M.E.P.-C.E.F., 1971) pp. 217–22.

37 *Israel Economist*, vol. XXXII, no. 4–5 (April–May 1976) p. 33. For a discussion of whether a country in such a dependent economic state can enjoy any political autonomy, as economic and political factors relate, see Maxime Rodinson, *Israel: A Colonial-Settler State?* (New York: Monad, 1973) Chapter 3, p. 35 ff. especially.

CHAPTER 5

1 *World Bank Atlas* (Washington, 1977), pp. 28–30.
2 For a description of the first years of oil in Kuwait see Violet Dickson, *Forty Years in Kuwait* (Allen & Unwin, 1970) Chapters 6 and 7, p. 144 ff. A brief assessment of oil's economic impact is given in the IBRD report on *The Economic Development of Kuwait* (Baltimore: John Hopkins Press, 1965) pp. 53–6.
3 6880 square miles, including the Kuwaiti-administered portion of the neutral zone dividing Kuwait and Saudi Arabia.
4 For a historical account of oil development in the emirates see K. G. Fenelon, *The United Arab Emirates: An Economic and Social Survey* (Longman, 1973) Chapter 5, pp. 32–43.
5 There is little economic literature exclusively devoted to Qatar. For a brief account of its oil industry see Peter Kilner and Jonathan Wallace (ed.), *The Gulf Hand-book 1976/77* (Bath: Trade and Travel Publications, and London: Middle East Economic Digest, 1976) pp. 399–401.
6 Ralph Shaw, *Kuwait* (Macmillan, 1976) p. 37.
7 Fenelon, op. cit., p. 56. See also Donald Hawley, *The Trucial States* (Allen & Unwin, 1970) pp. 195–7.
8 They have become quite valuable as antiques, especially as they are no longer made.
9 H. V. F. Winstone and Zahra Freeth, *Kuwait: Prospect and Reality* (Allen & Unwin, 1972) p. 90; Michael Tomkinson *The United Arab Emirates* (Michael Tomkinson, 1975) p. 29.
10 Unfortunately, as there was no real difference in appearance or quality between cultured and natural pearls, it was impossible to charge a premium for the latter.
11 Saad Andari, *Kuwait: Development of a Mini Economy*, M.A. thesis, University of Durham (1976) Chapter 3, p. 39 ff., discusses foreign trade dependence and the question of instability of export earnings.
12 For a brief review of the absorptive capacities in the Gulf see Yusuf J. Ahmad, *Oil Revenues in the Gulf: A Preliminary Estimate of Absorptive Capacity*: (OECD, Paris, 1974): Kuwait is discussed on pp. 50–69; the UAE on pp. 70–92; Bahrain on pp. 93–101; and Qatar on pp. 102–10.
13 Kilner and Wallace (eds.), op. cit. p. 303.
14 Ibid, p. 398; *Financial Times* Survey of Qatar (28 October 1970) p. 26; *The Times* Special Report on Qatar (15 May 1972) p. 3.
15 Fenelon, op. cit., pp. 48–51.
16 *Focus on the United Arab Emirates*, Progress International Survey (London, July 1975) pp. 18–19.
17 Fenelon, op. cit., pp. 58.
18 Kilner and Wallace (eds.), op. cit., p. 304.
19 Fenelon, op. cit., pp. 59–60.
20 Shaw, op. cit., p. 96.
21 Kilner and Wallace (eds.), op. cit., p. 27.
22 Roger Vielvoye 'Oil: The Long Goodbye', *The Times* Special Report on Qatar (3 September 1976) p. 3.
23 Kilner and Wallace (eds.), op. cit., p. 298.

24 Details of progress are given in the OAPEC Secratary-General's *Annual Reports*. See for example the second annual report (Kuwait, November 1975) pp. 73–4.
25 Colin Chapman, 'Industrial Progress – Fast and Visible', *The Emirates No. 6* (London: U.A.E. Embassy, December 1976) p. 8.
26 Smelters in Western Canada using hydro-electric power, which are much longer-established and more efficient, were running well below capacity by the mid-1970s.
27 For details see *Middle East Economic Digest*, Special Report on Qatar (April 1977) p. 11.
28 Kilner and Wallace (eds.), op. cit., p. 500.
29 Pipes for the oil industry are another Kuwaiti success, as although these were only made for domestic requirements at first, most of the production is now exported throughout the Middle East. Here again Kuwait, as a monopoly producer, has been able to take advantage of the economies of mass production.
30 For an appraisal of this, see Ragaei H. Mallakh, *Economic Development and Regional Co-operation: Kuwait* (University of Chicago Press, 1968) Chapter 5, p. 133 ff.
31 I.M.F. *International Financial Statistics*, vol. XXX, no. 5 (May 1977).
32 Anthony Pearson, '65 Banks Follow Oil Trade,' *Guardian* Special Report on the United Arab Emirates. (24 April 1975) p. 20.
33 Rodney Wilson, 'Banking: Competition for Beirut's Role', *Middle East Yearbook* (*Middle East Magazine*, 1978) p. 90–3.
34 For a summary of banking operations in the UAE see Nicholas Fallon, *Middle East Oil Money and its Future Expenditure* (Graham & Trotman, 1975) pp. 79–81.
35 The only published study on the economic impact of this migration is A. M. Farrog, 'Migration between Arab Countries', in I.L.O. *Manpower and Employment in Arab Countries: Some Critical Issues* (Geneva, 1976) pp. 84–108.
36 A major study of migration in the Middle East is being undertaken by C. Sinclair and J. S. Birks under I.L.O. sponsorship. See their article 'Towards Planned Migration in the Middle East: An Evaluation of Patterns and Processes of Labour Movement', *British Society for Middle Eastern Studies Bulletin*, vol. 4, no. 1 (1977) pp. 28–31.
37 Galal A. Amin, *The Modernization of Poverty: A Study in the Political Economy of Economic Growth in Nine Arab Countries 1945–1970* (Leiden: Brill, 1974) p. 83.
38 Kuwait Ministry of Planning Central Statistical Office, *Annual Statistical Abstract* (1976) Table 140, p. 190.
39 Ibid., Table 159, pp. 230–31.
40 Ibid., Table 23, p. 40.

CHAPTER 6

1 P. Wittek, *The Rise of the Ottoman Empire*, Royal Asiatic Society Monograph no. 23, (London, 1938) Chapters 1 and 3 especially.

2 Z. Y. Hershlag, *Turkey: The Challenge of Growth* (Leiden: Brill, 1968) p. 52.

3 Ibid., pp. 16–27, where an account is given of the economic implications of the Lausanne Treaty.

4 O. C. Sarc, 'Economic Policy of the New Turkey', *Middle East Journal*, vol. 2, no. 4, (October 1948) pp. 430–46.

5 S. C. Wyatt, 'Turkey: The Economic Situation and the Five-Year Plan, *International Affairs* (November–December 1934).

6 Z. Y. Hershlag, op. cit. Chapter 10, pp. 97–107, discusses some of the difficulties in the industrial sector.

7 Useful economic data on this period are provided by Max Weston Thornburg, *Turkey: An Economic Appraisal* (New York: Twentieth Century Fund, 1949). The trade data on p. 277–84 illustrate how, with imports falling over much of 1930s, import substitute industries had a major role to play.

8 Population census of Turkey, *One Percent Sample Results* (Ankara, 1975) p. 6.

9 State Planning Office, *Gelir Davilimi, 1973* (Ankara, 1976), pp. 18 and 38.

10 See Oddvar Aresvik, *The Agricultural Development of Turkey* (New York: Praeger, 1975) Chapters 1 and 4 especially. Also Z. Y. Hershlag, op. cit., chapter 17, pp. 157–68 for a summary of agricultural developments. For statistical data on trends in agriculture at this time see Edwin J. Cohn, *Turkish Economic, Social and Political Change* (New York: Praeger, 1970), p. 18.

11 Ceval Karatas, *Contemporary Economic Problems in Turkey*, unpublished paper presented at British Society for Middle Eastern Studies Conference in Durham (July 1976) p. 3 ff.

12 For details of state assistance to industry see Mete Durdag, *Some Problems of Development Financing: A Case Study of the Turkish First Five Year Plan 1963–1967* (Dordrecht, Holland: Reidel, 1973). Also Maxwell J. Fry, *Finance and Development Planning in Turkey* (Leiden: Brill, 1972).

13 See *Middle East Economic Digest*, vol. 20, no. 42 (15 October 1976), pp. 23–34, which outlines the problems faced by Turkey over its trade relations with the EEC.

14 EIB, *Activities of the European Investment Bank in Turkey* (Luxemburg, 1975).

15 John Bridge, *The EEC and Turkey: an Analysis of the Association Agreement and its Impact on Turkish Economic Development*, unpublished paper (Durham University, 1974).

16 Rodney Wilson, 'Strained Relations with EEC', *The Times* Special Report on Turkey (20 December, 1976) p. 8.

17 Two useful case studies of the impact of migrant workers on the host countries of Western Europe and the resultant strains are Jonathan Power, *Western Europ's Migrant Workers*, Minority Rights Group Report no. 28 (London 1976) and OECD, *The Effect of the Employment of Foreign Workers,* (Paris, 1974).

18 For useful statistical information up to 1972 see Besir Hamitogullari, *La Planification du Dêveloppement Économique en Turquie*, Faculty of Political Sciences Publication no. 266 (University of Ankara, 1968) pp. 308 and

310. A useful study of Turkish trade has been undertaken by Ann Kruegar, *Foreign Trade and Economic Development* (New York: Columbia University Press, 1974) Chapters 6 and 7 especially.

19 *Middle East Economic Digest*, vol. 20, no. 42 (15 October 1976) p. 27 ff.

20 For an appraisal of total capital transfers into Turkey see Nelson Arditi, *Les Investissements Étrangers en Turquie* (Geneva, Droz, 1970).

21 Susan Paine, *Exporting Workers; The Turkish Case*, Department of Applied Economics Occasional Paper 41 (Cambridge University Press, 1974).

22 See *Economist* Intelligence Unit, *Quarterly Economic Review of Turkey* Annual Supplement (1976), pp. 22–3.

23 An interesting discussion of these issues is given in an OECD report, *The OECD and International Migration* (Paris, 1975) p. 22 ff. The report questions the values of the skills acquired in European industry.

CHAPTER 7

1 A standard source on economic planning in Syria is Khaled A. Shair, *Planning For a Middle Eastern Economy: Model For Syria* (Chapman & Hall, 1965). Chapter 1, on the economic background, discusses the basic problems on pp. 3–19. For an account of planning in Iraq up to 1965 see Ferhang Jalal, *The Role of Government in the Industrialisation of Iraq 1950–1965* (Cass, 1972) Chapter 3, p. 32 ff., especially.

2 In Iraq between 1957 and 1965 there were 265 armed attacks, and in Syria 9 coups in the first 25 years of independence after 1946. See Galal A. Amin, *The Modernisation of Poverty* (Leiden: Brill, 1974) pp. 45–6.

3 The Iraqi population of Kuwait alone numbered almost 40,000 according to the Kuwait Central Statistical Office 1970 Population Census (Table 4, p. 9). Since then the number has increased substantially, although the exact figure will not be known until the next census results become available.

4 E. R. J. Owen, 'The Economic Aspects of Revolution in the Middle East', in P. J. Vatikiotis (ed.), *Revolution in the Middle East* (Allen & Unwin, 1972) p. 49.

5 For analysis of their impact on the Iraqi economy see Abbas Alnasrawi, *Financing Economic Development in Iraq* (New York: Praeger, 1967) Chapter 3, pp. 35–94; IBRD, *The Economic Development of Iraq* (Baltimore: John Hopkins Press, 1952) Chapter 3, p. 33 ff. especially; K. Haseeb, *The National Income of Iraq, 1953–1961* (Oxford University Press, 1964) Chapter 5, p. 79 ff.

6. For an account of the economic history of Iraq's oil industry written from the official point of view of the Baghdad government see *Iraq Today*, vol. II, No. 27 (October 16–31 1976) pp. 8–15.

7 Ibid, p. 13.

8 *Economist* Intelligence Unit, *Quarterly Economic Review of Iraq*, Annual Supplement (1976) pp. 9–10.

9 Ibid., p. 12.

10 *Iraq Today*, vol. II, no. 27, (16–31 October 1976) p. 14.

11 Brief details of the subsequent negotiations are given in the *Quarterly Economic Review of Iraq*, Annual Supplement (1976), pp. 11–12.

12 For an analysis of the trends see K. S. McLachlan, 'Development and Oil Revenues', *Focus Research* Report on Iraq (London, May 1975) pp. 24–6.

13 A useful account of the characteristics of Iraq's foreign trade sector was provided by United Nations, *Planning The Foreign Trade Sector of Iraq*, UN Studies on Development Problems in Selected Countries of the Middle East, (New York, 1972) p. 12 ff.

14 Nasir Gaylani, *The Capital Absorptive Capacities of Iraq and Kuwait: A Comparative Study*, M.A. thesis, University of Durham (1977) Chapter 4, provides details of Iraqi government revenue.

15 *Economist* Intelligence Unit, *Quarterly Economic Review of Syria, Lebanon and Cyprus*, no. 1 (1977) p. 9.

16 Ibid.

17 *Flash of Damascus*, no. 53 (June 1976) p. 21.

18 *Flash of Damascus*, nos 44–5 (June–July 1975) p. 22.

19 Ziad Keilany, 'Socialism and Economic Change in Syria', *Middle Eastern Studies*, vol. 9, no. 1 (January 1973).

20 Jawad Hashim, *Development Planning in Iraq: Historical Perspective and New Directions* (Baghdad: Planning Board, July 1975) pp. 14–16. For a detailed description of landownership in Iraq and Syria prior to the reforms see Doreen Warriner, *Land Reform and Development in the Middle East* (Oxford University Press 1957) where Syria is discussed on p. 82 ff, and Iraq on p. 139 ff.

21 For details of the reforms see the reports by both countries to the United Nations 1966 World Land Reform Conference in Rome: Syrian Report, UN Document RV:WLR–C/66/39 (in French, 23 pp.); Iraqi Report, UN Document RV:WLR–C/66/46 (in English 24 pp.)

22 Keilany, art. cit., p. 63.

23 For an uncritical account of the 1958 reform see A. W. M. Al-Dahiri, *The Introduction of Technology into Traditional Societies and Economies* (Baghdad: Al-Ani Press, 1969) p. 178 ff., which uses Iraq as a case study.

24 Hashim, op. cit., pp. 19–20.

25 *Past Developments and Growth Prospects in the Agricultural Sector of Syria*, UN Studies on Development Problems in Selected Countries of the Middle East (New York, 1972) p. 37.

26 *Economist* Intelligence Unit, *Quarterly Economic Review of Syria, Lebanon and Cyprus*, no. 1 (1977) p. 8.

27 Kielany, op. cit., p. 61.

28 For details see *Flash of Damascus*, no. 39 (December 1974) p. 12 ff.

29 *Flash of Damascus*, nos 44–5 (June–July 1975) p. 21.

30 *Iraq Today*, vol. II, no. 27 (16–31 October 1976) pp. 16–17.

31 Ibid.

32 It is notable that no mention is made of the question of farm prices in the 1975–80 plan, despite all the emphasis put on helping agriculture. See *Iraq Today*, vol. 2, no. 29 (16–30 November, 1976) pp. 23–5. See also *Iraq Today* vol. II, no. 33 (16–31 January, 1977) pp. 19–21.

33 Ministry of Planning, *Annual Abstract of Statistics*, (1975) Table 7/13, p. 188; Table 7/1, p. 176; and (1971) Table 91, p. 154. The official indices have 1963 = 100 for consumer prices, and 1962 = 100 for wholesale prices.

34 Ministry of Planning, *Annual Abstract of Statistics* (1973) Table 141, p. 271 ff.

35 United Nations, *Past Developments and Growth Prospects in the Agricultural Sector of Syria*, Tables 10 and 11, p. 39. The predecessor of the Agricultural Co-operative Bank was the Agricultural Bank. For details of its activities in the 1950s see Edmund Y. Asfour, *Syria: Development and Monetary Policy* (Harvard University Press, 1959) Table 32, p. 118.

36 Yet Arab Socialism is supposed to be 'against the democracy of the privileged, for the democracy of the people'. See A. R. Kelidar, 'Iraq, OPEC and Arab Socialism', *Focus Research* Report on Iraq (London, May 1975) p. 13.

37 Syrian Arab Republic Central Bureau of Statistics, *Statistical Abstract* (Damascus, 1976) Table 31/17, pp. 926–37, and 32/17, p. 928–9.

38 I.M.F., *International Financial Statistics* (Washington, May 1976) pp. 420–1.

39 For a brief account of Iraq's religious and ethnic divisions see Uriel Dann, *Iraq Under Qassem: A Political History 1958–1963* (Jerusalem: Praeger/Pall Mall, 1969) pp. 1–2.

40 They do enjoy greater control over local affairs than the Kurds in Iran or Turkey do, however. See *Iraq Today*, vol. II no. 3 (16–31 January, 1977) pp. 22–3. Although this is a sponsored publication, it does quote independent sources.

41 A point the Kurds themselves naturally emphasise. See Information Department of the Kurdistan Democratic Party, *On the Kurdish Question at the United Nations* (Helsinki, June 1974) pp. 15–17.

42 For a useful account of the economic interpretation of Arab Socialism see Z. Y. Hershlag, *The Economic Structure of the Middle East* (Leiden: Brill, 1975) p. 56 ff. Iraq's experience is outlined on pp. 64–6, and Syria's on pp. 66–7.

CHAPTER 8

1 Wendell Phillips, *Oman: A History* (Longmans, 1967) Chapters 2 and 3, p. 24 ff., especially.

2 Hugh Scott, *In the High Yemen* (Murray, 1942) Chapters XVIII and XIX, p. 195 ff.

3 Simone Mondesir, 'Yemen Arab Republic', in *Middle Eastern Yearbook* (*Middle East Magazine*, 1977), p. 280.

4 Arab World File (*Fiches du monde arabe*): South Yemen, Sheet 1 – SY1 (Beirut, 1974); Sheet 1 – 05 (Beirut, 1977).

5 *Middle Eastern Yearbook 1977* People's Democratic Republic of Yemen, p. 286, and Oman, p. 210.

6 Data from Arab World File: South Yemen Sheet 1 – SY6 (Beirut, 1975); Oman Sheet 1 – 04 (Beirut, 1974); North Yemen Sheet 1 – NY6 (Beirut, 1978).

7 Erich W. Bethmann, *Yemen on the Threshold* (Washington: American Friends of the Middle East, 1960) p. 57 ff.

8 Its effect on the trade deficit can be judged by the fact that the Yemini riyal sunk from 6·60 South Yemini shillings in 1964 to 1·40 shillings by 1970. See

Fred Halliday, *Arabia Without Sultans* (Harmondsworth: Penguin, 1974). 136. Three years of drought (1967–9) lowered food output still further.

9 For a critical account of British rule in South Yemen and the Aden economy, see Halliday, op. cit., Chapter 6, p. 153 ff.

10 Even in the 1950s there was considerable unrest, however. See D. C. Watt, 'Labour Relations and Trade Unionism in Aden, 1952–60', *Middle East Journal*, vol 16, no. 4, (1962) pp. 43–56.

11 See Halliday, op. cit., p. 207 ff. He provides a useful account of the differences between FLOSY and the NLF.

12 For a brief account of Teymour's rule see James Morris, *Sultan in Oman* (Faber & Faber, 1957) p. 151 ff. A comprehensive account of the Sultans of Oman up to the nineteenth century is given by Sahl-Ibri-Razik, *History of the Imans and Seyyids of Oman* (New York: Burt Franklin, 1871), translated by G. P. Badger.

13 Halliday, op. cit., gives a detailed account of the factors that lead to the emergence of the guerrilla war in Dhofar. See Chapter 10, p. 304 ff. For an account by the rebels themselves see *Documents of the National Struggle in Oman and the Arabian gulf*, Gulf Committee of 9th June Studies (London 1974) p. 7 ff.

14 See the *Middle East Economic Digest* Special Report on Oman (June 1976) p. 2. Also Peter Kilner and Jonathan Wallace (eds), *Gulf Handbook* (London, Middle East Economic Digest, 1976 and Bath, Trade and Travel Publications, 1977) p. 374, where the figures for 1973 and 1974 are given.

15 For a brief summary of the Iranian-Omani agreements see Arab World File, op. cit., Sheet 1 – 01.

16 *Middle East Economic Digest*, Special Report on Oman, pp. 24–6.

17 Though comparisons of this type can be particularly misleading unless similar groups in both countries gain from the economic growth. Few may benefit from rapid economic growth if income distribution remains concentrated, which the South Yemenis argue is the case in North Yemen.

18 *Middle East Yearbook*, op. cit. North Yemen's communications are discussed on p. 282, South Yemen's on p. 286.

19 Arab World File, op. cit., Sheet 1 – NY4.

20 *Arab Economist*, vol. IX, no. 90 (March 1977) pp. 22–3.

21 Which stood at $210 in 1975. See *World Bank Atlas* (Washington 1976).

22 Hence the title of the *Arab Economist* article: 'South Yemen Softens its Marxist Line'. Details of assistance from Kuwait and Saudi Arabia are given pp. 1–2.

23 Thus there was a threefold increase in dollar reserves, and a substantial rise in deutschmark deposits by the Yemeni Central Bank, as the Saudi assistance was made available in convertible currency. See Central Bank of Yemen, *Annual Report 1974–75*, pp. 46–7.

24 See James A. Sockrat and Clive Sinclair, *An Estimate of Yemen's Total Population and Workers Abroad* UNDP/ILO Working Paper (Sanaa, November 1975) p. 2 ff. for an analysis of the census results.

25 On p. 23 of *Arab Economist*, vol. IX, no. 90 (March 1977), the number estimated was more than 1 million, but this does seem too large.

26 The Kuwait-based Arab Fund for Economic and Social Development has prepared a tabulated summary of investment laws in Arab countries, in-

cluding that of North Yemen (Law no. 18 of 1975).

27 The interest rate increases were made early in 1976.

28 Central Bank of Yemen, *Annual Report 1974–75*, p. 72. The situation improved slightly in 1974/75 compared with 73/74, as the proportion of foodstuffs imported declined to 42·7 per cent.

29 Admittedly the migrants are obtaining experience in Saudi Arabia and the Gulf States which they could scarcely obtain in North Yemen. The problem for the North Yemini authorities is to attract the experienced people back for the projects they are implementing, as they seem in no hurry to return.

30 For an account of life in the PFLO-controlled areas in the early 1970s, and the liberation movement's ideology, see Halliday, op. cit., Chapter 10, p. 304 ff., and Chapter 11, p. 361 ff.

31 At least according to legal experts in Saudi Arabia and elsewhere on the peninsula, but in the rest of the Arab world this law does not appear to be applied.

32 Paradoxically the Koran itself stresses equality. See Stephen Goode, *The Prophet and the Revolutionary: Arab Socialism in the Modern Middle East* (New York: Franklin Watts, 1975) p. 19.

33 Halliday, op.cit., p. 250.

34 Ibid.

35 Especially in view of the strained relations with the Gulf States and Saudi Arabia. Paradoxically, socialist nationalisation measures would have made the South Yeminis more directly dependent on these conservative oil suppliers.

36 Arab World File, op. cit., Sheet 1 – SY9.

37 Ibid., Sheet 1 – SY1.

38 Even those who migrate because they cannot obtain an adequate living for themselves or their families on the land, almost all of whom hope to return to their local villages when they have accumulated sufficient unds.

39 Apart from the Gulf Coast, the fisheries potential of the seas around the Arabian peninsula have yet to be seriously exploited. Japanese and Russian fishermen have benefited more in the past than local coastal residents.

40 Not surprisingly, for normally the communists have assisted industrial development in fields where they themselves have experience as a consequence of being major producers. In this respect it could be argued that private investment is preferable, for the Western multinationals only enter fields where they can identify a ready market.

CHAPTER 9

1 Figures from OECD, *Development Co-operation* (Paris, 1976) Statistical Annex, Table 46, p. 270.

2 Provisional results from the 1973 census indicated that the total Sudanese population numbered under 15 million, but serious doubts have arisen about the accuracy of this census. The projection of 18 million from earlier and more reliable data would seem a more likely figure. See *Sudannow* (Khartoum, June 1976) pp. 9–11.

3 Ministry of Planning and Scientific Research, Libyan Arab Republic, *The Plan of Economic and Social Transformation 1976–1980*, (Tripoli, 1976) p. 39. For accounts of what Libya's non-oil sector has developed from see Rawle Farley, *Planning for Development in Libya: The Exceptional Economy in the Developing World* (New York: Praeger, 1971) Chapter 7, p. 132 ff. Also the IBRD report, *The Economic Development of Libya* (Baltimore: John Hopkins Press, 1960) Chapter 8, p. 130 ff., Chapter 9, p. 179 ff.

4 See Bank of Sudan, Sixteenth Annual Report (Khartoum, 1975) Appendix 2, Table 3, p. 101. For a recent study of the structure of the Sudanese economy see F. A. Lees and H. C. Brooks, *The Economic and Political Development of the Sudan* (Macmillan, 1977).

5 Confederation of British Industry (CBI), *Market Study: Sudan* (London, May 1977) p. 13.

6 For brief details of the takeover see Ruth First, 'Libya', *Middle East Annual Review* (London, 1977) pp. 237–8.

7 The IMF compiles an index of the volume of Libyan oil exports. See its *International Financial Statistics* vol. XXX, no. 8 (August 1977) pp. 226–7.

8 For details of recent infrastructure improvements see *Middle East Economic Digest*, Special Report on the Sudan, (26 August 1977) pp. 5–7. An historical account of the importance of Sudanses trade with its neighbours is given by P. F. Martin, *The Sudan in Evolution: A Study of the Financial and Administrative Conditions of the Anglo-Egyptian Sudan* (New York: Negro University Press, 1970), p. 100 ff.

9 The roads on the Kenya side are unsurfaced, so communications with East Africa will remain difficult.

10 For details of its economic implications see *Middle East Economic Digest*, Special Report on the Sudan, p. 17.

11 Ibid.

12 Apart from welfare considerations, on grounds of efficiency there is a case for deploying funds in regions such as the south, rather than concentrating funds in agricultural projects along the Nile. This point is made in the ILO report, *Growth, Employment and Equity: A Comprehensive Strategy for the Sudan* (Geneva, 1976) p. 32 ff.

13 *Sudannow* (Khartoum, April 1977) p. 41. Also (June 1977) p. 27.

14 *Sudannow* (Khartoum, August 1977) p. 37.

15 Unfortunately not all of the aid inflows have been coming on schedule, which may delay the plan. See Peter Kilner, 'Sudan: Devaluation and Spending Cuts Loom as Aid Inflows Falter', *Middle East Economic Digest*, vol. 21, no. 40 (7 October 1977) pp. 3–5.

16 Louis Eaks, 'Agriculture: The Desert Comes Alive', *Arab Dawn*, vol. 1, no. 12 (September 1975) p. 10.

17 Atef Sultan, 'Agriculture: Population Growth Spurs Self-Sufficiency Plans', *Middle East Economic Digest*, Special Report on Libya (18 February 1977) p. 7.

18 Eaks, op. cit., pp. 10–11.

19 Libyan Arab Republic, *The Plan of Economic and Social Transformation 1976–1980*, p. 31.

20 See 'Special Report on Kenana' in *Sudannow* (Khartoum, October 1976) p. 24.

21 See 'Kenana: Exit Lonrho', *Sudannow* (Khartoum, August 1977) p. 32.
22 For details of some of the delays see James Buxton and Margaret Reid, 'Lonrho's Kenana Project: The Crumbling of an Ambitious Dream', *Financial Times* (24 May, 1977) p. 6. Sudan's existing agricultural schemes such as that in the Gezira had taken years to develop, unlike Kenana. For a history of this earlier scheme see A. Gaitskell, *Gezira: A Story of Development in the Sudan*, (Faber & Faber, 1959) Part 2, p. 99 ff. especially.
23 *Sudannow* (Khartoum, August 1977) p. 28.
24 For a history of the company, and the Tiny Rowlands financial empire, see Suzanne Cronje, Margaret Ling and Gillian Cronje, *Lonrho: Portrait of a Multinational* (Julian Friedman, 1976) Chapter 7 discusses the 'unacceptable face' (p. 134 ff.), while Chapter 9 p. 178 ff., deals with the Sudan.
25 For a complete list of industrial projects, and brief details, see Ministry of Information and Culture, *The First of September Revolution Achievements 1969–1974: 5th Anniversary* (Tripoli, 1974) pp. 64–9.
26 A brief account of the Sudanese communist party and the 1971 abortive coup is given in Arab World File (*Fiches du monde arabe*) (Beirut 16 April, 1975) Sheet 1 – Sn 10.
27 Arab Fund For Economic and Social Development, Investment Services and Promotion Unit, *Tabulated Summary of Investment Laws in Arab Countries: Sudan* (Kuwait, 1977) p. 1.
28 CBI, *Market Study: Sudan*, p. 35. A survey has been carried out of small industrial establishments and their attitudes towards these laws. See K. A. Hammeed, *Enterprise: Industrial Entrepreneurship in Development*, (Sage Publications, 1974). Chapter 3 gives details of establishments covered by the survey (p. 56 ff.).
29 Ibid.
30 Libyan Arab Republic, *The Plan of Economic and Social Transformation 1976–1980*, p. 17.
31 *Middle East Economic Digest*, Special Report on Libya, p. 12. For a detailed acount of Libya's labour laws see M. A. Nafa, *Libya: Company and Business Law* (Arab Consultants, 1976) Chapter 5, p. 208 ff.
32 Nafa, op. cit., p. 257.
33 *Arab Dawn*, vol. 1, no. 27 (December–January 1977) p. 19.
34 *Arab Dawn*, vol. 1, no. 32 (June 1977) p. 19.
35 *Financial Times* (2 December 1976) p. 1.
36 *Arab Dawn*, vol. 1, no. 28 (February 1977) p. 18.

CHAPTER 10

1 This figure is an estimate, as there has not been an official census for over forty years. The Christians feared that any census might reveal a Moslem majority, which would upset the country's delicate political and social balance.
2 Hashemite Kingdom of Jordan, *Statistical Yearbook* (Amman, 1975) Table 2.
3 The West Bank is still partially covered by Jordanian statistical sources, but Israeli data is more reliable as they are, after all, in control of the area.

4 For a useful profile of King Hussein see Peter Snow, *Hussein: A Biography* (Barrie & Jenkins, 1972) Part 3 deals with Hussein and the Palestinians (pp. 161–249).

5 According to UNRWA (United Nations Relief and Welfare agency) figures, the 212,800 are refugees registered as qualifying for UNRWA support in the Lebanese camps in 1977.

6 Provisional estimates for the costs of reconstruction in Lebanon total $3000 million. Quoted in *The Middle East*, no. 28 (London February 1977) p. 34. See also *Middle East Economic Digest*, vol. 20, no. 49 (3 December 1976) p. 3.

7 The private census is cited in the Economist Intelligence Unit, *Quarterly Economic Review of Syria, Lebanon and Cyprus*, (London, 4th quarter 1976) p. 17.

8 The Hashemite Kingdom of Jordan, National Planning Council, *Five Year Plan 1976–80* (Amman 1976) Chapter 7, pp. 166–90 deals with mining and industry.

9 For a brief account of the history and development of the Jordanian phosphates industry up to 1974 see Arab World File (*Fiches du monde arabe*) (Beirut, 27 November 1974) no. 138. Sheet 1-JZ. For more recent developments see Rodney Wilson, 'Rapid Growth is Daunting Target', *The Times* Special Report on Jordan (25 May 1976) p. 2. See also Rami G. Khouri, 'Phosphate Wealth', *Financial Times* Survey of Jordan (21 April 1976) p. 15.

10 Jordan has long had a liberal trade policy. See US Department of Commerce Overseas Business Report, *Foreign Trade Regulations of Jordan*, Report no. 15 Washington, May 1969, pp. 1–6.

11 Rami G. Khouri, 'Amman's Emergence', *Financial Times* Survey of Jordan (21 April 1976) p. 14.

12 Yusif A. Sayigh, *Entrepreneurs of Lebanon* (Harvard University Press, 1962); Arthur E. Mills, *Private Enterprise in Lebanon* (American University of Beirut Press, 1959).

13 Z. Taky, *Monetary Policy in an Open Developing Economy: A Case Study of Lebanon*, Ph.D. thesis, American University, Washington D.C. (1971).

14 *Arab Economist*, vol. VI, no. 66 (July 1974) p. 28 ff.

15 J. N. Bridge *Financial Growth and Economic Development: A Case Study of Lebanon*, Ph.D. thesis, Durham University (1975) For details of the monetary controls since 1967 see p. 248 ff.

16 Samira Harfouche, *Lebanese Handicraft*, no. 1, (Lebanon, August 1971) p. 19 ff.

17 For a discussion of the scale issue see Nadim G. Khalaf, *Economic Implications of the Size of Nations with Special Reference to Lebanon* (Leiden: Brill, 1971). The occupational structure of Lebanon is considered on p. 181 ff.

18 Although the banking system has been criticised for not playing a more active role. See J. N. Bridge, *Development in the Lebanese Economy, 1950–1973*. David Horowitz Institute for the Research of Developing Countries, Tel Aviv University, Paper No. 5 (1974) pp. 26–33.

19 Elias T. Ghantus, 'Lebanon', *The Times* Supplement on the Arab Renaissance (20 March 1975) p. 6.

20 The Hashemite Kingdom of Jordan National Planning Council, *Five Year*

Plan 1976–1980 (Amman, 1976) pp. 170–1. For details of Jordan's small-scale industries see Industrial Development Bank, *The Small Scale and Handicraft Industries in Jordan* (Amman, 1976) p. 4 and pp. 11–60 especially.

21 Peter Hopkirk, 'Better Days After 25 Hard Years', *The Times* Special Report on Jordan (25 May 1976) p. 1. See also *Economist* Intelligence Unit, *Quarterly Economic Review of Jordan and Saudi Arabia* (4th Quarter 1976) p. 11.

22 *Middle East Economic Digest*, vol. 20 no. 48, 26 November 1976, p. 9.

23 Ibid.

24 A useful analysis of the previous union between Lebanon and Syria, and its trade implications, is provided by Elias S. Saba, *The Foreign Exchange Systems of Lebanon and Syria,* (American University of Beirut Press, 1961) pp. 177–201.

25 Syria does not have the financial capacity to play a major role in Lebanese economic reconstruction itself, in any case. See *The Middle East* no. 28, (London, February 1977) pp. 30–3.

26 Despite this, the old regime was not without influential supporters, even amongst academic economists. See for example Elie Abid Salem, *Modernization without Revolution: Lebanon's Experience* (Bloomington: Indiana University Press, 1973). This study gives a very different picture of the Lebanese government's record to that presented here.

27 Agriculture, in fact, received less attention in the 1960s and 1970s than it did earlier in the 1950s. For information on this earlier period see Georges G. Corn, *Politique Économique et planification au Liban* (Paris: Librairie de Medicis, 1964) pp. 8–18. There was no shortage of planning models, however, integrating agriculture with the rest of the economy. See for example Muntasir M. Labban, *A Development Planning Model for an Underdeveloped Economy with Special Reference to Lebanon.* Ph.D. thesis, State University of New York, Binghamton (1972).

28 *Economist* Intelligence Unit, *Quarterly Economic Review of Syria, Lebanon and Cyprus* (London, 4th quarter 1976) p. 25.

29 One prophetic work was Naaman Azhari, *L'Evolution du système économique libanais où la fin du laisser-faire*, (Paris: Pichon et Durand-Auzias, 1970). Part 3 gives an analysis of the contradictions in Lebanon (pp. 41–67).

Index